THE AVENGERS

COMPANION

BAY
BOOKS

First published by Huitième Art Editions. First published in English by Titan Books. North American Edition published 1998 by Bay Books & Tapes, Inc., by arrangement with Titan Books, 42-44 Dolben Street, London, SE1 0UP, England.

For information, address: Bay Books & Tapes, 555 De Haro Street, No. 220, San Francisco, CA 94107.

Publisher: James Connolly
Art Director: Jeffrey O'Rourke
American edition designed by Cabra Diseño
Cover design: Cabra Diseño / Scott DiGirolamo & Jeremy Stout
Book design: Cabra Diseño / Jeremy Stout
Original UK edition designed by Darren Clark, based on a design by P.J. Oswald

For Cathy (not Gale!) with all my love. J.-L. P. ⊕

Acknowledgments:
To Gérard Biard, Jean-Christophe Carbonel, Philippe Ferrari, Jean-Marc Palland, Pascal Pinteau and, above all, to Dominique Seigneur, for having kindly placed at our disposal their personal collections. To Christophe Casa-Zza, Philippe Danon, David Fakrikian and Chrisophe Petit, for the kind help they have given us. To the British Film Institute, who provided the beautiful color photographs in this book. And, finally, to Dave Rogers, whose work has been of particularly valuable help to us. Titan would also like to thank Alex J. Geairns, Paul Buck, Sarah Barker and Mark Kent for their help in the preparation of the British edition of this title.

Library of Congress Cataloguing-in-Publication Data

Carrazè, Alain.
    [Chapeau melon et bottes de cuir. English]
    The Avengers companion / Alain Carrazè & Jean-Luc Putheaud, with
Alex J. Geairns ; translated by Paul Buck.
        p.   cm.
    ISBN 0-912333-61-8
    1. Avengers (Television program) 2. New Avengers (Television
program) I. Putheaud, Jean-Luc. II. Geairns, Alex J. III. Title.
PN1992.77.A923C3713   1998
791.45'72--dc21   98-9188
                                                   CIP

Printed in Hong Kong

ISBN 0-912333-61-8

10 9 8 7 6 5 4 3 2 1

Distributed to the trade by Publishers Group West

7 6 5

4

THE AVENGERS
COMPANION

ALAIN CARRAZÉ AND JEAN-LUC PUTHEAUD
WITH ALEX J. GEAIRNS

FEATURING EXCLUSIVE INTERVIEWS WITH PATRICK MACNEE, DIANA RIGG, LINDA THORSON AND BRIAN CLEMENS.

Articles by Christophe Casa-Zza, David Fakrikian, Grant Morrison, François Rivière and Dave Rogers.

With the collaboration of Bruno Billion and Catherine Szczepanski.

Translation by Paul Buck.

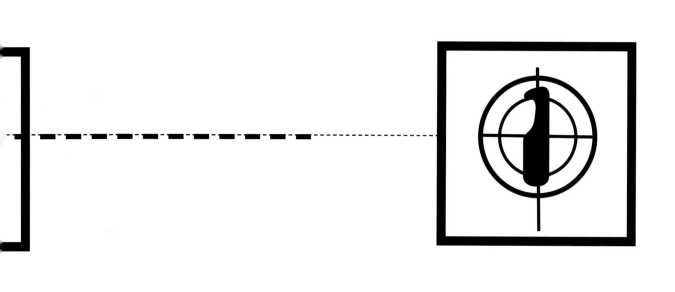

TABLE OF CONTENTS

In the ground-breaking 1960s, the television industry was revolutionised by artists as innovative as their musical colleagues, producing work both admired and imitated by today's generation. Instead of the current obsession with nostalgia and the retro explosion, perhaps we should be looking at the qualities which make such programmes as relevant and appealing today as they were thirty years ago—what makes a style timeless?

Two 'cult' British television series are perfect examples of a timeless work: *The Prisoner* and *The Avengers*. They seem to have little in common, however, except quality. *The Prisoner* had a short life but made a real impact—a "fixed explosion", to use a metaphor from another ageless art form, surrealist poetry. Condemned in its time, it was met with outrage and misunderstanding. *The Avengers* survived for much longer, and was launched to immediate popular success. What the two series shared was the long wait for proper critical evaluation.

The subversive and sometimes violent message of *The Prisoner* is clear and direct, as instantly apparent now as it was originally. *The Avengers* has a more subtle, gradual impact. The devastating humour was aimed at old-fashioned establishment figures as well as at the excesses and absurdities of the modern world, provoking the audience with its disrespect and sharpness. Beneath the apparent lightness of the programme there were always positive values; the individuality, grace, courage and discretion embodied by Steed and his assistants. Above all, simple good taste was upheld, neither imposed by society nor dictated by fashion, combining the progressive and the proven. Two apparently contradictory words come to mind: popular aristocracy!

If the Avengers are on their way to becoming a classic (John, Emma, Tara and the others, we will *always* need you!), it's because of their style above all else. The unique flair of the programme—dazzling, inimitable and unequalled—was maintained by its creators throughout the original series, and is also there beneath the gritty tone of *The New Avengers*.

Like Patrick McGoohan with *The Prisoner,* Brian Clemens had the skill and invention to turn a brilliant idea into a timeless series. The delirious storylines that unfolded told of villainous secret agents, mad scientists, deadly computers and megalomaniac murderers in surreal, displaced settings where fashions collided and wit prevailed. The female actresses, who drove ultra-modern vehicles and wore breathtakingly avant-garde clothes, were perfectly balanced by John Steed, the gentleman driver of the series, wearing elegant suits from the same classic period as his vintage cars.

The Avengers was also uniquely able to resist 'Americanisation' in order to conquer the international market, achieving success on its own terms. It is the unmistakably English, eccentric style of the series that has won countless devotees on both sides of the Atlantic.

The aim of this book is not to dissect the series and attempt to explain its success, but to show some of its many different facets, primarily through numerous photographs, both in black and white and colour. The first part of this book is comprised of interviews and opinions, and as an introduction we have asked Patrick Macnee, Diana Rigg and Linda Thorson (thanks to whom *The Avengers* will remain forever in our hearts) for their thoughts.

The second part of the book is made up of episode listings and synopses, presenting the different adventures experienced by the couple—later the trio—of heroes throughout their successive incarnations. Perhaps those who are new to *The Avengers* will be surprised to discover that there were six series produced, followed later by two series of *The New Avengers*.

For a detailed view of the programme, we also focus at length on some episodes that we judge to be particularly representative of the style of *The Avengers,* and we haven't hesitated in making a subjective choice! Readers are of course free to choose their own favourites.

In the last part we focus on the technical side of the programme. Brian Clemens shares with us a fascinating insiders look at the series he produced and scripted many times. We also include several detailed articles on the actors, vehicles and costumes which made *The Avengers* the phenomenon it is today. ◉

A.C./J.-L.P.

the AVENGERS REMEMBERED

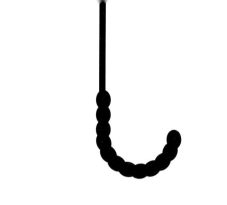

12

PATRICK MACNEE
MANY YEARS LATER...

In September 1990, Patrick Macnee was in Luxembourg filming the television miniseries Sherlock Holmes and the Leading Lady, in which he played the part of the good Dr Watson, alongside Christopher Lee as Sherlock Holmes. It was there that he welcomed us and related his memories of the series that made him famous, and the impressions that he has of it...many years later.

Everything began in November 1960. For some time I had been working as a producer in Canada, having decided to abandon my career as an actor, which at the time was not profitable enough for me to make a living. When I returned to England, and had just finished working on a series about Winston Churchill, I was contacted by Sydney Newman, with whom I had already worked in Toronto. He was preparing a new series, and was searching for an actor to serve as assistant to the principal character in *The Avengers*. He immediately thought of me for the role, which I accepted 7 for one pure and simple reason: it paid me £150 a week, and I was not in a situation to be disinterested.

At that time the series was filmed entirely live. At ten in the evening, on a Saturday, Ian Hendry and I were launched into the homes of the viewers in order to resolve our latest investigation. I had already experienced live television in Toronto, and I knew how testing it could be on the nerves. To shoot *The Avengers* was far from being easy, but was nevertheless gratifying. The creative team, made up of Peter Hammond, Ian Hendry and—to some degree—myself, contributed largely to providing the new ideas. It was certainly not always conscious, but we got into the habit of saying: "Wouldn't it be amusing to do..." Then we reread the script asking ourselves how, without completely changing it, one could make it 'different'. In fact, it was terribly pretentious on our part, for, after all, these scripts bore the signature of very competent people, using ideas from the whole history of 'cops and robbers'. But what was lacking in them was that spark of madness that we all possessed. All those who revolved around the series at that time were caught by the same sweet madness: Sydney Newman, from *Armchair Theatre,* and the others, like the director Ted Kotcheff. All that team gathered in a place called Teddington to produce a bizarre series, barely using any furniture beyond an improbable looking armchair which was pushed about from scene to scene, surrounded by a field of cameras.

Ian Hendry was an extraordinary actor. I remember he used to take the script and rewrite it to give it a new dimension. In those days we had barely ten days to rehearse, then two days to shoot. As for Peter Hammond, he knew how to control his remarkable talent to see things clearly, but it was as if he was looking through the wrong end of a telescope, coming up with the craziest images and giving the series an amazing style. *The Avengers* was all that. Everything, including the photography, the writing and the excellent theme music by Johnny Dankworth, was realised with fervour and enthusiasm. In fact, for most of the time in that period complete panic reigned on the studio floor...and that consumed energy! But on the other hand, since it was shot live, the creative team exercised total control on what was made, and the least element became immediately thrilling. No, it was not very easy, but the public reacted to it very quickly: "Bloody hell, finally, here's something different!" Actually, it was not so different, it just had a fresh approach!

I would say that *The Avengers* lost that style from the moment the series began to be filmed in 35mm, in part, of course, because it needed to take the financial aspect more seriously. The change was not brutal; on the whole it was spread out over the years. When Honor Blackman appeared, in 1962, the style was still the same, with the same team. However, they took a decision that would change the course of *The Avengers*' history. Without doubt, the main reason for its ultimate success was the arrival of a woman!

And not just *any* woman! Not one of them was simply 'a woman'. Each would have been able to be an Admiral of Her Majesty's fleet, or leader of any society. All possessed enormous capacities of imagination, and knew how to take control no matter what the situation. Furthermore, the characters were played by excellent actresses. They all played the roles of women who were able to fight as well as seduce a man, and from which an aura of sensuality radiated, and this became the mark of the series. But no representative of the feminine sex would have succeeded without disposing of the potential autonomy which had characterised the initial partnership of Keel and Steed.

We had to give my female partners as much impact as possible. I had been raised by women, and I thought I was able to say that I knew them. I knew, for example, that if you allow total freedom to a woman, she becomes extravagant, mad, delightful, attractive, and, of course, it is then easier to work with her. That is what I did with Diana Rigg, and it worked out well. As for Honor Blackman, she had no need to be helped, she worked very well by herself! She was an extraordinary woman, very beautiful, and extremely feminine. As a contrast to her leather look, the production team decided I would be dressed close to the fashion of the start of the century, and with the bowler hat which became, eventually, one of the distinctive signs of the series. That led to numerous discussions. We asked ourselves if it was necessary that I keep the bowler in all situations. I told the production team that wherever he went, John Steed must remain true to himself. After all, when the Pope travels to a foreign country, he does not change his clothes!

In any case, it was this type of approach that ended up becoming very important to the series. Later, when *The Avengers* began to interest the Americans, the production team asked Diana Rigg to stop wearing her miniskirts, as people were very puritanical across the Atlantic. Diana instantly refused, and her way of dressing launched a new fashion: she was the first heroine on television to appear in miniskirts! That characterises the spirit with which the series was produced. We decided to make something without caring about the eventual consequences. Sometimes nothing came of it, but we did it all the same! Certainly, to my mind, it was one of the many reasons for the show's success.

In fact, it is a gathering of small details like that one which made *The Avengers*. The show found its sources in the perversion of reality. It is something that David Lynch has completely understood in his excellent hit series *Twin Peaks*. One discovers the same tendencies, with the inhabitants of that small town where everyone knows each other, where everyone comes together innocently in the restaurant to talk, whilst behind all that is hidden the repressed phantasms which Lynch reveals with a stroke of genius. That's a bit like what we did in *The Avengers*, but from another angle: by showing everything in daylight, from the humour to the sexuality, passing through the nature of the characters and their ambiguities.

But, from the moment when the Americans showed interest in the series, the shooting conditions worsened. Sometimes it was like working on an assembly line. The episodes in black and white with Diana are the exception. They still had a part of the originality of the series, and everyone still felt dedicated. But for me it no longer seemed as interesting as at the start.

However, the atmosphere on the studio floor always remained good. I had never had anything but an excellent relationship with Ian Hendry and, later, with the women in the series. In fact, we only had problems with the producers. From the moment when the episodes were no longer shot live, we were in perpetual conflict with them.

Nevertheless, one must say that Brian Clemens was an exceptional and highly creative man. He is marvellous, and knew how to surround himself with extraordinary people like James Hill, Sidney Hayers and above all, Charles Crichton, the director of *A Fish Called Wanda*. (At the time of the series, we were persuaded that he was approaching seventy, when he was in fact bordering on fifty!) All those directors brought much to the series, each with their slice of genius, but they were all surpassed by the talented Diana Rigg, who, in my opinion, is certainly one of the five best actresses in the world. Linda is also an excellent actress. Simply magnificent! It's a shame that at the time, Clemens and Fennell did not give her the chance she merited. Nevertheless, she has remained in the hearts of numerous fans of the series. As for Honor, she has remained very beautiful. All together, we comprised a formidable group of individuals!

When we were in the process of making the series, we did not suspect that, thirty years later, it would still have such success. At the end of 'Bizarre' we had really thought it was finished! Personally, I had worked for nine years with the same character and it was time that it finished. However, six years later, Clemens made *The New Avengers,* which did not work like the old series, quite simply because it lacked an original point of view on things. The new characters established some interest, but, except for a few rare episodes in the purest *Avengers* style ('The Eagle's Nest', for example), they were not allowed the time to show what they were capable of. Without original ideas, the new series was condemned to become repetitive and tedious. I do not like to employ the term repetitive, but I really believe that the essential problem of that series was that it was impossible to make a remake.

As for knowing if Patrick Macnee is or is not John Steed, I'll answer that question by telling you a small anecdote. Whilst I was shooting the new series, one day I met Peter O'Toole in a lift in Toronto. He asked me what had become of me, and what was I working on. I replied that I was shooting *The New Avengers*. He looked at me and said: "But, Patrick, you're *always* doing *The Avengers!*" Is that a good answer? ♥

Patrick Macnee

DIANA RIGG
AN INTERVIEW WITH...

In July 1990, David Fakrikian met up with Diana Rigg in San Francisco, at the theatre where she was appearing in Love Letters with Stacy Keach. Learning of our plans to produce an 'art' book about The Avengers, she was happy to participate when, three months later, she kindly answered these questions.

Q *The Avengers* went through many changes of style and characters. What do you think you brought to the series with the character of Emma Peel? You portrayed a different kind of heroine, feminine and strong, not a damsel in distress type. Did you agree with that? Did you have some input in the characterisation? Is Diana Rigg Emma Peel in some ways?

A Emma Peel was definitely a different type of character for television. For the first time a woman in a TV series was intelligent, independent and capable of looking after herself. That is why the show became such a success—it reflected what was happening to women throughout the world in the 1960s.

Q The series quickly became a classic. Some years after, it was recognised as being truly unique and perfect in every way. Did you have this feeling during the filming? Why do you think it is still such a critical and popular success more than twenty-five years later? Did you ever dram that all this would be taken seriously, being featured in an 'art' book?

A One had no idea during the filming that it would be such a success. The reason why it has remained so is that it was well ahead of its time.

Q You have had an important career, but how do you feel now, regarding *The Avengers?* Are you tired of the character of Emma Peel? To most people your best known role was Emma Peel, but which do you consider to be the most important character you've portrayed? What part has *The Avengers* played in your life and in your profession?

A Emma Peel was extremely important in my life and I will always be grateful to her. I had been regarded simply as a classical actress prior to doing the series and Emma catapulted me into the homes of people all over the world. Of course, I am very fond of her character, but she is in the past and an actor's life must be to constantly try new things.

Q What were the most difficult things you had to do as Emma Peel? What is the hardest part of filming a television series? The relationships with the people involved? Or is it the physical aspect?

A The most difficult things in the series were the speed with which one had to work and learn one's lines. It was extremely hard as our hours were often very long. However, we built a good relationship with the crew and the producers and, for the most part, enjoyed it hugely. The fights were not at all difficult because I was, of course, helped by extremely good stuntmen. Occasionally I was asked to do things that were a little dangerous, but in those days I had no fear and went ahead.

Q What was Patrick Macnee like to work with?

A Patrick Macnee was wonderful to work with, always generous, and we shared the same sense of humour, so we laughed a great deal together.

Q Why did you leave the show? Did the pressure become too much, so it was no longer fun doing it? Had the character become a little bit empty? Now, twenty-five years later, do you regret leaving?

A The reason I left the show was because I had been with it for two years and I believe an actor must keep learning. I was no longer learning anything and, although I was extremely fond of Patrick and many of the people involved in the show, felt it was time to move on. I have never regretted my decision to leave the show. I look back on it with much gratitude and fondness. ◉

LINDA THORSON

THE CHANCE OF MY LIFE

> At the end of September 1990, Linda Thorson was in Paris for a few days' holiday. Speaking about The Avengers was a pleasure for her. And, for us, it was a joy to meet and listen to her.

At that time, I was supposed to have the main role in the film *Sinful Davey,* alongside John Hurt. It had been promised to me, but it turned out that I was far too tall. So, by way of recompense, John Huston, the director, told me they were looking for someone to succeed Diana Rigg in *The Avengers.* He made me register for the casting. I arrived to face 200 girls…I was chosen, with two other actresses, and was sent to a health farm for a week because they thought I was too fat! On the day they came to inform me that I had the part, I was so exhausted and famished that I said just one thing: "I don't care! Give me food and send me home!"

Then, I realised that it was the chance of my life: to play in the most famous British series. However, for the entire duration of the shoot, I was petrified. I was reproached for being Canadian and the artists' agents looked disapprovingly on the fact that a foreigner had been chosen. The media took me for a kind of Greta Garbo…only because I was not confident enough of myself to give interviews. The public adored Diana Rigg and I was afraid that I would not be accepted. Patrick Macnee, at the start, was not very happy. I was young and he was afraid of appearing old beside me. Furthermore, I had been chosen by John Bryce. We were living together and, when he quit the series, it was a difficult decision for me to decide to stay. "If you leave, I'll be very upset," he said to me. "You must stay." That's how I made up my mind, and then the problems with Brian Clemens and Albert Fennell started. All of that made my life not very easy at the beginning. I often left production meetings in tears, as I was so overwhelmed by unpleasant remarks.

I talked about it to Patrick and from then on he became a bit like my 'valiant knight in shining armour', who was there to save my life. He took me under his wing, took care of me and, from then on, I could never imagine working with a more marvellous actor. We were the opposite of Bruce Willis and Cybill Shepherd on *Moonlighting.*

When an actor entered the studio, we used to invite him or her to come and drink a glass of champagne, or to accompany us to the restaurant. And I've understood since that the best way to work is to be relaxed. Thanks to that attitude, everyone wanted to act in the series.

Fortunately, from the first broadcasts, I knew the public liked me. I soon realised that everything was going to be fine and that I would soon be able to enjoy working on *The Avengers.*

It was a lot of work, and nothing else, after that, could ever appear harder. At 5.30am a car used to pick me up to drive me to the studios. Sometimes, when the shoot had been delayed, and the broadcast dates were approaching, the pressure was really on. So we had to shoot several episodes *simultaneously!* I would play one scene, then change my clothes and rush to another studio where I would play opposite other actors. And all of that in ignorance of the script, as I was given the text with the latest rewrites and I didn't even know what the episode was about! It was a bit like everyday life: one doesn't know what's going to happen the next minute…When the series ended, I went to Sicily and slept for two weeks!

I quite sincerely believe that I had a great influence on the character. I had chosen the name myself, with reference to Tara, the estate in *Gone with the Wind.* Besides, at the beginning, I had to be Mrs King, because it had been Mrs Peel and Mrs Gale. But I thought: "What is worse, that Tara is single and spends a night with John Steed, or that she has a husband and does the same?" So Mrs King became Miss King! For me, Tara is in love with Steed. It didn't have to be obvious at each moment but… she is young, and he is brave, elegant, and they work together all the time. She could *only* fall in love with him.

I was too young to be able to bring to the character the fruit of experience, but I did my best, because I think one has to bring a little bit of oneself into the creation of a character.

Linda Thorson

19

Even if the series could have gone on and on, Patrick Macnee and I knew that the vogue for secret agents was about to end. We often talked about it and we believed that the series was about to end as well, one day or the other. However, when it happened, I was really upset. I had improved my character and interpreted it now with much more ease. I would willingly have carried on for two more years, because I wasn't finished with Tara King. But Patrick wouldn't have been happy to do another season.

At the time, I didn't realise that the role was going to pursue me all through my career. On the contrary, I was saying to myself that it was only a beginning and that several opportunities would present themselves offering a place for 'the *Avengers* girl'.

I think that one of the reasons why people have appreciated the series is the perfection with which it was produced: the settings, the costumes, the scripts, the guest stars, the tremendous directors (by the way, my favourite episodes are 'Pandora', 'Game' and 'Look—(stop me if you've heard this one) But There Were These Two Fellers…'), and, above all, the time we had at our disposal. To have a week to shoot an hour of television has become unthinkable! Today I shoot an hour in a day! *Everything* was exceptional. And then there was the money. But not too much, just enough to excel in every field.

I also think that the public appreciated the criticism of British society the series made. But there were more important matters: that man/woman relationship that was never clear. Are they living together? Are they sleeping together? Or are they only working together? Of course the man was very strong, but Emma Peel and Tara King knew very well how to take care of themselves, while remaining very feminine…and while also needing Steed. However, the impression was always that Steed came running to Tara's aid without hesitation, and that he was very concerned by the possibility that something could happen to her. The series came before the 'feminist movement', which didn't really exist at the time. It showed that relationships between man and woman could be more equal than they had ever been before. Furthermore, we were agents of the government's secret services. The role of *The Avengers* was on a totally different scale from that of simple detectives. And those agents were very clever and highly trained.

Examples of longevity on television are rare. *The Avengers* had something really special. I get confirmation of that by reading the fan letters I still receive, as well as at all the conventions I take part in. But, now the Berlin Wall has fallen and the KGB is no longer a threat, the world of espionage has far less reason to exist. Of course there will always be enemy countries, but all of that is far away. We tried to show a better world, without irrational violence, and my son will perhaps one day understand what a spy was by watching *The Avengers*.

Linda Thorson

GRANT MORRISON
A WORLD OF MIRACULOUS TRANSFORMATIONS

When I was young, my family used to have an old, broken television set in the bedroom. For years it lay there gathering dust, with its strange, small screen and its cabinet doors. That television set fascinated me; I was convinced that, if I could get it to work, it would display not the current TV shows of the day but programmes that were old and long-forgotten, the ghosts of shows that were running when the set was new. One of the programmes I'd hoped to see was the first *Avengers* series.

I mention this broken but infinitely mysterious television set because, although part of the attraction of *The Avengers* is purely nostalgic, it seems to me that the series deserves to be remembered and recognised for reasons other than mere nostalgia. Like my old TV, *The Avengers* hinted (and still seems to hint) at a world of miraculous transformations hidden beneath the ordinary and the overlooked. I can't speak for anyone else, but when I dredge up my childhood memories of the series, it's always the same potent images that recur: the giant, lethal game of Snakes and Ladders; the deadly black box in the episode 'Thingumajig'; the London bus, whose top deck has been converted into a mobile office for Mother in 'False Witness'; the murderous golf ball in 'The Thirteenth Hole'. These memorable images confirm for me my contention that shows like *The Avengers,* and later *The Prisoner,* were instrumental in identifying and popularising a tradition which I can only describe as English Surrealism.

As is well documented, the original Surrealist Movement of the 1920s picked up and developed a number of ideas which emerged out of the work of the pre-war Futurists and Dadaists. One of the most important of these ideas involved the transformation of ordinary objects by placing them in extraordinary settings. (Duchamp's urinal, Magritte's bowler-hatted men, etc.)

English Surrealism, as a popular aesthetic, was defined and embodied in television series like *The Avengers* and *The Prisoner.* Unlike its continental precursor, English Surrealism was distinguished by an element of dark whimsy, which can probably be traced back to Lewis Carroll. What was more unusual and, indeed, more radical was the fact that here was surrealism taken out of the galleries and placed in the living rooms of millions of television viewers. In *The Avengers,* supremely mundane elements of British life and culture, which had been taken for granted for years, suddenly assumed a new and sinister significance. Undertakers in top hats and frock coats; bus stops and country inns; train stations and toy shops; all were viewed through the magic looking glass of *The Avengers* and transformed. In the world of John Steed and his partners, country vicars nurtured secret dreams of conquering the world, stately homes were revealed to be Pandora's boxes of amok technology and children's game boards could become the gigantic playgrounds of megalomaniac killers. Even Steed himself, the very epitome of the bourgeois English gentleman, concealed behind his conservative façade the skills of a highly-trained secret agent. It was as though someone had lifted the lid off of the drably cozy familiarity of post-war Britain and revealed a world of vivid delights seething underneath.

It was even more appropriate that all this should occur at a time, in the 1960s, when people were beginning to use chemical means to effect their own transformation of the ordinary. In the series' heyday, the development of *The Avengers'* style ran almost parallel to (and, in many cases, predated) the changes that were taking place in popular culture. Boundaries were being stretched and broken down by new designers, new musicians, new film-makers and, as the black and white world of Merseybeat evolved into Technicolor psychedelia, so too did *The Avengers* mutate from an urban crime drama into a dazzling hyper-real parody of the entire spy genre. The world of *The Avengers* became no longer the world we know but a kaleidoscopic reflection in a funhouse mirror. Style was *everything* and, in its pace and colour, in its fashions and imagery, *The Avengers* offered a weekly distillation of the mood of the times.

As a child in front of a television screen, of course, none of this mattered to me. I was simply swept up by the dazzle and flair of the images and bowled along by the vitality of the stories. (When I was six years old, I was given a toy 'John Steed swordstick'. It became a prized possession and lasted for years until it vanished to that place where all interesting toys ultimately go. I'm told now that the swordstick is a rare collectors item!) Watching the series now, I can see that beyond the wit and the imagination, beyond the sixties nostalgia, lies the true appeal of *The*

Avengers as a window into a world where even the most conventional things might suddenly reveal themselves to be miraculous. Using only the everyday elements of British daily life, *The Avengers* constructed a fantasy world that remains as distinctive and intriguing today as it ever did.

In the end, I think that's one of the major reasons for the continuing popularity of *The Avengers*. Like my magic television set, the series serves as a reminder of the possibilities for transformation that exist in even the most mundane of objects and situations. It shows us a world where the astonishing and the commonplace are indistinguishable and then reminds us that that world, as ever, is our *own*. ◉

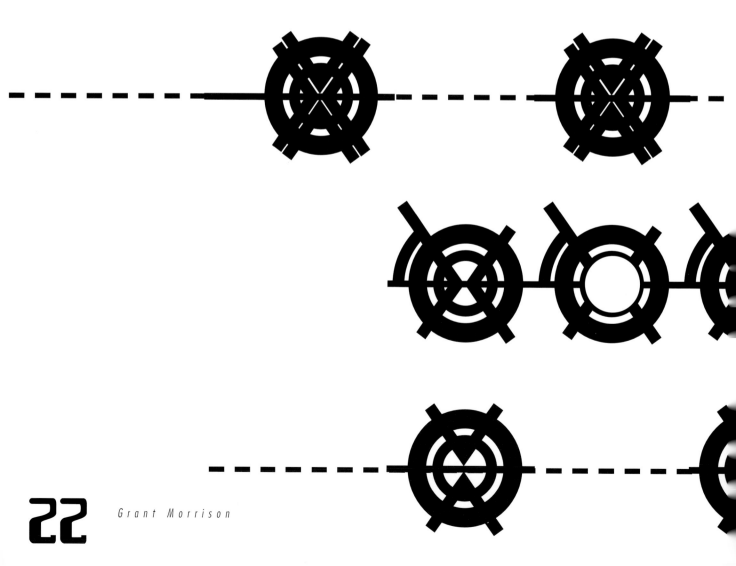

Grant Morrison

A crash. A tall stack of wooden warehouse crates falls towards the camera. (We are viewing an earlier *Avengers* episode—'The Cybernauts'—a clip of the final attack on Emma in Armstrong's warehouse.) The camera pulls back to reveal a TV screen. Emma is seen, recumbent and resplendent sitting on a sofa. She is watching the screen with a wistful smile. Suddenly, her mouth purses in annoyance as the sound fades and the picture dissolves into a distorted pattern of wavy lines. As Emma leans forward to adjust the set, John Steed magically appears on the screen, complete with brolly and bowler.

"Mrs Peel...!" Emma's eyes widen with amused astonishment. "We're needed!"

With those words, Steed and Mrs Peel were off on another bizarre adventure. Fifty-two minutes of cleverly plotted TV mayhem was in store. One hour's worth of delightful, wacky entertainment. There was nothing like it then, and it's debatable that we will ever see its like again. *The Avengers,* you see, was that rarity among television shows, a series that was destined to indelibly stamp its mark on the plinth in the Television Hall of Fame.

My involvement with the series (although I didn't know it at the time) began with the very first story, 'Hot Snow'. A lifetime couch potato, I took to this new 'thriller' series like Italians take to pasta. The Ian Hendry/Patrick Macnee partnership (in those days, Macnee took second billing) was a giant step away from the, as it was then, 'kitchen sink'-orientated TV fare. I found the stories infinitely more enjoyable than the run-of-the-mill cops-and-robbers shows of the period. It's true that the plots lacked subtlety, but the good-humoured style was already there, giving Keel and Steed the opportunity to run rings around their nearest competition.

Enter Honor Blackman as Mrs Cathy Gale, the leather-clad blonde bombshell who would change the face of television heroines forever. No wilting daisy this lady. She would just as soon toss you over her shoulder as give you a smile. Thugs ran shy of her, those that didn't regretting their mistake. Viewers (not to mention yours truly) found themselves captivated by this emancipated young woman, this ice-cool blonde with a PhD in anthropology, whose character gave the series the kick it needed to jolt it towards more spy-laden adventures. Needless to say, the series reached a new high, and *The Avengers* was but a few steps away from 'overnight success.' With the entrance of Cathy Gale, the gritty, down-to-earth thriller-style became more sophisticated, well-paced, better conceived. The thugs-versus-the-angels approach of the earlier stories was flipped slightly askew and replaced with an off-beat formula, the like of which television had never seen before. The baddies were given their come-uppance with a wink of the eye, the victims of crime treated in a more sympathetic manner. The camaraderie between Steed and Mrs Gale was to be taken with a pinch of salt: despite Steed pursuing her (with thoughts of getting her beneath the sheets), Cathy remained inviolate, preferring to ward off her partner's advances with a smile (and, perhaps, the knowledge that *one day*...). By now I was well and truly hooked.

Imagine my anxiety when I read that Honor Blackman was quitting the show. I accepted the news with mixed emotions. 'Emma is the new Avenger,' screamed the newspaper headline when introducing auburn-haired Diana Rigg, as the girl most likely to step into Cathy Gale's boots. Horror of horrors. They get rid of my favourite TV heroine, and dare to replace her with an upstart. I waited for the première of the latest series with bated breath. Who was this newcomer? Would she evoke the same feeling as her predecessor? Would her relationship with Steed be as tender and teasing? I need not have worried. Zip, and we were back into another *Avengers* season. The new girl, a five-foot-nine nymph-like beauty, was unleashed in a whirlwind of punch-ups and *haute couture*. The new series (made on film for the first time, in an attempt to break into the lucrative American market)

was an amalgam of all that was best from the previous series, and, the biggest surprise of all, actually surpassed what had gone before. True, the format was still the same: two slick crime-fighters serving out their own brand of justice against a bizarre assortment of villains, each intent on taking over Britain for their own nefarious ends. True, Steed was back, wielding his brolly in defence of the nation. But Emma. Here was a lady who had all the trappings of a strong, sexy, independent woman. A flippant approach when dealing with the plug-uglies (but could come on strong when the occasion called for fisticuffs), and an inborn sense of fair play. Like Cathy Gale before her, Emma handled her assailants with nonchalant ease. Flip, and another male bit the dust. Splat, and her attacker would spin over backwards, the breath knocked out of his lungs by Emma's perfectly-timed karate chop. At the beginning I viewed her as cautiously as a child learning to swim. She, too, was in at the deep end and had something to prove. She did so, in her own inimitable way. I was, by now, a convert.

With the arrival of Linda Thorson as Tara King—sans judo, karate or kung fu—I expected the show to totter on the precipice and plunge downward into extinction. How on earth could I accept a heroine who wore neither black leather jerkins or man-made cat-suits, and whose only defence against the bad guys was a brick stuffed into her handbag!? Having convinced myself that the party was over, I tuned in for my first glance at the new girl. Guess what? I was pleasantly surprised. Tara was a tough cookie in her own right. (Given the fact that her predecessors were experts in the martial arts, and the new girl had to use her own devices to ward off attacks, Tara was probably tougher than the two of them combined!) Tara King was a different *Avengers* heroine: a young trainee agent who, when plucked from obscurity by Steed, is sent out into the field and is expected to prove herself. She did so, and was soon vying for my affection towards her predecessors.

But you already know this, of course. Anyone who has read any (or all) of my reference books on the subject is already aware of the affection I have for the show. My current status as the 'Avengers guru' is, I suppose, well founded (although, it must be said, is something of an albatross around my neck). Watching *The Avengers* now, three decades after they were made (which I do, regularly), leads me to confess that nothing has changed.

I still get a kick from watching the (unintentional) clangers dropped by Honor Blackman and Patrick Macnee in the videotaped series. (There's no disgrace in that. They were, after all, 'live' transmissions, recorded onto videotape—and part of its appeal lay in its devil-may-care approach to the gremlins that infected *all* live television transmissions.) Great satisfaction is gained from the slick writing abilities of the series' scriptwriters, who made the op-and-pop world of *The Avengers* such a wild, wacky wonderland. Its frills and spills, titillating attire and bonhomie, have become entrenched in television legend. I love it, without reservation.

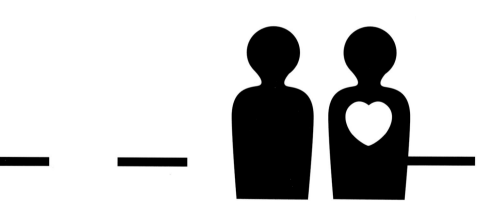

DAVID FAKRIKIAN

EVERYTHING IS PERMITTED

In the rigorously planned world of television programmes, *The Avengers* series symbolises irreverence, disrespect and originality. The apparently conformist appearance of the programme, which was without doubt one of the keys to its immense success, hides one of the most effective jokes in the history of the small screen. John Steed, the pivot of the series, is apparently the perfect British gentleman. But if one looks closer, the veneer cracks…

His cool exterior can be pushed to the limit. With three dead bodies lying in his living room, he gravely asks his visitor to "excuse the disorder". His sense of patriotism is always at attention—when he pursues a villain, one can't miss the miniature Union Jacks fixed to the bonnet of his green 1928 Bentley.

Steed's vintage means of transport are certainly not very effective for catching criminals equipped with fast, modern vehicles! When he fights, his clothes remain immaculate. He is dressed, naturally, by the most expensive tailors, only reads *The Times* and always allows women to go first.

To make this caricature credible, the producers, scriptwriters and directors had to create an original world around him, functioning according to his criteria, where logic has very little space. Thus the most unbelievable and extravagant events occur: in one episode, a scientist drowns in the rain; in another, a man sneezes so hard that he dies; in a third, a Lord, arriving at the scene of a murder and asking who has been killed, receives the response "You" from a detective who proceeds to kill him…and his body falls perfectly into the chalked silhouette on the ground. A veritable theatre of the absurd takes shape before our astonished eyes. A cartoon with real characters! To reinforce the surreal look, all walk-on parts unnecessary to the action are excluded, and one comes across dead bodies by the dozen without ever seeing the smallest drop of blood. Besides that, the death scenes are as absurd as they could be: a man working at his desk says good morning to his colleague quite pleasantly, shoots him, and returns peacefully to his occupation.

The idea of contrast, the bending of rules and codes, of foundation and form, is constant. In the course of enquiries by Steed and his charming and lethal partners, one encounters so many eccentric characters, often disturbingly normal in appearance, that it seems as if the doors of all the asylums in England have been flung open. A mountaineer descends by rope from his window to reach the ground floor. A breeder of cats laps up the milk in his glass. A comic artist thinks he is a superhero and administers his justice disguised as a bird…

More megalomaniacal and twisted than the villains pursued by James Bond, Steed's adversaries have an evil ingenuity unsurpassed before or since. Some transform their toy shops with thermonuclear bombs, others want to shoot and release a 35mm film featuring the death of their worst enemy. All are impeccably dressed, and take a perverse pleasure in tying up the heroines while reciting the most whimsical dialogue explaining their desire for world domination by means of their mad inventions.

Steed's female partners, a key element in the series' charm, represented in the sixties (and still today) a radical and welcome change: rather than being aided, seduced and consumed by the hero, they are independent women, experts in combat, and often even more intelligent than their male counterparts. The first, Cathy Gale, laced into her black leather outfit and high boots, threw her adversaries over her shoulder. The second, Emma Peel, seems to have been created specifically for the series' unique world, so perfectly does her physique lend itself to it. Wearing the most fashionable clothes, driving the most modern cars, she represents the future, whereas Steed is a stickler for the values and traditions of the past. And thus the alchemy works.

The settings of each episode use the most audacious and unpredictable *mise en scène.* The most unusual objects fill the screen. Strange décors and music combine to create a soft, sensual ambience which has no equivalent in any other television series. The dialogue is intelligent and cutting, with a bite and an off-handedness which are the hallmark of *The Avengers.* "I keep thinking I'm a horse," says Steed to a psychiatrist whom he is supposed to consult, "must be something to do with my name. It distresses my friends terribly. I'm given to cantering across the quiet room of my club!" "Sit down," replies the psychiatrist, "and relax. Smoke if you like." "No thanks," retorts Steed, "I'm a healthy horse!"

The scripts parody an incredible amount of filmed and televised works, to the point that it is difficult, unless one shares the same cultural references as the scriptwriter, to discern all of the sources.

Each episode catches the viewer unawares. Unlike ordinary series, the genre can change from one week to the next. A story of espionage follows a science fiction episode, followed by a military story, which could itself be succeeded by a story in the horror tradition, straight out of a Hammer film. As long as the common denominator of *The Avengers'* style is respected, everything is permitted!

By subverting the narrative codes of the thriller, by bending the rules of censorship to its advantage, *The Avengers* asserts itself as a series apart, beyond classification. An inexplicable anomaly that survives to this day is that certain people, as one of its first producers, John Bryce, says, "still insist on taking it seriously."

One cannot imagine of a better compliment: it required an unbelievable convergence of talents to create a television series that is still, more than thirty years later, able to make its viewers believe that the moon is made of green cheese.

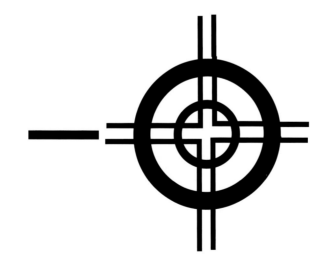

David Fakrikian

CHRISTOPHE CASA-ZZA

EMMA, TARA, THE OTHERS AND ME

The Avengers undoubtedly had an important influence on the burgeoning of my telephile career. A delicate eight-year-old, I was completely susceptible to the influence of an adult world full of lies, degradation and other felonies. It had quite an impact when I first saw the black and white image of Emma Peel on the second channel of my goggle box, only one year before the student protest which shook France.

At the height of the era of bell bottoms and 'flower power' shirts from Frisco, Mrs Peel shot through my cathode-ray tube, gun in hand, moulded into a black leather suit, to torment the saint that I was. It seemed that women, contrary to what my father had tried to instil in me, were not all to be labelled as the weaker sex. Revolt raged in homes as the feminist movement moved beyond its infancy. I have never sought to determine if my devotion to that TV creation was due to her mistress-in-black-leather image, or whether I had succumbed to the only woman whom I thought capable of standing up to my august father.

Diana Rigg (for that was her name) was a tall, slim girl with auburn hair and big, dark, mischievous eyes (features I only discovered later, when my parents finally decided to get rid of our old black and white telly in order to enjoy the realism of colour). She moved with feline grace, and her futuristic style, contrasting with the 'old England' look of her companion John Steed, gave her silhouette a sex appeal which I responded to at once.

Gradually I became a TV addict. Faithfully watching each episode, defying my parents' wrath, I waited for the connection with the network and the appearance of the test card, the signal for a fresh meeting. My studies suffered:

mathematics was too pragmatic for my taste, but there was room in my heart for literature, which I found more romantic. Like Emma, I learned martial arts—when judo wasn't enough any more, I started kung fu. My through-the-screen affair lasted for years, until the day I saw the episode called 'The Forget-Me-Knot' in which she left me for her husband Peter Peel. She gave up her role alongside Steed to Tara King, played by a Canadian barely twenty years old and discovered by John Huston, who answered to the name of Linda Thorson.

Tara King had beautiful curves and a generous form: she was incredibly feminine and sexy. She had a different look. After the leather came the miniskirt and thigh boots, which did not fail to please. Only one thing upset me—she seemed closer to John Steed than Emma ever was. I pushed aside that detail, thinking times were changing and morals were evolving, and I became immersed once more in my daily routine and its televisual habits, making my life a pleasant erotomaniac nightmare.

First there had been Mrs Gale of course, but I had never seen her, as French TV was slow to catch up with that of our Anglo-Saxon friends.

Then came Emma Peel and Tara King…

I prefer to keep silent on the Purdey period, which saw my television set gradually gather dust. I had succumbed, like many of my contemporaries, to the appeal of the darkened halls, to the heroines on the giant screen, to their cries in Dolby stereo…and the small screen, with its mediocre programmes, no longer succeeded in satisfying my telephile's appetite.

FRANCOIS RIVIERE
A CONJURATION OF ELEGANCE

I've never been able to prevent myself from feeling that very tight bonds, albeit invisible ones, linked (and continue to link with an unequalled emotive power) two of my strongest fascinations as an adolescent in the sixties: The Beatles and *The Avengers*.

The exploits of The Fab Four were at first presented to me in the shape of fixed images—magazine illustrations and, of course, the covers of their singles and LPs. Moving between a strict, religious boarding school and a family who considered television to be the devil's instrument, it was not until much later in England that I saw the first footage of my idols actually moving.

It was the beginning of the psychedelic hippy period, a somewhat sad affair in France, but an altogether more sumptuous experience in England, with Carnaby Street and the flower children who moved slowly and delightfully through a cloud of smoke, which had a radically different effect on me to the incense of Sunday vespers! Two steps away, in Soho—my nirvana—behind the windows of the production houses of Wardour Street, images were lined up from the fantastic nightmare known as Hammer Films. Peter Cushing and Christopher Lee, under the authoritative direction of Terence Fisher, held out a 'helping hand' to me. Trying to make up for the lost years of slapdash secondary education, I began my non-stop viewing in a smoke-filled cinema near Victoria Station. First were the American horror classics (*House of Frankenstein, Son of Dracula,* etc). Then came Jimmy Sangster (*Jack the Ripper, Hysteria, The Nanny*), the first English screenwriter who specialised in horror to inspire me. Then I discovered Michael Reeves and my fascination peaked. Nose stuck to the famous windows of Wardour Street, I devoured the Hammer Films, then the Amicus ones, even before their release, unable to resist the sulphurous and impure appeal of those Technicolor visions. I liked the settings, but above all, I was captivated by the extraordinarily suggestive and symbolic costumes of those creatures of

dreams, creatures I naturally associated with my beloved Beatles, the Beatles of 'I am the Walrus' and 'Hey Jude'.

Naively, perhaps, I was falling into the dandified trap the films set for me. The astute mix of arrogant eighteenth century fantasy and the elegance of the Victorian period suggested, by its Britishness alone, very troubling feelings—frightening too. Small British production houses brought back to our perverted aestheticism what Hollywood, with a certain clumsiness, had sculpted in sporadically delectable bad taste despite enormous means. "All art is both surface and symbol," said Oscar Wilde.

The calamity was that I had to wait for years and years before being in a position to admire the masterpieces of black magic conjured by eminent directors like Fisher, Ward Baker, Sasdy, Sharp or the fabulous Michael Reeves (who was already dead by then—in the most mysterious way, too). In the meantime, however, a black and white television set had appeared in my parents' living room, and I had made an astonishing discovery. An English series entitled *Chapeau melon et bottes de cuir* ('Bowler Hat and Leather Boots'—at the time I didn't know the original title) was able to transmit as far as the south-west of France a programme which amazed me as much as the fetish films I had glimpsed (or imagined) in the course of those all too brief holidays in London. On the small screen, the lively characters, elegantly dressed, were breaking the unbearable torpor, not to say the rigor mortis, of French productions, with a stream of boldly drawn episodes, designed like real films, full of winks and nods at my favourite literary and cinematic worlds.

What appears to me, with hindsight, to be the major quality of a series I wouldn't have been at all surprised to see Paul McCartney and his friends turn up in (watch *A Hard Day's Night* to see what I mean) remains the audacity of its creators in making it the embodiment of the spirit of the time, in a youthful, aesthetic and culturally coherent way.

But perhaps there is nothing ultimately surprising in a fictional tradition that has never been suppressed in England, and about which French people generally understand nothing.

I soon noticed in the programme's credits the name of Brian Clemens, creator and scriptwriter. I associated him, to his credit, with his contemporaries Sangster, Elder and Hinds (but weren't they one and the same person?) and Subotsky, as well as the novelist John Burke, author of Hammer's *Horror Film Omnibus,* kept like a Bible on my night table. These nightmare-makers already figured, invisibly and hauntingly, alongside my idols from the collection "Angoisse", Marc Agapit and Kurt Steiner. And Clemens, capable of mixing in an audacious and precise way the most unbridled themes and a parade of spy stories, fully deserved my admiration.

The inspired protagonists of that secret service saraband, John Steed and Emma Peel (evocative names both sharp and velvety at the same time), were driving me mad! Diana Rigg, rumoured to be a consummate Shakespearean actress, featured in my wildest dreams as my ideal partner in romances set to the music of Lennon and McCartney. She passed smoothly from a setting curiously close to that of a Hammer thriller into a vision of footage accompanying a Beatles song. Then the tall silhouette of Christopher Lee loomed, guest-starring in an *Avengers* episode, and my imagination set off once again in another direction.

The wardrobe of my dream partners, as inspired as the scripts of Brian Clemens (I almost wrote Brian Epstein!), co-ordinated with the stable of luxurious cars (Bentley, Jaguar, M.G.), accommodating Steed and Mrs Peel's love of speed and providing their adventures with a touch of ostentation. McGoohan and 007, in the same period, shared an immoderate taste for sophisticated sports cars, a sumptuous and respectable drug for those fleeing the appalling slowness of life in the grip of middle-class prosperity.

Sharing a clever, daring, adventurous alchemy, Steed and Mrs Peel also represented the distinct worlds which made up their universe. Steed: a confirmed gentleman's club man, the dandy secret agent with a bowler, was the friend of characters played by Peter Cushing or Michael Gough in the films shot at Bray studios. It was Steed, lover of the refined leather and precious wood on the interiors of the limousines he drove (rather than in his library!), who assumed the secular tradition. Mrs Peel, authentic upper class sixties pin-up, preferred the E-type Jaguar and pretended to be a frivolous Twiggy peer, but was very attached to the ancestral values of her country all the same. What undetectably links our two Avengers, beneath the heavy unselfconsciousness of dandyism, is the firm conviction that they have to serve an ideal, one which was already that of their 'big brother', *The Thirty Nine Steps'* Richard Hannay.

As a frequenter of the Jermyn Street shops and Grosvenor Square clubs, John Steed never lost control in the face of danger; not only the threat of communism, for instance, but of the ill-used education which seems to characterise many of his opponents. The quality of the cloth and the excellence of the cut of his suits, the very shape of his tie knots—the tendency for half-Windsors—reveal, more tellingly than a long conversation beneath the ceilings of the Savage Club, his membership of the clan of heroes in the grand 'conservative' action novel. In that clan we can find the characters of P.G. Wodehouse (themselves heirs to a whole lineage of 'boys' heroes' from the end of the nineteenth century); Hannay and Leithen, creations of John Buchan; Anthony Morton's Baron and Leslie Charteris' Saint and, of course, Ian Fleming's Bond.

Even if, unlike James Bond perhaps, Steed plays to the more 'human' line, as typified by Gilbert and Sullivan's theatricals earlier in the century, Steed has fun, and amuses us with his wit, and his flirtations with women and danger. In short, he defuses situations, allowing the atmosphere to develop over the course of an episode, while his partners take care of the main confrontations of the plot. He looks after the mystery, with that pleasant insolence of the *Boys' Own* heroes he no doubt admired at Eton.

Steed is a man of ostentatious wit and verbal swordsmanship, a Scarlet Pimpernel epitomising, in his tailcoat, shining bowler and fresh butter-coloured gloves, the ideal representation of the lover of justice in modern times—times perhaps too modern in his eyes. Steed's indoor jackets, hunting or sporting suits, hats and canes, are the dress of a gentleman spy who is terribly nostalgic and tender, in the same way as the melodies Lennon and McCartney recorded in the Abbey Road studios are.

From the confrontational nature of this television phenomenon and a certain number of other English and American creations, my amazement grew into a recurrent pleasure. Almost Proustian, my desire to see *The Avengers* again and again remains intact. Reliving the disorder of its 'period', seeing Steed's progressive ageing and the addition of more sporty partners, almost Thatcherite in their militancy, but always sympathetic, didn't get the better of my fascination for the 'Bowler Hat and Leather Boots' myth. And, with the passing years, it seems to me increasingly to be the case that the chemically pure Anglomania distilled by the adventures of those elegant characters has in a way been fetishised, giving a ring of truth (subtle, for once) to the French title of their exploits.

the EPISODES:

"FOR ME, JOHN STEED WAS MORE THAN A ROLE, HE WAS AN EXTENSION OF MYSELF...
ALL MY ENTHUSIASM, MY IMAGINATION, MY SENSE OF HUMOUR, MY TALENT, WAS
PLACED IN THE BALANCE. I ENJOYED MYSELF AS NEVER BEFORE..."

PATRICK MACNEE

The Avengers was one of the most popular series of the 1960s, and it comes as no surprise that the original run clocked up an incredible 161 episodes, with twenty-six more *New Avengers* stories appearing in the following decade. Allowed to experiment and push back the frontiers of television, the programme's format constantly developed to take advantage of gradually expanding budgets.

By 1966, the involvement of an American television network allowed the series to move from videotape to film, then from black and white to colour, thanks to the massive bounty such a sale can deliver. The show gained the distinction of being the first British programme to be given a primetime network screening across the Atlantic.

The Avengers also became a major player in the battle of the sexes. When Ian Hendry's character Dr Keel, Steed's first partner, made way for a succession of female foils, actresses were at last dealt a winning hand by TV writers, directors and producers. These women were strong, independent and in control. This leap forward in equality was made acceptable at the time because it blended

seamlessly into a format that took escapism to new heights, with its fiendish villains and outlandish plots overseen by an extremely conscientious production team.

SEASON ONE
STEED GETS THE JOB DONE
KEEL BATTLES WITH HIS ETHICS

Thanks to his performance as Dr Brent in the 1960 ABC TV series *Police Surgeon,* Ian Hendry was already a bankable TV commodity. Although *Police Surgeon* hadn't quite set the rating figures alight, it had been extremely engaging and had many ardent fans writing letters of approval. The decision was taken to rework the format, and give the public something different from the standard 'cops and robbers' fare—something a little more light-hearted. Sydney Newman (who was also in at the start of another British television institution, *Doctor Who*) collaborated with *Police Surgeon* co-producer Leonard White to revamp the series. As a result, Dr Brent metamorphosed into Dr David Keel, with his own private practice and no direct links to the police. To act as a balance to Keel's compassion they brought in a dynamic character prepared to get the job done by any means necessary. His name was John Steed.

In the first episode, 'Hot Snow', Keel's fiancée Peggy is murdered. The duo's determination to right this wrong and seek justice provided the impetus behind both their mission and the show's title. Peggy's death must be avenged, and they soon become involved with a gang of drug smugglers, led by the evil Ronnie Vance…

During that first season, the scripts 'Brought to Book' and 'One for the Mortuary' came from the imagination of a young writer called Brian Clemens. He would play an important part in the evolution of the series.

In the beginning, the plots were fairly conventional. Our anti-heroes dealt with racketeers ('Brought to Book', 'The Frighteners', 'Toy Trap'), smugglers and thieves ('Diamond Cut Diamond', 'Double Danger'), counterfeiters ('Square Root of Evil') and several thrilling cases of espionage.

These spy stories were very popular, mainly because of the political climate at the time. The Burgess/Maclean case was fresh in everyone's minds, and there was a lingering distrust of Eastern bloc governments. Episodes such as 'Girl on the Trapeze', 'Tunnel of Fear', 'One for the Mortuary' and 'Death on the Slipway' played on such popular fears. The Avengers also became responsible for diffusing potential political flashpoint situations when foreign dignitaries visited British shores. Stories such as 'Crescent Moon', 'Yellow Needle' and 'Kill the King' demonstrated the thoroughly British preoccupation with maintaining the status quo in overseas countries. Dr Keel even travelled to Mexico in 'The Far-Distant Dead' to help keep the peace.

We were also introduced to Steed's boss. Known only as One-Ten, and played by Douglas Muir, he appeared in 'Diamond Cut Diamond', 'The Deadly Air', 'The Springers', 'The Tunnel of Fear' and 'Death on the Slipway', also cropping up in five season two episodes. He was a precursor of

Mother, who would be introduced in the Tara King season. Over the course of the first two years, we also met One-Six (Michael Gover), One-Seven (Frederick Farley), One-Twelve (Arthur Hewlett) and One-Fifteen (Eric Dodson).

There were already signs that the production team were keen to veer into the fantastic. 'Please Don't Feed the Animals' involved highly trained monkeys, while 'The Radioactive Man' and 'Dragonsfield' were science fiction in all but name. Suspended animation was used as a central theme for 'Dead of Winter', in which Nazis, another source of contemporary paranoia, planned to re-establish the Third Reich.

SEASON TWO
STEED ESCORTS A LADY
CATHY GAINS A FOLLOWING

A strike by Equity, the actor's union, prevented another thirteen episodes from being added to the first season. Several months passed before the issue was resolved, and by that time Ian Hendry had decided to move on to feature film projects. Deprived of one of their leads, but having already decided that a female co-star was something their audience would appreciate, the producers needed to fill the gap while they found the right woman for the part. In came Dr Martin King (Jon Rollason), another man of medicine, to keep the production wheels turning. Plans to introduce a second associate, night-club singer Venus Smith (Julie Stevens), were shelved until they had their new star lined up.

Enter Catherine Gale, played by Honor Blackman. By the time she was ready to join the cast, Steed had been repositioned as the main attraction following a positive reaction from the viewing public. However, if Steed represented a type of character new to a television audience, then Cathy proved even more of a departure. An expert at judo, she fought her way out of trouble and could certainly look after herself.

The episode themes were also becoming a little more out of the ordinary. While our heroes still had to deal with hired hitmen, drug smugglers and arms dealers ('The Removal Men', 'Death on the Rocks', 'Bullseye'), a fair share of traitors and double agents ('The Sell-Out', 'School for Traitors', 'Box of Tricks', 'Traitor in Zebra'), the Mafia ('Conspiracy of Silence') and the inevitable protection of a foreign dignitary ('The Decapod'), there were also unmistakable signs of what was to come.

'The White Dwarf' was reminiscent of a Tintin adventure, as Cathy and Steed investigated the possible collision of a star with the earth, and the occult featured heavily in the storyline for 'Warlock'. 'Immortal Clay' saw the first of a series of incredible scientific discoveries—in this case an unbreakable ceramic material.

The second season managed to establish a continuity that would sustain the show further down the line; the villains in the episode 'Intercrime' eventually reappeared in the Tara King story 'Homicide and Old Lace', and the episode 'Death of a Great Dane' was later revamped as the Emma Peel story 'The £50,000 Breakfast'.

SEASON THREE
STEED INVESTIGATES THE FANTASTIC
CATHY MAKES A FASHION STATEMENT

Finally, Mrs Gale became Steed's one and only partner. Petty criminals were gradually phased out as the evil super genius took centre stage, fine-tuning the format that would be followed throughout the Emma Peel era and beyond.

Duality began to emerge as a recurring theme, used as the main plot device in 'The Man with Two Shadows', in which Steed and Cathy have a new boss called Charles, played by Paul Whitsun-Jones. The shadow of the nuclear menace loomed large in 'November Five', and 'The Grandeur That Was Rome' addressed the issue of bacteriological warfare, with a madman about to release a bubonic plague to further his own ends. Our heroes were now facing the sort of criminals you would expect to see in a James Bond film rather than an ordinary spy series.

Brian Clemens wrote several season three episodes—'Don't Look Behind You', when Cathy finds herself the target of revenge; 'Brief for Murder', in which it looks like Steed has murdered Mrs Gale; 'Dressed to Kill', about a New Year's Eve party aboard a train, where someone is

killing off fellow revellers; 'The Charmers', where a charm school is used as a cover for the training of foreign agents (later reworked as the basis of the Emma Peel episode 'The Correct Way to Kill') and 'Build a Better Mousetrap', concerning an electronic jamming device wreaking havoc in a small village.

Espionage was the main ingredient of just three stories this season—'The Secrets Broker', 'Concerto' and 'The Nutshell'—but all had an intriguing twist to them. In a similar vein, smuggling was given an unorthodox angle with the trade in donor corneas used as a cover for a diamond shipment, in 'Second Sight'.

Cathy Gale announced she was off for pastures new in the episode 'Lobster Quadrille', the Bahamas being put forward as the ideal antidote to all the death and devastation she had seen. In fact, Honor Blackman did go there, but to start filming the James Bond adventure *Goldfinger!*

SEASON FOUR
STEED IS IMMORTALISED ON FILM
EMMA IS SHOWN THE ROPES

With Honor Blackman gone, it was time for a fresh start. A new producer, Julian Wintle, was installed and he immediately put Albert Fennell in charge of production. Brian Clemens was credited as associate producer, although he did his fair share of script editing during the season.

But who should their new heroine be? Naturally, they had to stick with the leather-clad fashion made famous by

Honor Blackman, but they had to avoid simply creating a clone of Cathy Gale. The character would be trained in some form of martial arts, in order to continue the tradition of exuberant fight scenes. After initial filming with actress Elizabeth Shepherd was deemed unsuitable, she was replaced by Diana Rigg. Mrs Emma Peel had arrived.

In order to improve on the already healthy overseas sales, the new season was to be filmed rather than videotaped. To make the series worthy of such expensive treatment and to maintain its high profile, the producers moved away from its classic espionage roots into somewhat more bizarre science fiction territory.

An early example of the SF genre making its mark was 'Man-Eater of Surrey Green', a case that Professor Quatermass would have been equally at home investigating. Carnivorous plants from outer space had never had to face the Avengers before! Meanwhile, the Cybernauts, robotic henchmen of a succession of criminals intent on world domination, became regular visitors throughout the show's run, and their popularity far oustripped that of any other villain.

You could never be sure quite what would happen next in *The Avengers*. 'Death at Bargain Prices' and 'Silent Dust' involved complex plots about madmen with desperate plans to hold the world to ransom, using department stores converted into atom bombs or a fertiliser that destroyed everything it came into contact with. Nothing was ever what it seemed to be, and elaborate threats contrived by enemy agents were continually being uncovered. 'The Hour That Never Was' was set on a military base where time appeared to stand still for Steed and Emma, and in 'The Thirteenth Hole' an enemy bunker transmitting secrets to satellites was hidden on a golf course.

There were always crackpot scientists with a lot to answer for. 'A Surfeit of H_2O' featured a rain-making device, and 'Small Game for Big Hunters' centred on a new strain of tsetse fly about to cause widespread devastation. The villains often used elaborate front offices to conceal sinister goings on: 'The Murder Market' provided assassins for hire in the guise of a dating agency; 'The Masterminds' were a crooked version of MENSA, strictly for felons with a high IQ; 'How to Succeed...at Murder' featured a keep-fit class fronting for a group of militant suffragettes; 'The Danger Makers' was a club especially for those who found mortal danger thrilling, as Emma discovered while undertaking one of their suicidal entry tests.

Humour was gradually coming to the fore as an important ingredient in the series' overall mix. The Soviet threat, for example, was sent up a little in 'Two's a Crowd', which introduced us to Warren Mitchell's comic Soviet Ambassador Brodny, who reappeared in 'The See-Through Man'.

A variety of unusual locations added to the unique style of the programme. 'Room Without a View' features unfortunate kidnap victims who wake up believing they are in the foreign country of Manchuria, but are in fact still in a London hotel. 'Castle De'Ath' is believed to be haunted by a mournful bagpipe player. 'Too Many Christmas Trees', 'A Touch of Brimstone' and 'The House That Jack Built' all feature ambiguous backdrops that blur the line between fantasy and reality.

The Avengers was always happy to acknowledge the opposition. In 'The Girl from Auntie', Emma has suddenly become a glamorous blonde, a joke at the expense of *The Man from U.N.C.L.E.* In season five, 'Mission: Highly Improbable' also tipped its hat to an illustrious American competitor.

The season finished with 'Honey for the Prince', which is a hoot, featuring gigantic honey jars, harems, magic carpets and Mrs Peel doing the extremely steamy 'dance of the six veils'. This inability to count didn't stop the American networks wanting a piece of the action...

SEASON FIVE
STEED SWITCHES TO COLOUR
EMMA CHANGES OUT OF HER LEATHERS

A deal was struck with America's ABC network to secure sufficient finance to produce the show in colour. England only had monochrome at the time, and that wouldn't change for a couple of years, but the United States had already begun to make the switch. In 1966, the NBC network had vowed to go completely to colour, much to the benefit of one particular show called *Star Trek*. The producers of *The Avengers* were eager to see a good return on their previous season's outlay (changing to film stock from videotape) and so, with the condition that the purchase of the monochrome episodes was part of the package, ABC took the bait. This provided the capital necessary for the fifth season's 'upgraded' adventures, plus a network deal guaranteeing that the entire United States would know who the Avengers were!

With such financial backing, the series was able to deliver even the most outlandish concepts. As on other contemporary shows (*Batman, Lost in Space, The Monkees*), the chance to move beyond black and white was seized with both hands, utilising an incredibly rich variety of colours—almost as if to demonstrate that the new colour TV sets were working properly! And to justify such vivid imagery, there had to be incredible stories…

In 'From Venus with Love' it looked as if we were about to be invaded from the heavens, but fortunately there was a very human explanation. 'The Fear Merchants' discovered the ability to play on people's fears and used them to manipulate their victims. The classic theme of man being able to control animals was addressed in a couple of episodes: 'The Bird Who Knew Too Much' had pigeons acting as aerial photographers, and a parrot as a secret messenger; 'The Hidden Tiger' featured domestic cats being controlled by electronic kitty collars, and included an excellent performance by comic genius Ronnie Barker as feline fan Cheshire.

In an effort to give the two leads a break, 'Who's Who' saw them swap bodies with two Soviet agents, using a dastardly machine in the hands of the enemy. Unfortunately, the double agents are not too good at imitating the mannerisms of our heroes, and it's not long before people start to suspect that something's wrong. Writer Philip Levene and director John Moxey help make the switch plausible with touches such as Steed rubbing chins with Emma and savouring cigars, while the phoney Mrs Peel dances to some funky tunes and is seen chewing gum!

Another genre altogether was tackled in 'The Superlative Seven', which took several leaves out of Agatha Christie's books. When Steed is kidnapped he discovers that he and his fellow abductees have a killer in their midst. This story saw Emma coming to Steed's rescue, subverting what had become the norm in 'The Joker' and 'The House That Jack Built'.

Somewhat out of place in the season was 'The £50,000 Breakfast', a revamp of a Cathy Gale story which didn't quite have the fabulous eccentricity found in the other episodes. 'Dead Man's Treasure', in contrast, starts out as what seems to be a 'race to the booty' caper, until the thrilling finale with Emma at the wheel of a motor racing simulator that will administer a fatal electric shock should she fail to keep on the road. 'Death's Door' had many similarities to the previous season's 'Too Many Christmas Trees', but this time the objects people think they have dreamed do actually exist, if only as mock-ups.

Guest stars of a high calibre helped to make certain stories extra special. The presence of Christopher Lee in 'Never, Never Say Die' as the mastermind behind a collection of super-strong robotic doubles who are gradually infiltrating the establishment contributed to a memorable episode.

'Mission: Highly Improbable' was the final programme filmed this season, providing a fitting end to the high jinks that had epitomised this particular run of episodes. The plot was firmly entrenched in science fiction, a tale

of miniaturising rays used as a way to smuggle military weapons and vehicles. Building a telephone three times the size of Steed must have taken a lot of effort on the part of the prop department!

SEASON SIX
STEED GAINS A MOTHER
TARA IS THROWN IN AT THE DEEP END

Although *The Avengers* had been a huge success in America, there was a feeling amongst the upper echelons of the production company's hierarchy that the stories had become a little too outlandish the previous year. It was decided that the services of Mr Clemens and Mr Fennell were no longer required. John Bryce, who had been a story editor at the very beginning of the programme's history and produced the last season and a half of Honor Blackman's run, was re-employed. However, the format had moved on in the three years he had been away from the series, and the medium of film was entirely different from the videotape system he had been used to.

Technical hitches aside, there was one big problem to be resolved right away. Once again, *The Avengers* had lost its

leading lady to James Bond. Diana Rigg moved on to star in *The Assassination Bureau,* and then marry 007 in *On Her Majesty's Secret Service,* leaving Steed without a partner for a third time. At one point it was touch and go as to whether even Patrick Macnee was going to stay with the production. Ultimately, of course, Steed gained a new protégée in the form of Agent 69, the voluptuous Tara King (Linda Thorson). It was hoped the audience would accept that the agents were both too professional and too many years apart to become romantically involved. Tara was a thoroughly modern woman, relying on her own resources and any objects that came to hand to overcome opponents.

Almost from the beginning, it was apparent that there would be problems. The first episode shot, 'Invitation to a Killing', has never been shown in its entirety (although footage was used in the later episode 'Have Guns—Will Haggle'). Two other stories, 'Invasion of the Earthmen'

and 'The Great Great Britain Crime', were deemed unsuitable for transmission in their original form as episodes of *The Avengers*. It was during the filming of 'The Curious Case of the Countless Clues' that Clemens and Fennell were re-employed to bring back the sparkle that had made the series such a success. They did just that, resulting in some of the best stories ever.

Immediately, Clemens set to work writing 'The Forget-Me-Knot', the hand-over episode showing Mrs Peel's husband returning (dressed in the same manner as Steed and played by Patrick Macnee), after being presumed dead in the Amazon jungle. In the classic farewell scene there is a hint that maybe, just maybe, Steed and Emma's relationship had been a little more than platonic. Mother (Patrick Newell), Steed's superior, was introduced in this episode, and the torch was passed to Tara King.

Paralysed in the prime of his career as an active field agent, you were never quite sure where Mother and his extremely portable office would turn up next—in the middle of a swimming pool, on top of a double-decker bus, even navigating a car through dense fog in the manner of a submarine! In several episodes he was aided by a very tall and buxom female assistant, Rhonda (Rhonda Parker), who never uttered a word. Another series regular provided another target for attempted assassinations, as Mother found out in 'Stay Tuned'. 'Homicide and Old Lace' gave Mother a couple of elderly aunts, to whom he relates the tale of how Steed and Tara stopped all Britain's art treasures being stolen at once.

Time was even taken to introduce another temporary partner for Steed, in the episode 'Killer'. Jennifer Croxton, who had already appeared in 'Invitation to a Killing', found herself re-cast to play Lady Diana Forbes-Blakeney, an agent from Special Forces assigned to help Steed foil a computer with murder as part of its program.

The plots were once again as bizarre as ever. In 'You'll Catch Your Death', people were sneezing their way to an early grave, all caused by an empty envelope. 'Whoever Shot Poor George Oblique Stroke XR40?' showed attempts to murder a computer. In 'Invasion of the Earthmen', soldiers prepared to take over outer space. 'Thingumajig', 'The Rotters', 'Have Guns—Will Haggle', 'Get-A-Way!' and 'They Keep Killing Steed' featured fiendish scientific developments that were part of megalomaniacal plots for world domination. 'The Morning After' saw Steed handcuffed to a villain he was bringing in, while the rest of London had been put to sleep by a group of thieves. Not all plots were on such a grand scale, though—Tara is kidnapped by a pair of brothers who want to learn the whereabouts of their family legacy in 'Pandora', while 'Love All' featured a book that hypnotised people into love at first sight, and 'False Witness' demonstrated that a pint of milk a day makes you into an outrageous liar.

Several episodes paid homage to other characters from fiction and history. 'Legacy of Death' (*The Maltese Falcon*), for instance, as well as 'The Curious Case of the Countless Clues' (Sherlock Holmes) and 'Fog' (Jack the Ripper), with perhaps even a nod to fellow TV export *The Prisoner* in 'Wish You Were Here'.

If all else failed, they could always go back to the Cold War. 'Split' showcased another Soviet plot to kill Steed, starring a foreign agent with the ability to transfer his mind into other people's heads. Meanwhile, 'The Interrogators' were thought to be trainers at a secret service school, but in the bar afterwards the Russians would find out what they wanted to know from their victims.

The final episode of all was 'Bizarre', and not only in name. The ultimate service a funeral director can provide is giving you an afterlife when everyone believes you to be dead, and paradise can be found beneath a graveyard. Having put this particular case to rights, Steed and Tara accidentally blast off in a space rocket. Only one of them was destined to return several years later…

THE NEW AVENGERS
STEED WOOS THE FRENCH AND CANADIANS
PURDEY'S HAIRCUT CAUSES A STIR
GAMBIT BECOMES AN ACTION MAN

A French champagne commercial featuring Patrick Macnee and Linda Thorson triggered off the return of *The Avengers* in the mid-1970s. The producer responsible was amazed that the show was no longer being made. The truth was that the final season of the original series had been scheduled against *Rowan and Martin's Laugh-In* in America, which was the country's most popular programme at that time. The duel was one of the few *The Avengers* couldn't win! ABC announced they would not be commissioning any further episodes, and without American backing there was no way the series could continue. It was the involvement of French and Canadian interested parties that brought the series back seven years later, and

their desire for 'hands-on' production meant *The New Avengers* headed off in a grittier, more realistic direction.

On the face of it, it seemed a logical progression to turn *The Avengers* from a traditional duo into a trio. The relationship could be further complicated by their interaction. Gambit was smitten with Purdey. Purdey much admired the experienced Steed. Steed liked the idea of having a protégé like Gambit. Gambit knew he could learn a lot from Steed. Steed realised Purdey was a very attractive woman. As long as everything remained platonic, things would work out. But there was always the possibility…

The series got off to a traditional start with 'The Eagle's Nest' and 'Last of the Cybernauts…?', but was dragged back to earth by such standard spy fare as 'House of Cards', 'Tale of the Big Why' and 'To Catch a Rat' (Ian Hendry returned to the series in the latter, albeit in a different role). The spirit of the original show did occasionally raise its head above the parapet, in 'The Midas Touch', 'Faces', and particularly 'Cat Amongst the Pigeons', which managed to incorporate the level of menace Hitchcock achieved in *The Birds*.

Other stories weren't without clever plot twists, however. 'Target' employed a shooting range that shot back, and 'Dirtier by the Dozen' featured a commando unit for the worst recruits in the army, while 'Gnaws' let a giant flesh-eating rat loose in the sewers!

By the time the second season went into production, there were too many factions involved in the production of *The New Avengers*. The foreign backers didn't think Purdey looked or dressed sexily enough and they wanted episodes filmed abroad rather than all in Britain, whilst money contracted for production costs was apparently not forthcoming. These backers also thought that there should be more romantic liaisons for our heroes, which brought intense objections from Patrick Macnee. It didn't help that in Britain, the ITV network decided to schedule the series at different times in different regions, rather than giving it a simultaneous nationwide transmission.

'Angels of Death' was one of the best episodes from the second season, with its ladykillers proving a truly traditional threat. 'Trap', however, has the trio teaming up with the CIA to battle a Chinese mandarin, not really in keeping with the style of the classic Rigg and Thorson series.

The final seven episodes saw the financial backers getting their way and the show moving overseas, but sadly leaving the spirit of the series behind. Three episodes were filmed in France ('The Lion and the Unicorn' and 'K is for Kill', parts one and two), and four in Canada ('Complex', 'The Gladiators', 'Forward Base' and 'Emily'). The final programme credited Hugh Marlow and Jim Handley as producers, rather than Albert Fennell and Brian Clemens. *The Avengers* swan-song was a damp squib—not a fitting curtain call for such a ground-breaking and exciting series.

44

THE AVENGERS

Filmed in black and white
With Ian Hendry, Patrick Macnee
Produced by Leonard White
Music by Johnny Dankworth
Designed by Alpho O'Reilly, Robert Fuest,
Patrick Downing, Paul Bernard, James Goddard, Dou-
glas James, Robert Macgowan, Voytek

1 HOT SNOW

Written by Ray Rigby & Patrick Brawn
Directed by Don Leaver
With Catherine Woodville, Philip Stone,
Murray Melvin

Dr David Keel, assisted by the mysterious Steed, searches for the killer of Keel's fiancée, mistakenly gunned down when a drug trafficking operation went wrong. Vance, the gang leader, proves a difficult man to entrap.

2 BROUGHT TO BOOK

Written by Brian Clemens
Directed by Peter Hammond
With Lionel Burns, Redmond Bailey,
Carol White, Neil McCarthy
And Ingrid Hafner

Still on the trail of Vance, Keel and Steed infiltrate rival gangs in order to bring him to justice. At the end of the episode, they decide to continue their crime-fighting partnership.

3 SQUARE ROOT OF EVIL

Written by Richard Harris
Directed by Don Leaver
With Michael Robbins, Alex Scott,
Delphi Lawrence, Vic Wise
And Ingrid Hafner

Steed takes the place of a counterfeiter in a gang that's planning to circulate forged banknotes. Whilst the gang leader, Hooper, is taken in by the ruse, a henchman called 'The Cardinal' sets out to prove that Steed is an imposter.

4 NIGHTMARE

Written by Terence Feely
Directed by Peter Hammond
With Helen Lindsay, Michael Logan,
Gordon Boyd, Robert Bruce
And Ingrid Hafner

Dr Keel is asked by one of his patients to seek out her missing husband, a task which lands Keel in hospital after an attempt on his life. It is up to Steed to come to his rescue.

Hot Snow

John Steed and Dr Keel (Ian Hendry)

The Episodes **45**

5 CRESCENT MOON

Written by Geoffrey Bellman & John Whitney
Directed by John Knight
With Patience Collier, Roger Delgado,
And Eric Thompson

Steed goes to the Caribbean, to investigate the kidnapping of the daughter of dictator General Mendozza, a man believed to be dead. Steed rescues the daughter, Carmelite, and Keel finds out he's treating the General!

6 GIRL ON THE TRAPEZE

Written by Dennis Spooner
Directed by Don Leaver
With Kenneth J. Warren, Nadja Regin,
Delena Kidd, Ian Gardiner
And Ingrid Hafner
(Without Patrick Macnee)

A dying girl gives a clue to her murderers after being dragged from the Thames. Dr Keel and his assistant Carol follow the clues to a touring Eastern Bloc circus, which has kidnapped a defector's daughter.

7 DIAMOND CUT DIAMOND

Written by Max Marquis
Directed by Peter Hammond
With Sandra Dorne, Hamlyn Benson,
Joy Webster, Ingrid Hafner
And Douglas Muir

Steed and Keel are trying to break a diamond smuggling ring, but the criminals have the assistance of two beautiful women, who are an obstacle that only Steed can conquer.

8 THE RADIOACTIVE MAN

Written by Fred Edge
Directed by Robert Tronson
With George Pravda, Christine Pollon
And Ingrid Hafner

Marko works as a cleaner in a medical research laboratory, and he's acquired a capsule containing radioactive material. It will kill him, and anyone else he comes into contact with, within hours if Dr Keel cannot locate him with a Geiger counter.

9 ASHES OF ROSES

Written by Peter Ling & Sheilagh Ward
Directed by Don Leaver
With Olga Lowe, Mark Eden, Peter Zander
And Ingrid Hafner

Convinced that several recent fires have been started deliberately, Steed asks Carol to investigate a hairdressing salon, unaware that he is sending her into mortal danger at the hands of arsonists.

10 HUNT THE MAN DOWN

Written by Richard Harris
Directed by Peter Hammond
With Maurice Good, Melissa Stribling,
Susan Castle and Ingrid Hafner

A convict is released from jail after doing time for robbery. When he goes to claim his booty, he is attacked by two hoods who are in league with his wife. When the same men kidnap his receptionist, it's up to Keel and Steed to bring them all to justice.

11 PLEASE DON'T FEED THE ANIMALS

Written by Dennis Spooner
Directed by Dennis Vance
With Carole Boyer, Tenniel Evans,
Harry Ross, Mark Baker
And Ingrid Hafner

Felgate, a Whitehall civil servant, has become a victim of blackmail. Steed and Keel stalk him, following him to a zoo. He passes on his latest information to his contact there, who turns out to be a monkey in the employ of the real villain— the zoo's owner!

12 DANCE WITH DEATH

Written by Peter Ling & Sheilagh Ward
Directed by Don Leaver
With Caroline Blakiston, Angela Douglas,
Dudley Sutton and Ingrid Hafner

After an assassination attempt on the owner of a dance school, Dr Keel tries to discover who is responsible. Next time, however, the dance teacher is killed and Keel is framed for her murder.

13 ONE FOR THE MORTUARY

Written by Brian Clemens
Directed by Peter Hammond
With Peter Madden, Ronald Wilson,
Dennis Edwards, Frank Gatliff
And Ingrid Hafner

Dr Keel unwittingly transports a secret medical formula for Steed, as a microdot on an invitation card. Unfortunately, he gives it away to a girl he meets on a plane, and Steed has to recover it.

14 THE SPRINGERS

Written by John Whitney & Geoffrey Bellman
Directed by Don Leaver
With David Webb, Brian Murphy,
Charles Farrell and Douglas Muir

At Steed's request, Keel goes undercover as a crook, sent to jail to find out how one particular criminal will make his escape from prison.

15 THE FRIGHTENERS

Written by Berkely Mather
Directed by Peter Hammond
With Philip Locke, Willoughby Goddard,
Stratford Johns, Doris Hare
And Ingrid Hafner

Steed and Keel are on the trail of a new band of criminals, whose speciality is protection rackets, raising money through threats of violence. A little deception makes one victim lead our heroes to the kingpin, known only as 'The Deacon'.

16 THE YELLOW NEEDLE

Written by Patrick Campbell
Directed by Don Leaver
With Andre Dakar, Eric Dodson,
Margaret Whiting
And Ingrid Hafner

Lungi is the president of Tenebra, an African country, and old friend Dr Keel meets up with him in London while he's in town negotiating the country's independence. An assassination attempt on Lungi sees Steed and Keel jump into action, but Lungi's diabetes and reliance on insulin give the killers another way to carry out their mission.

17 DEATH ON THE SLIPWAY

Written by James Mitchell
Directed by Peter Hammond
With Peter Arne, Nyree Dawn Porter,
Frank Thornton, Sean Sullivan
And Douglas Muir

Going undercover as a metallurgist, Steed infiltrates a shipyard where a nuclear submarine is being built and a fellow agent has already been killed. Steed's quarry knows him only too well, and arranges an accident for him.

18 DOUBLE DANGER

Written by Gerald Verner
Directed by Roger Jenkins
With Charles Hodgson, Robert Mill,
Peter Reynolds and Ingrid Hafner

Steed is trying to find those responsible for a recent diamond robbery, unaware that the new patient Dr Keel is treating for gunshot wounds is one of the duo he is looking for.

19 TOY TRAP

Written by Bill Strutton
Directed by Don Leaver
With Hazel Graeme, Nina Marriott,
Sally Smith, Brian Jackson

Steed and Keel find themselves on the trail of a prostitution racket, where the penalty for not co-operating is death. Their search leads them to a well-heeled department store, where several female workers have disappeared.

20 THE TUNNEL OF FEAR

Written by John Kruse
Directed by Guy Verney
With Stanley Platts, John Salew,
Murray Mayne, Douglas Muir
And Ingrid Hafner

Steed and Dr Keel investigate a fun fair, following the capture of an alleged criminal who had been hiding out there. The duo realise they have stumbled upon a drop-off point where foreign agents pick up top secret information.

Dance with Death

The Episodes **47**

21 THE FAR-DISTANT DEAD

Written by John Lucarotti
Directed by Peter Hammond
With Katherine Blake, Francis De Wolff,
Tom Adams, Reed De Rouen
(Without Patrick Macnee)

Dr Keel is off to Mexico, to help the victims of a recent cyclone. He meets a fellow doctor, Alverez Sandoval, and they realise that people are not just dying from the natural disaster—the 'cooking oil' they are using is in fact hydraulic engine oil.

22 KILL THE KING

Written by James Mitchell
Directed by Roger Jenkins
With Burt Kwouk, Patrick Allen,
Lisa Peake, Peter Barkworth
And Ingrid Hafner

Steed is called in to protect the leader of an Arab state, in London to negotiate an important oil contract. Unbeknownst to him, the threat is in the hotel across the road, in the form of a sniper.

23 DEAD OF WINTER

Written by Eric Paice
Directed by Don Leaver
With Carl Duering, Michael Sarne,
David Hart, John Woodvine
And Ingrid Hafner

After the discovery of a Nazi war criminal frozen in the cargo hold of a freighter, Steed and Keel find themselves trying to stop the formation of a new political party keen to found the Fourth Reich.

24 THE DEADLY AIR

Written by Lester Powell
Directed by John Knight
With Ann Bell, Allan Cuthbertson,
Geoffrey Bayldon, Richard Butler,
Ingrid Hafner and Douglas Muir

At a bacteriological research establishment, humans are dying from a new vaccine, even though lab monkeys survive. Steed and Keel volunteer as the next guinea pigs, only to be nearly killed by an airborne virus. The partners believe someone is trying to discredit the vaccine for their own gain.

John Steed with Dr Keel

25 A CHANGE OF BAIT

Written by Lewis Davidson
Directed by Don Leaver
With Victor Platt, John Bailey,
Robert Desmond, Gary Hope
And Ingrid Hafner

Steed and Keel are asked to investigate an insurance fraud that's based at the local docks. Unusually, the centre of attention is a cargo of bananas!

26 DRAGONSFIELD

Written by Terence Feely
Directed by Peter Hammond
With Alfred Burke, Barbara Shelley,
Ronald Leigh-Hunt, Eric Dodson

Steed is on his own for this mission, investigating a scientific research centre manufacturing a new radioactive shield to be used in the space programme. Unfortunately, there's double-crossing all around...

⟫⟫⟫ SECOND SEASON — 1962/1963

Filmed in black and white
With Patrick Macnee
Produced by Leonard White, John Bryce
Music by Johnny Dankworth
Designed by Terry Green, Paul Bernard, Robert Macgowan, Patrick Downing, Philip Harrison, James Goddard, Anne Spavin, Robert Fuest, Richard Harrison, Douglas James, Maurice Pelling, Stephen Doncaster
Story Editors: John Bryce, Richard Bates

27 MR TEDDY BEAR

Written by Martin Woodhouse
Directed by Richmond Harding
Starring Honor Blackman
With Tim Brinton, Bernard Goldman,
Michael Robbins
And Douglas Muir

Steed and Cathy investigate a series of ingenious murders, carried out by an assassin known only as 'Mr Teddy Bear'. One-Ten, meanwhile, orders Cathy to hire the assassin to kill Steed as part of a trap.

28 PROPELLANT 23

Written by Jon Manchip White
Directed by Jonathan Alwyn
Starring Honor Blackman
With Justine Lord, Catherine Woodville,
Geoffrey Palmer

Steed and Cathy must recover a container of a new rocket fuel, after it goes missing at an airport.

John Steed and Cathy Gale (Honor Blackman)

Bullseye

29 THE DECAPOD

Written by Eric Paice
Directed by Don Leaver
Starring Julie Stevens
With Philip Madoc, Paul Stassino,
Pamela Conway, Wolfe Morris

Steed and Venus Smith are given the mission of protecting a foreign diplomat on a visit to London. The diplomat's bodyguard is killed, and all the evidence points to a wrestler known as 'The Decapod'.

30 BULLSEYE

Written by Eric Paice
Directed by Peter Hammond
Starring Honor Blackman
With Mitzi Rogers, Judy Parfitt,
John Frawley, Bernard Kay

Cathy Gale joins the board of directors of a weapons manufacturing company believed to be selling arms illegally to unstable third world countries.

31 MISSION TO MONTREAL

Written by Lester Powell
Directed by Don Leaver
Starring Jon Rollason
With Patricia English, Mark Eden,
Gerald Sim, Alan Curtis

Steed and Dr King help protect a famous actress from spies hunting for a microfilm containing details of America's early warning defence system.

32 THE REMOVAL MEN

Written by Roger Marshall & Jeremy Scott
Directed by Don Leaver
Starring Julie Stevens
With Reed De Rouen, Edina Ronay,
Edwin Richfield, Donald Tandy
And Douglas Muir

Steed and Venus Smith go undercover to save a film actress from assassination by a new crime organisation calling themselves 'The Removal Men'.

33 THE MAURITIUS PENNY

Written by Malcolm Hulke & Terrance Dicks
Directed by Richmond Harding
Starring Honor Blackman
With Alfred Burke, Richard Vernon,
David Langton, Alan Rolfe

A very rare stamp is being sold at a ridiculously low price through a conventional stamp catalogue. His suspicions raised, Steed discovers the stamps are a way for secret codes to be passed from one part of a mysterious organisation to another. He and Cathy must stop them from achieving their goal: to take over the country by force, and establish a fascist state they describe as 'New Rule'.

34 DEATH OF A GREAT DANE

Written by Roger Marshall & Jeremy Scott
Directed by Peter Hammond

The Mauritius Penny

Starring Honor Blackman
With Leslie French, Billy Milton,
Herbert Nelson

Steed and Cathy are in pursuit of diamond smugglers, and the trail leads to a pet's grave—which contains the owner rather than the dog itself. (The Diana Rigg episode 'The £50,000 Breakfast' is a revamp of this story.)

35 THE SELL-OUT

Written by Anthony Terpiloff & Brandon Brady
Directed by Don Leaver
Starring Jon Rollason
With Carleton Hobbs, Frank Gatliff,
Anthony Blackshaw
And Arthur Hewlett

A United Nations representative is the victim of an assassination attempt. Dr King assists Steed, knowing that there has to be a traitor in One-Twelve's department. All the clues point to Harvey, the security chief, who turns the tables and implicates Steed as a traitor!

36 DEATH ON THE ROCKS

Written by Eric Paice
Directed by Jonathan Alwyn
Starring Honor Blackman
With Annette Kerr, Hamilton Dyce,
Richard Clarke, Gerald Cross

Steed and Cathy pose as husband and wife to infiltrate another diamond smuggling ring, which is using rock salt containers as its method of getting the jewels into the country.

37 TRAITOR IN ZEBRA

Written by John Gilbert
Directed by Richmond Harding
Starring Honor Blackman
With Noel Coleman, William Gaunt,
Michael Browning, Ian Shand

Steed and Cathy investigate a naval base in order to establish the identity of a traitor who is leaking secret documents to the enemy.

38 THE BIG THINKER

Written by Martin Woodhouse
Directed by Kim Mills
Starring Honor Blackman
With David Garth, Walter Hudd,
Tenniel Evans, Penelope Lee

Plato is the most sophisticated computer ever built, but someone's trying to sabotage it. Dr Clemens(!) finds the identity of the villain and is killed, but not before he reveals the secret to Plato.

39 DEATH DISPATCH

Written by Leonard Fincham
Directed by Jonathan Alwyn
Starring Honor Blackman
With Gerald Harper, Richard Warner,
Alan Mason And Douglas Muir

The Mauritius Penny

A courier is assassinated, but the papers he was carrying are hidden before his death. Steed is charged with finding the bag, which he does successfully, although there seems to be nothing of importance in it. When he takes over the role of courier, an attempt is made on his life.

40 DEAD ON COURSE

Written by Eric Paice
Directed by Richmond Harding
Starring Jon Rollason
With Trevor Reid, Peggy Marshall,
Elisabeth Murray, Bruce Boa

Steed and Dr King investigate an aircrash. Behind the tragedy is a fraudulent convent and a ruthless Mother Superior.

41 INTERCRIME

Written by Terrance Dicks & Malcolm Hulke
Directed by Jonathan Alwyn
Starring Honor Blackman
With Alan Browning, Kenneth J. Warren,
Donald Webster

Cathy takes the place of assassin Hilda Stern in an international crime syndicate, but the real Hilda Stern has escaped custody...

42 IMMORTAL CLAY

Written by James Mitchell
Directed by Richmond Harding
Starring Honor Blackman
With Gary Watson, Paul Eddington,
James Bree, Bert Palmer
And Douglas Muir

Steed and Cathy are sent by One-Ten to investigate the claims of Allan Marling, who reckons he has invented an indestructible ceramic material.

Box of Tricks

43 BOX OF TRICKS

Written by Peter Ling & Edward Rhodes
Directed by Kim Mills
Starring Julie Stevens
With Ian Curry, Maurice Hedley,
Jacqueline Jones

NATO secrets are being passed to the enemy, and Steed believes a girl's death may be linked to that of a magician's female assistant at the club where Venus Smith works.

44 WARLOCK

Written by Doreen Montgomery
Directed by Peter Hammond
Starring Honor Blackman
With Peter Arne, John Hollis, Pat Spencer,
Philip Mosca and Douglas Muir

A scientist who has manufactured a new type of fuel is found mysteriously comatose. Steed begins to be convinced that black magic is involved and investigates a group who worship the occult...

Warlock

45 THE GOLDEN EGGS

Written by Martin Woodhouse
Directed by Peter Hammond
Starring Honor Blackman
With Donald Eccles, Peter Arne,
Gordon Whiting, Louise Haslar

Steed and Cathy are out to rescue a couple of crooks who have stolen two golden eggs, for one of them contains a deadly virus...

46 SCHOOL FOR TRAITORS

Written by James Mitchell
Directed by Jonathan Alwyn
Starring Julie Stevens
With Melissa Stribling, John Standing,
Reginald Marsh

Steed and Venus Smith look into the apparent suicide of a lecturer, and uncover a spy circle at the highest level of the university.

47 THE WHITE DWARF

Written by Malcolm Hulke
Directed by Richmond Harding
Starring Honor Blackman
With Philip Latham, Peter Copley,
Vivienne Drummond, Paul Anil

An astronomer is killed in his observatory, and his notes reveal that he had found a star on a collision course with Earth.

48 MAN IN THE MIRROR

Written by Geoffrey Orme & Anthony Terpiloff
Directed by Kim Mills
Starring Julie Stevens
With Ray Barrett, Julian Somers,
Daphne Anderson

Steed and Venus Smith investigate the suicide of a cypher clerk, whom Venus had just taken a picture of in a hall of mirrors at a circus.

49 CONSPIRACY OF SILENCE

Written by Roger Marshall
Directed by Peter Hammond
Starring Honor Blackman
With Alec Mango, Sandra Dorne,
Roy Purcell, John Church

Steed and Cathy help an assassin disguised as a circus clown, who is on the run from the Mafia. Unfortunately, the target of his latest contract is Steed!

50 A CHORUS OF FROGS

Written by Martin Woodhouse
Directed by Raymond Menmuir
Starring Julie Stevens
With Eric Pohlmann, John Carson,
Frank Gatliff

Steed is off to Greece on holiday, but finds himself teaming up with Venus to investigate the death of a deep-sea diver. Their hunt leads them to a millionaire's yacht.

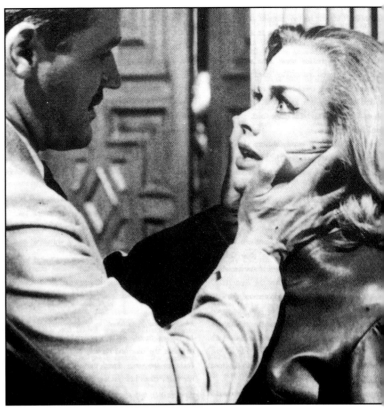

Warlock

51 SIX HANDS ACROSS A TABLE

Written by Reed R. de Rouen
Directed by Richmond Harding
Starring Honor Blackman
With Guy Doleman, Edward De Souza,
Philip Madoc

Cathy is invited to a party for an old friend. Expecting a weekend of peace and quiet, Steed soon becomes involved when an attempt is made on her life.

52 KILLERWHALE

Written by John Lucarotti
Directed by Kim Mills
Starring Honor Blackman
With Patrick Magee, Morris Perry,
Kenneth Farrington

Steed and Cathy are introduced to a young boxer, who leads them into breaking up a smuggling operation based at a local gymnasium.

))))))) THIRD SEASON — 1963/1964

Filmed in black and white
With Patrick Macnee, Honor Blackman
Produced by John Bryce
Music by Johnny Dankworth
Designed by James Goddard, David Marshall,
Paul Bernard, Philip Harrison, Douglas James,
Robert Macgowan, Terry Green, Anne Spavin,
Richard Harrison
Story Editor: Richard Bates

53 BRIEF FOR MURDER

Written by Brian Clemens
Directed by Peter Hammond
With Alec Ross, Fred Ferris,
John Laurie, Helen Lindsay

Steed and Cathy are out to nail two lawyer brothers. They are sure the legal eagles are bad news when a man accused of treason walks away from a charge despite all the evidence. The duo hatch a plot which makes it look like Steed has murdered Cathy, and the brothers arrange for him to be acquitted. Meanwhile, Cathy poses as a businesswoman who wants her two partners framed for fraud, proving one case too many for the bent barristers.

54 THE UNDERTAKERS

Written by Malcolm Hulke
Directed by Bill Bain
With Howard Goorney, Patrick Holt,
Lee Patterson, Mandy Miller

A retirement home for millionaires unexpectedly takes in a scientist. Steed has been working with the boffin on the promotion of his latest invention, and his sudden departure leaves Steed baffled. Cathy goes undercover as an Assistant Matron, and discovers a pensions scam designed to allow the millionaires to avoid paying death duties—by having actors replace them for five years after their death. It's not long before Cathy's cover is blown and Steed has to come to the rescue.

55 THE MAN WITH TWO SHADOWS

Written by James Mitchell
Directed by Don Leaver
With Terence Lodge, Daniel Moynihan,
Philip Anthony

Secret agents within the Ministry of Security are being replaced by exact doubles, and an eminent scientist is going to be the next victim of the scheme. The clues lead to a holiday camp, and while investigating a car crash in which the scientist was involved, Steed finds out he is also to be replaced. It's up to Cathy to discover who is the real Steed, and who is the fake.

56 THE NUTSHELL

Written by Philip Chambers
Directed by Raymond Menmuir
With Edina Ronay, Patricia Haines,
John Cater, Ian Clark

The Nutshell is the name of an underground shelter to be used in the event of World War Three, and presently it contains confidential documents. A young girl gets through the complicated defences and escapes with some microfilm containing information about double agents. Steed acts very strangely, and is seen leaving a rehearsal room after a liaison with the thief. When the girl is later found murdered, all the evidence seems to suggest that it is Steed who is the traitor.

57 DEATH OF A BATMAN

Written by Roger Marshall
Directed by Kim Mills
With Katy Greenwood, Andre Morrell,
Philip Madoc, David Burke

Wrightson, a former batman of Steed's, leaves almost half a million pounds in his will to his wife. He was only a draughtsman, so foul play is suspected. Could it be that he was using his skills in the noble art of forgery? The trail leads to a swindle involving counterfeit share certificates being used to save an electronics firm from a foreign takeover. Despite Steed's silent support for such a move, he has no choice but to have the culprits arrested.

58 NOVEMBER FIVE

Written by Eric Paice
Directed by Bill Bain
With Gary Hope, Aimee Delamain,
John Murray Scott, Ric Hutton

The winning candidate in a local by-election is assassinated just as he promises to expose a national security scandal. Cathy stands for election in the man's place, just as a ransom demand arrives for a stolen nuclear warhead. It turns out that the dead candidate is not in fact dead at all—his faked murder was part of a bigger scheme to blackmail the Government for £500,000. Steed exposes the dastardly plot, just in time to stop the man from blowing up the Houses of Parliament and becoming a latter-day Guy Fawkes.

59   THE GILDED CAGE

Written by Roger Marshall
Directed by Bill Bain
With Patrick Magee, Neil Wilson,
Norman Chappell

When Cathy reveals to Steed that a gold vault she is working in could be robbed by just six men, he sees this as ideal bait to trap a millionaire believed to be the mastermind behind several recent gold robberies. They visit the man, announcing their intention to steal the gold with his help, but the millionaire is not convinced. Later, the man is found dead, and the police arrest Cathy for the crime. This turns out to be a ruse to test Cathy, and, convinced of her sincerity, the villains proceed to plan the theft. But they are still not sure about Steed, and an assassin is sent to dispose of him...

60   SECOND SIGHT

Written by Martin Woodhouse
Directed by Peter Hammond
With John Carson, Steven Scott,
Peter Bowles, Judy Bruce

A millionaire called Halvarssen is intending to have an operation to restore his sight, involving cornea grafts from a live donor flown in from Switzerland. Halvarssen's assistant, Anstice, is setting up the procedure. Steed is suspicious, and sends Cathy and an eminent surgeon to observe the operation after he is refused access. The operation is revealed to be a sham, and Anstice is the kingpin behind it—with precious diamonds being smuggled in the container that was supposed to be for the corneas!

61   THE MEDICINE MAN

Written by Malcolm Hulke
Directed by Kim Mills
With Peter Barkworth, John Crocker,
Joy Wood

An important pharmaceuticals manufacturer has a major problem—fake versions of its drugs are appearing overseas, and damaging its reputation. Behind it all is a plot to send poisoned drugs to Arab countries, to discourage them from signing a new oil treaty with Britain. Steed and Cathy find the printing company responsible for the bogus packaging and add the word 'poison' to the latest print run, thus making the whole consignment useless.

62   THE GRANDEUR THAT WAS ROME

Written by Rex Edwards
Directed by Kim Mills
With Hugh Burden, John Flint,
Colette Wilde, Ian Shand

Sir Bruno Lucer is the chairman of a food company and has a fascination for the lifestyle of ancient Rome. He is also the leader of a radical political party which has plans for world domination hinged on releasing a bubonic plague into the food chain. With reports of the outbreak of illnesses in both people and animals all over the world, Steed and Cathy check out a distributor of fertilisers and insecticides. The trail leads to Lucer, but Cathy is captured and the chairman concocts a way of utilising her to test his next project...

November Five

63 THE GOLDEN FLEECE

Written by Roger Marshall & Phyllis Norman
Directed by Peter Hammond
With Warren Mitchell, Robert Lee,
Tenniel Evans, Lisa Peake

A Chinese restaurant, owned by the suave Mr Lo, is in fact the nerve centre of a smuggling operation involving British servicemen. Steed and Cathy discover that one particular arms shipment contains bullets tipped with gold. The arms are being smuggled to fund 'The Golden Fleece', which supports deserving ex-military personnel. When Steed finds this out, he is left with a difficult decision...

64 DON'T LOOK BEHIND YOU

Written by Brian Clemens
Directed by Peter Hammond
With Janine Gray, Kenneth Colley,
Maurice Good

Cathy is invited to spend the weekend at the country manor of an expert in mediaeval clothing. She arrives to find only a young woman, Ola, at home. Ola makes her excuses and leaves Cathy alone, except for an unseen psychotic madman she helped arrest a few years earlier. His intention is to drive her to the edge of madness before killing her, in his twisted game of revenge. (This story was revamped in the Diana Rigg episode 'The Joker'.)

65 DEATH A LA CARTE

Written by John Lucarotti
Directed by Kim Mills
With Henry Soskin, Robert James,
Paul Dawkins, Ken Parry

Emir Akaba, an Arab head of state, is in London for his annual medical check-up. While Steed takes a job in the kitchen serving the VIP, Cathy takes responsibility for the supervision of the visit. An extremist group is planning an assassination attempt, but everyone is foiled by Akaba dying of natural causes. This panics the assassin as his superiors are not ready to mount their coup, and it's up to Steed and Cathy to make sure their plan does not succeed...

66 DRESSED TO KILL

Written by Brian Clemens
Directed by Bill Bain
With Leonard Rossiter, Leon Eagles,
Peter Fontaine, Richard Leech

It's New Year's Eve, and Steed has been invited to a fancy dress party aboard a train. The British secret agent, dressed as a cowboy, is in fact investigating why early warning defence systems had given a false alarm of an impending attack. The partygoers all seem to be interested in buying land next to defence base stations. Cathy, dressed as a highwaywoman, hitches a ride as an uninvited guest. As the train thunders along, one by one the revellers are murdered...

67 THE WHITE ELEPHANT

Written by John Lucarotti
Directed by Laurence Bourne
With Judy Parfitt, Bruno Barnabe,
Martin Friend

Cathy is given what is seemingly a very banal mission—searching for a stolen white elephant! What Cathy doesn't know is the animal may be the only one who can identify an ivory smuggler called Lawrence, who is trying to re-establish himself in the illegal trade, having been presumed dead. The elephant's keeper is found murdered, and Cathy goes undercover as a zoologist. Steed uncovers the scheme to smuggle ivory within the framework of cages, and after bringing the culprits to justice, returns the elephant to a very grateful zoo.

68 THE LITTLE WONDERS

Written by Eric Paice
Directed by Laurence Bourne
With Lois Maxwell, Tony Steedman,
David Bauer, Harry Landis

The arrest of a member of the Church is cause for concern. The Reverend Harbottle was stopped at an airport, and his suitcase contained a gun, ammunition and a doll. The toy has a loose head, and Cathy takes it to a doll's hospital for repair. She is asked for £20,000 in order for the repair to be carried out. Cathy refuses to pay, but is still allowed to take the doll away with her. The doll is found to contain microfilm with details of top British secret agents. Steed switches the microfilm, and a criminal organisation called 'Bibliotek' then reveals its interest in the information...

69 THE WRINGER

Written by Martin Woodhouse
Directed by Don Leaver
With Peter Sallis, Barry Letts,
Paul Whitsun-Jones, Gerald Sim

Steed is accused of treason by Anderson, an agent who has been missing for six weeks. The chief of the Secret Service employs 'The Wringer', an expert in interrogation, to gain the truth from Steed. But he's committed a grave error, as The Wringer is part of a group which is trying to create mistrust and suspicion amongst the ranks of the Secret Service. Only Cathy can save the day by stopping Steed from being fed with false information through brain-washing, and revealing The Wringer to be the real traitor.

70 MANDRAKE

Written by Roger Marshall
Directed by Bill Bain
With George Benson, John Le Mesurier,
Philip Locke, Robert Morris

A village cemetery in Cornwall arouses the suspicions of Steed, there to attend the funeral of an old friend. Contained within the cemetery are the bodies of several millionaires, all recently buried and not local to the area. Cathy finds that the soil within the grounds contains high levels of arsenic from the mandrake plants growing there. If post mortems were carried out after burial, and arsenic had been the murder weapon, nothing could be proven. Steed and Cathy arrange some bait to bring out the villains, one of their suspects being the owner of the local cracker factory...

71 THE SECRETS BROKER

Written by Ludovic Peters
Directed by Jonathan Alwyn
With Patricia English, Avice Landon,
Jennifer Wood, John Stone

Cathy is investigating a research facility which is developing a prototype underwater tracking device, while Steed is looking into the activities of a wine shop. Both locations seem to be linked to the murder of one of Steed's friends, a fellow secret service agent. Their enquiries lead them to a fake medium, who is blackmailing people to get hold of military secrets, which are then smuggled abroad within microdots printed onto wine lists.

72   TROJAN HORSE

Written by Malcolm Hulke
Directed by Laurence Bourne
With Derek Newark, Lucinda Curtis,
Geoffrey Whitehead

Steed is asked to protect a racehorse belonging to a wealthy Shah, following allegations of betting swindles. Instead, Steed uses the horse, Sebastian the Second, to gain access to the stable behind the rigging. Bookmakers, jockeys and owners are all involved, and will stop at nothing to make sure their scheme can continue undiscovered.

73   BUILD A BETTER MOUSETRAP

Written by Brian Clemens
Directed by Peter Hammond
With Donald Webster, John Tate,
Nora Nicholson, Athene Seyler

In a village near an atomic research station, reports emerge of the 'jamming' of mechanical and electrical devices within the area. Cathy joins a motorcycle gang for some scrambling, and raises the hackles of two elderly ladies who are far from pleasant to her. Our duo realise they are the daughters of an eminent scientist, now long dead, and believe they may well hold the answer to the mystery...

74   THE OUTSIDE-IN MAN

Written by Philip Chambers
Directed by Jonathan Alwyn
With Ronald Mansell, Ronald Radd,
Virginia Stride

A hero in the country of Abarain, Sharp is considered a traitor by his native country for spreading negative propaganda about the British. Who but Steed, therefore, would be asked to look after the man on a forthcoming visit to England! Things are not going to be easy, as Steed will also have to deal with a British agent who has returned from imprisonment in Abarain. The reason for his journey there was to assassinate Sharp, and his spell of detention may not have weakened his resolve to carry out his mission...

75   THE CHARMERS

Written by Brian Clemens
Directed by Bill Bain
With Warren Mitchell, Fenella Fielding,
John Greenwood

Steed and Cathy discover that agents from both sides of the Iron Curtain are being killed. Steed suggests a truce with the opposition to find out who is responsible, and an exchange of agents takes place as an act of good will. However, Steed has been given an actress, Kim Lawrence, instead of an agent, and Cathy has been unknowingly paired with the killers' ringleader. The base for their operations turns out to be a charm school. (This story was revamped in the Diana Rigg episode, 'The Correct Way to Kill'.)

Dressed to Kill

The Little Wonders

The Town of No Return

76 CONCERTO

Written by Terrance Dicks & Malcolm Hulke
Directed by Kim Mills
With Geoffrey Colville, Nigel Stock,
Sandor Eles, Valerie Bell

Anglo-Soviet cultural exchanges are taking place, but not
without their problems. There are attempts being made to
discredit famous Iron Curtain pianist Stefan Veliko. A young
girl has accused him of assault, and subsequently turns up
dead. The girl worked at a strip club, and Steed goes there
for clues, arriving just in time to stop Veliko being photo-
graphed in a compromising position! The pianist is forced by
the enemies working against him to try and assassinate a
Soviet trade minister, and it's up to Cathy to save the day.

77 ESPRIT DE CORPS

Written by Eric Paice
Directed by Don Leaver
With John Thaw, Roy Kinnear,
Douglas Robinson, Hugh Morton

A firing squad, commanded by Captain Trench, kills an unfortunate Corporal. Steed begins an investigation into the High-
land Guards and their activities when the Corporal's murder is
logged as an accident. Behind it all is Major General
Bollinger, who has used family trees to discover that his step-
son is the rightful heir to the throne of Scotland. Steed throws
a spanner in the works by revealing Cathy's family tree, which
shows that she should be Queen of England!

78 LOBSTER QUADRILLE

Written by Richard Lucas
Directed by Kim Mills
With Gary Watson, Burt Kwouk,
Corin Redgrave, Jeanie Linden

An agent is assassinated, his body turning up in the burnt
remains of a seaside hut. Steed and Cathy follow the trail to
a lobster-fishing business owned by Captain Slim. The duo
find out that his son, Quentin, who is feared drowned, in fact
faked his demise to avoid dope smuggling charges. Cathy
locates his hideout, and the panicked Quentin ends up
killing himself in a fire rather than murdering Cathy as was
his intention. Cathy decides this will be her final case, and
heads off to the Bahamas.

⟩⟩⟩⟩⟩⟩⟩ FOURTH SEASON — 1965/1966

Filmed in black and white
With Patrick Macnee, Diana Rigg
Produced by Julian Wintle
In Charge of Production: Albert Fennell
Associate Producer: Brian Clemens
Script Editor: Brian Clemens (uncredited)
Music by Laurie Johnson

79 THE TOWN OF NO RETURN

Written by Brian Clemens
Directed by Roy Baker
With Patrick Newell, Jeremy Burnham,
Robert Brown

The Gravediggers

The Episodes

Bazeley-by-the-Sea is a remote village on the Norfolk coast. Seemingly tranquil, four agents have mysteriously disappeared there in quick succession. Steed and his new partner, Mrs Emma Peel, visit the location, but no one seems particularly keen on talking to them... they are faced with a conspiracy of silence. The corpse of one visitor, Jimmy Smallwood, turns up near the beach having been savaged to death by dogs. The two agents soon uncover massive bunkers at a nearby airfield, containing a very heavy arsenal of weaponry. The entire village has been infiltrated by foreign agents, who aim to take over the country by force. Steed and his new colleague soon have the imposters trapped in their own bunkers.

The Gravediggers

80   THE GRAVEDIGGERS

Written by Malcolm Hulke
Directed by Quentin Lawrence
With Ronald Fraser, Paul Massie,
Steven Berkoff, Victor Platt

Britain's radar defences look like they are being jammed by enemy powers, but the Government boffins reckon a device strong enough to do this does not yet exist. A scientist called Marlowe, apparently recently deceased, was working on such a device. However, Marlowe is alive and well and in the sanctuary at a rest home for retired railwaymen, and the exhumation of his coffin, arranged by Steed, causes panic. Marlowe has been burying jamming devices in graveyards all over the county, and now a nearby radar station is completely surrounded by them. Emma finds herself captured and tied to a railway line, but will there be enough time to save her as the oncoming train edges its way over the horizon...?

81   THE CYBERNAUTS

Written by Philip Levene
Directed by Sidney Hayers
With Michael Gough, Burt Kwouk,
Frederick Jaeger, John Hollis

(A detailed synopsis of this episode is contained in a later section.)

82   DEATH AT BARGAIN PRICES

Written by Brian Clemens
Directed by Charles Crichton
With Andre Morell, George Selway,
John Cater, Peter Howell

Pinter's, a large London department store, attracts the attention of the Secret Service when an agent on a top secret mission is found dead, with a receipt from the store on his person. Emma is employed as an assistant in the lingerie department, while Steed poses as an efficiency expert. Kane, the new owner, keeps arranging night-time meetings for many of the staff. Emma uncovers a laboratory, in which an atomic scientist is being held against his will. Before she can escape, Emma is captured, leaving Steed to find out that the till receipts are in fact punchcards for a computer, and the whole building has been converted into a huge atomic bomb!

83   CASTLE DE'ATH

Written by John Lucarotti
Directed by James Hill
With Gordon Jackson, Robert Urquhart,
Jack Lambert

Death at Bargain Prices

Death at Bargain Prices

Emma Peel visits a sinister Scottish castle. Posing as a representative of the tourist industry, she is actually there to investigate the mysterious death of a frogman, who was washed ashore four inches taller than when he was alive. There's another visitor, too—a certain 'John McSteed', who says he's researching the family history of Black Jamie, a thirteenth century Laird. A phantom appears to play the bagpipes at night, but is actually there to cover the noise made by a set of turbines, part of the machinery involved in cornering the local fishing market by trapping the fish using submarines.

84　THE MASTERMINDS

Written by Robert Banks Stewart
Directed by Peter Graham Scott
With Laurence Hardy, Patricia Haines,
Ian McNaughton

A high-ranking government official is caught and kept in custody following his attempt to steal top secret papers. Steed and Emma discover he is part of the 'Ransack Club', a group of intellectuals who pool their collective wisdom. With a little help from Emma on his written paper, Steed is accepted as a member of the club. He soon discovers that Holly Trent, who club members thought was just an innocent archery instructor, is brainwashing them into carrying out acts of sabotage. Steed is caught, and someone will need to carry out his liquidation. A seemingly mesmerised Emma, who has been undercover as the club's secretary, volunteers to carry out the task...

85　THE MURDER MARKET

Written by Tony Williamson
Directed by Peter Graham Scott
With Patrick Cargill, Peter Bayliss,
Naomi Chance, John Woodvine

A series of murders seem to have only one common thread to them—all the victims had dealings with the 'Togetherness Marriage Bureau'. Emma speaks with the latest victim's widow, while Steed sees if Mr Lovejoy, the frontman of the operation, can set him up with someone suitable. Having been told that one cousin stands between himself and a huge inheritance, the bureau suggests one of its more unusual services—they will dispose of the cousin for Steed, if he will carry out a murder for them. The person they have in mind has begun to be a nuisance, and her name is Mrs Peel!

86　A SURFEIT OF H₂0

Written by Colin Finbow
Directed by Sidney Hayers
With Noel Purcell, Sue Lloyd,
Albert Lieven, John Kidd

A small village is being subjected to freak and sudden rainstorms, which are not predicted in the weather forecasts. Many of the villagers are preparing for the worst, thinking that the Great Flood is about to come again. The village carpenter has almost completed his ark in readiness! Soon, a poacher drowns in the middle of a field, bringing Steed and Emma to investigate. Emma realises that the storm clouds emanate from a wine-making factory, a theory confirmed by a meteorologist friend of hers, who then also mysteriously meets his death. Emma is captured and strapped to a wine press, as the dastardly plan to use the rain-making device as a weapon is revealed. Steed must find a way of coming to the rescue.

Castle De'Ath

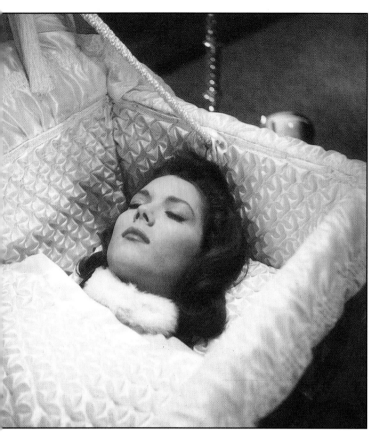

87   THE HOUR THAT NEVER WAS

Written by Roger Marshall
Directed by Gerry O'Hara
With Dudley Foster, Roy Kinnear,
Gerald Harper, Roger Booth

Invited to a closing down party for one of his former RAF regiments at a military base, Steed and his guest Emma have to crash their car to avoid hitting a dog in the road. When they eventually find their way to the base, time is frozen at 11.00am and the place seems deserted. The bizarre atmosphere intensifies as the duo witness the shooting of a milkman. Steed loses Emma, and after an encounter with a drunken tramp is knocked unconscious. When he wakes he is back at the wheel of his car, and there is still no sign of Emma. On reaching the base a second time, everyone who should be there has returned, and an hour has passed. The only thing that makes Steed sure that the incident really happened is the discovery of the tramp's dead body. The clues point to the camp's new dentist, who has captured Emma and is busy extracting secrets rather than teeth from his patients.

88   DIAL A DEADLY NUMBER

Written by Roger Marshall
Directed by Don Leaver
With Clifford Evans, John Carson,
Gerald Sim, Peter Bowles

Numerous sudden deaths are happening throughout the financial world. Steed detects a link between all the dead men and Boardman, a banker who was in business with every one of them. He discovers a criminal scheme to kill off people via the telephone—sophisticated electronic bleepers that all the dead men had carried in fact concealed a lethal hypodermic needle that would be triggered by a particular phone call. Placing fake devices on all his suspects, Steed waits to see who will reveal themselves to be the real villain.

89   MAN-EATER OF SURREY GREEN

Written by Philip Levene
Directed by Sidney Hayers
With Derek Farr, Athene Seyler, Gillian Lewis

Several botanists have disappeared, and Steed and Emma are called in to investigate. Their hunt takes them to a little village where work is being carried out on a new shrub. Unfortunately, the plant in question is a man-eater and can control minds! Having come down from space by hitching a ride on a spacecraft, it now has the entire village hypnotised. Steed calls on his friend, Dr Sheldon, to assist in dealing with the problem. Discovering that scientists with hearing aids were immune to the power of the plant, the trio go in all wired up themselves, with a powerful acidic plant poison for protection. But can they overpower the alien vegetation?

90   TWO'S A CROWD

Written by Philip Levene
Directed by Roy Baker
With Warren Mitchell, Julian Glover,
Maria Machado, Alec Mango

The Soviet Embassy is the base for a plot to infiltrate a meeting of defence chiefs in London. Ambassador Brodny thinks he has found the perfect double for Steed in a male model he sees on the street, and begins to train him to take over from Steed at the conference. Emma uncovers the scheme, but Steed

The Murder Market

Man-Eater of Surrey Green

Two's a Crowd

Too Many Christmas Trees

Too Many Christmas Trees

Room without a View

The Thirteenth Hole

The Girl from Auntie

The Girl from Auntie

does not take her warning seriously. After finishing off the schooling of the fake Steed, it is arranged for him to see Emma at a cocktail party. But Emma realises straight away that this is the double, which leads to her detention by the Soviets. During her confinement she hears the double assassinate Steed via a radio transmitter placed in Steed's apartment, the fake promptly returning to base with some secret microfilm...

91   TOO MANY CHRISTMAS TREES

Written by Tony Williamson
Directed by Roy Baker
With Mervyn Johns, Alex Scott,
Barry Warren, Robert James

Steed is falling victim to some terrible nightmares centred around Father Christmas! Emma thinks the best thing to cheer him up is to invite him along to a party given by her publisher, where everyone must turn up in costumes with a Charles Dickens theme. Two telepaths who bluff their way into the function are able to further influence Steed's thoughts, introducing images of a former colleague who was killed by similar attempts to extract information from him. Will Steed succumb to their continuing efforts, or will Emma realise what is going on and save him from either revealing secrets or cracking up entirely?

92   SILENT DUST

Written by Roger Marshall
Directed by Roy Baker
With William Franklyn, Isobel Black,
Jack Watson, Norman Bird

When an experimental new fertilizer known as 'Silent Dust' doesn't work out as planned, it leaves a large area of the English countryside ravaged and uninhabitable. Steed and Emma investigate the strange behaviour of a landowner called Omrod, finding out that the daughter of the fertilizer's inventor has joined forces with him to hatch a plan to extort money from the Government. If their demands are not met, Silent Dust will be used to devastate the whole of Britain.

93   ROOM WITHOUT A VIEW

Written by Roger Marshall
Directed by Roy Baker
With Peter Jeffrey, Philip Latham,
Paul Whitsun-Jones

A scientist reappears on the scene, after being listed as missing for over two years. Government officials believe he's been held captive in a foreign concentration camp, where he has been brainwashed. The trail leads to a London hotel, where Emma takes a job as a receptionist, and Steed goes undercover as a famous food critic assessing the hotel's cuisine. But what is the secret of room 621, mentioned by the brainwashed scientist? The hotel owner, Chessman, is the mastermind behind a scheme to establish a world-wide chain of hotels, with the scientists being captured and used as bargaining tools to achieve his aims. The concentration camp is in fact at the hotel and there is no foreign country involved. But now Chessman has found out Emma's true identity, and she is taken to the camp to undergo the procedure...

94   SMALL GAME FOR BIG HUNTERS

Written by Philip Levene
Directed by Gerry O'Hara

With Bill Fraser, James Villiers,
Peter Burton, Liam Redmond

A man is found with a tribal dart in his back, suffering from a type of sleeping sickness. It seems the condition has been caused by a new strain of tsetse fly. Entomologist Professor Swain tries to cast a tribal spell to save the man, without success. Steed then investigates an ex-serviceman's association run by Colonel Rawlings, who spends a lot of time in a mock-up of a tropical jungle. The eccentric has lost his grip on reality and actually believes he is still abroad in the country of Kalaya. His assistant, Trent, turns out to be the villain of the piece, with a plan to conquer Kalaya by releasing thousands of the new strain of insecticide-immune tsetse fly over the land, leaving it desolate and ready to be taken over...

95   THE GIRL FROM AUNTIE

Written by Roger Marshall
Directed by Roy Baker
With Liz Frazer, Alfred Burke,
Bernard Cribbins, David Bauer

Steed, returning from vacation, finds Emma's apartment occupied by a stunning blonde who claims that she is, in fact, Mrs Peel! Pressing the girl for the truth, he finds that she is an actress, who got the job through an advert in a newspaper. She is unwittingly part of a scheme devised by a gang of international kidnappers, who are responsible for Emma's abduction. Finding the person who hired the blonde dead, stabbed in the back by a poisoned knitting needle, Steed gets himself involved in an auction, where the principal lot is the real Mrs Peel!

96   THE THIRTEENTH HOLE

Written by Tony Williamson
Directed by Roy Baker
With Patrick Allen, Victor Maddern,
Francis Mathews, Peter Jones

Another friend of Steed's is murdered, and he and Emma find themselves investigating a golf course. Why is it that no one ever seems to complete the thirteenth hole? A club member named Reed has hidden a satellite monitoring system beneath the hole, which is about to make contact with the Soviet space orbiter, Vostok 3. Emma is captured by Reed after asking one difficult question too many. The plot is revealed to her—the criminals will be transmitting scientific secrets to the satellite as it orbits overhead. Unfortunately for the crooks, they haven't yet succeeded in eliminating Steed.

97   THE QUICK-QUICK-SLOW DEATH

Written by Robert Banks Stewart
Directed by James Hill
With Eunice Gayson, Maurice Kaufmann,
Larry Cross, Michael Peake

Enemy agents are carrying out their activities behind the facade of a dance school. The school's director, Lucille Banks, employs Emma as a dance instructor. Novices with two left feet are allowed to graduate, which seems strange to her. Steed assumes the cover of a lonely man who wants dancing lessons. The scam is that single men whom no one will miss are being replaced by foreign spies, assuming their identities with no friends or family to question the exchange. Lucille announces that there is to be a grand ball, where dancing diplomas will be awarded. Could it be that Steed is going to find himself replaced at the event? Not if Emma has anything to do with it...

A Touch of Brimstone

98   THE DANGER MAKERS

Written by Roger Marshall
Directed by Charles Crichton
With Nigel Davenport,
Douglas Wilmer, Moray Watson

Several high-ranking military personnel are being injured or killed in various stunts they are carrying out; climbing St Paul's Cathedral, for instance, or playing a game of 'chicken' on public highways. Steed and Emma are led to Manton House, a military museum, when a postcard of the place is found on the dead body of a lieutenant who had promised our heroes information. Manton is the base for the 'Danger Makers', a society for those who like placing themselves in extreme danger and live for the rush that high risk activities give them. Harold Long, the leader of the group, will use his members to carry out Operation Grand Slam—an attempt to steal the crown jewels. Emma sets herself up as a potential new member of the society, but in order to join she must place herself in mortal danger...

99   A TOUCH OF BRIMSTONE

Written by Brian Clemens
Directed by James Hill
With Peter Wyngarde, Jeremy Young,
Carol Cleveland, Colin Jeavons-

A sinister criminal organisation, run by the cynical Cartney, bases its activities on those of the eighteenth century Hellfire Club, whose ultimate aim was to overthrow the Government. Emma is introduced to Cartney's entourage, and at a meeting of the club witnesses several acts of debauchery. Steed decides to try and join the club himself after the murder of one of its members, which Emma thinks is down to the inner circle that runs the group. They uncover a plot to bomb a country house currently occupied by three foreign Prime Ministers, but not in time to avoid Steed being challenged to a duel, and Emma being confronted by Cartney...

100   WHAT THE BUTLER SAW

Written by Roger Marshall
Directed by Bill Bain
With John Le Mesurier, Thorley Walters,
Howard Marion Crawford

Military secrets are being passed to the opposition and Steed has three suspects: one from the army, one from the navy, and one from the air force. Steed's barber may have the answer, but is despatched by a pair of scissors in the back before he can reveal the truth. A common thread seems to be that they have all had household servants recently replaced, their new staff being supplied by the 'Butlers and Gentlemen's Association'. They also offer a laundry service, which cleans out the secrets of the employers by the use of bugs in returned clothing. Can Steed and Emma ensure that the scheme runs out of steam?

101   THE HOUSE THAT JACK BUILT

Written by Brian Clemens
Directed by Don Leaver
With Michael Goodlife,
Griffith Davies, Michael Wynne

(A detailed synopsis of this episode is contained in a later section.)

A Touch of Brimstone

A Touch of Brimstone

A Sense of History

What the Butler Saw

How to Succeed at Murder

102 A SENSE OF HISTORY

Written by Martin Woodhouse
Directed by Peter Graham Scott
With Nigel Stock, Jacqueline Pearce,
Patrick Mower, John Barron

Broom, a brilliant economist, is found dead, killed by an arrow in the back. Papers in his briefcase reveal a link to the University of St Bodes, and a revolutionary economic theory called 'The Europa Plan', which sells itself as a way to eliminate world poverty. Steed, along with Emma, who has taken a job as a lecturer at the university, discover a group of student reactionaries with revolution on their minds. At a costume ball, Steed dresses as the Sheriff of Nottingham, while Emma becomes Robin Hood, and the leader of the sect, an archivist called Grindley, previously believed murdered, reveals himself and vows to stop those who wish to thwart his plans...

103 HOW TO SUCCEED... AT MURDER

Written by Brian Clemens
Directed by Don Leaver
With Sarah Lawson, Angela Browne,
Jerome Willis, Robert Dean

There seems to be no real link between the murders of various highly regarded city executives, all major players in the world of commerce. Just one clue is enough for Steed—the distinctive smell of perfume. Taking a sample to an eminent expert in all types of scent, Emma smells success as the expert recognises the aroma as one of his own, and promises to write out a list of all the clients who have purchased it. Before he can supply the list, the expert is murdered, and his singularly unhelpful secretary has taken charge. Women taking over the businesses of the murder victims becomes a common thread, which leads to a keep-fit school run by Henry and Henrietta Throgbottom. Steed's research shows that Henrietta died twenty years previously, and Emma's infiltration reveals that the classes are a cover for a bunch of revivalist suffragettes, who have the sole intention of eliminating men from the world. Everyone thinks that Henrietta is alive and well, but it's really Henry that wears the skirt in this relationship...

Honey for the Prince

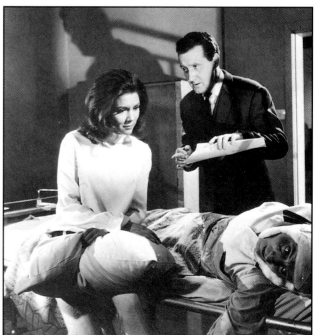

The Danger Makers

104 HONEY FOR THE PRINCE

Written by Brian Clemens
Directed by James Hill
With Ron Moody, George Pastell,
Bruno Barnabe, Ken Parry

Steed takes over an investigation after an agent associate is murdered. A postal clue sent by the agent before his death leads to a honey emporium owned by B. Bumble. Could it be that the Bahrainian Embassy's love of the amber nectar is tied into the mystery? Steed finds out they are close to signing a deal involving the exchange of oil for military protection. Emma is nearly assassinated after she goes to visit Mr Bumble, who is found dead when she makes a hasty return to his shop. A membership form for Q.Q.F. (Quite Quite Fantastic) at the crime scene leads Emma to investigate the company that makes people's fantasies come true. They are involved in making a dream of assassination reality, and only Emma can search the man-sized pots of honey within the sheik's harem. That means she must become a dancing girl at the sheik's disposal...

FIFTH SEASON—1967

Filmed in colour
With Patrick Macnee, Diana Rigg
Produced by Albert Fennell, Brian Clemens
Executive Producer: Julian Wintle
Music by Laurie Johnson
Designers: Wilfred Shingleton, Robert Jones

105 FROM VENUS WITH LOVE

Written by Philip Levene
Directed by Robert Day
With Barbara Shelley, Philip Locke,
Jon Pertwee, Jeremy Lloyd

After observing the planet Venus, an astronomer dies in a sudden flash of light—his hair turning completely white. Steed and Emma seek the assistance of Venus Brown, director of the British Venusian Society, a group of amateur astronomers whose objective is to land a satellite on Venus. Steed becomes a member of the society, but this doesn't stop the inexplicable deaths from occurring. Could it be extra-terrestrial intervention? Venus Brown and her society have unwittingly been responsible for funding a devastating laser weapon, and Emma may have uncovered its location...

106 THE FEAR MERCHANTS

Written by Philip Levene
Directed by Gordon Flemyng
With Patrick Cargill, Brian Wilde,
Andrew Keir, Annette Carell

Leading figures in the ceramics industry are being driven crazy for no apparent reason. Evidence points to Raven, who was trying to get all the men to agree to a merger with his company. He has employed a market research organisation, headed by a man named Pemberton, to try and improve the profitability of his company. The researchers have found a way to play on people's secret fears, and use the technique to break them. Steed sets himself up as a travel agent wishing to improve his profits, and tells Pemberton that his main business rival is a certain Mrs Peel...

From Venus with Love

The Fear Merchants

Escape in Time

The Bird Who Knew Too Much

107   ESCAPE IN TIME

Written by Philip Levene
Directed by John Krish
With Peter Bowles, Judy Parfitt,
Imogen Hassall, Nicholas Smith

(A detailed synopsis of this episode is contained in a later section.)

108   THE SEE-THROUGH MAN

Written by Philip Levene
Directed by Robert Asher
With Warren Mitchell, Roy Kinnear,
Moira Lister, Jonathan Elsom

Confidential information about a crackpot inventor has been stolen from two Government buildings. The Secret Service reckons it to be the work of the Soviets, and Ambassador Brodny, last seen in the episode 'Two's a Crowd', thinks he has stumbled on an excellent weapon for use in espionage— the secret of invisibility. When Steed and Emma visit the inventor, he tells them the formula has been sold to a drug company. Unfortunately, the invention is a hoax, and the drug company is a cover for two top Soviet agents, whose objective is to kidnap Emma Peel, while keeping Brodny in the dark!

109   THE BIRD WHO KNEW TOO MUCH

Written by Brian Clemens & Alan Pattillo
Directed by Roy Rossotti
With Ron Moody, Kenneth Cope,
John Wood, Anthony Valentine

Two agents are murdered—one is found in a field with a bag of bird seed next to him, another turns up cased in concrete, pictures of a secret missile base still in his pocket. A third agent, shortly before his death, tells them that secrets are being smuggled by Captain Crusoe, who Steed and Emma conclude must be at Heathcliff Hall, as the address has been left on the agent's desk. They find themselves attending a rare bird exhibition, where they discover Crusoe is in fact a parrot, but he's already flown the roost! The bird has been taught to memorise and repeat confidential information when it hears the sound of a triangle. Carrier pigeons are being used by the villains to take photographs of the missile base, but Crusoe knows his value and is soon asking for political asylum!

110   THE WINGED AVENGER

Written by Richard Harris
Directed by Gordon Flemyng & Peter Duffell
With Jack MacGowran, Roy Patrick,
Nigel Green, Colin Jeavons

(A detailed synopsis of this episode is contained in a later section.)

111   THE LIVING DEAD

Written by Brian Clemens & Anthony Marriott
Directed by John Krish
With Julian Glover, Howard Marion Crawford,
Jack Watson

The Duke of Benedict seems to have acquired a ghost in his private chapel. Steed and Emma are invited to investigate, and are joined on their quest by two members of rival supernatural societies that conduct research into the paranormal.

The quartet are not made to feel welcome by the Duke's estate manager, Masgard. After a night's ghost hunting, Emma goes missing. Little do they know that beneath the wine cellar is an underground city, designed to house survivors after a nuclear bomb is dropped on Great Britain. Masgard and his fellow foreign countrymen will then be able to take over what remains. Things look bleak as Steed, too, is captured, and is about to face a firing squad...

112 THE HIDDEN TIGER

Written by Philip Levene
Directed by Sidney Hayers
With Ronnie Barker, Gabrielle Drake,
Lyndon Brook, John Phillips

A series of savage murders are put down to big cats on the rampage. Steed and Emma investigate a society for abandoned moggies, PURRR (Philanthropic Union for the Rescue, Relief and Recuperation of cats). The manager of the group is Cheshire, who is aided and abetted by his assistants Dr Manx and Angora. When PURRR committee members begin to be killed, Steed discovers that the murders are being committed by domestic cats fitted with electronic collars that turn them into savage beasts. A Siamese cat has just been delivered to Emma, and it too wears one of the killer collars...

113 THE CORRECT WAY TO KILL

Written by Brian Clemens
Directed by Charles Crichton
With Michael Gough, Anna Quayle,
Philip Madoc, Terence Alexander

Steed and Emma are accused of murdering opposition agents when two dead bodies turn up. The duo are paired up with rival agents when a third murder occurs, and together the two teams work on the case. Emma investigates a chiropodist and finds her new partner has disappeared, while Steed finds himself at an umbrella shop, where the missing partner is spotted in a packing case being carried away by four hoods in bowler hats. Steed's partner also disappears when they check on things back at the chiropodist's. A finishing school for gentlemen, called Snob, is the final destination for the packing cases, and we discover that a top foreign agent is using the establishment as a way to make money by selling secrets to the highest bidder...

114 NEVER, NEVER SAY DIE

Written by Philip Levene
Directed by Robert Day
With Christopher Lee, Jeremy Young,
Patricia English

Why won't one particular corpse die? It decides to make its own way out of a mortuary, to be involved in a second accident, this time with the car that had brought it to the hospital. Once again, it comes to life, breaking its way forcibly out of the ambulance taking it back to the morgue. Steed and Emma find out that such survival has been quite commonplace in the area, and decide to investigate a nearby research unit. They discover that work is underway to create virtually indestructible duplicates of people, who then do their creators' evil bidding. Steed and Emma learn that the replicas can be disabled with certain radio transmissions, and try to close down the operation.

The Bird Who Knew Too Much

The Hidden Tiger

Never, Never Say Die

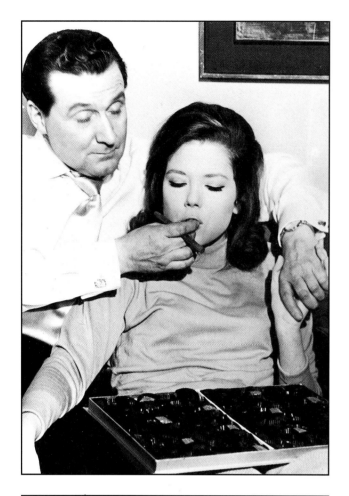

115 EPIC

Written by Brian Clemens
Directed by James Hill
With Peter Wyngarde, Isa Miranda,
Kenneth J. Warren, David Lodge

(A detailed synopsis of this episode is contained in a later section.)

116 THE SUPERLATIVE SEVEN

Written by Brian Clemens
Directed by Sidney Hayers
With Charlotte Rampling, Donald Sutherland,
Brian Blessed

Steed receives an invitation for a surprise costume party. The party is a little unusual as it is going to be held on an aeroplane, and all those who have been invited are experts in some sort of weaponry or fighting art. While in flight, they are all stunned to find that the plane has no pilot. They land on a desert island, and are informed by radio that they must all use their skills to survive in what proves to be a very hostile environment. One of them has been trained to be the ultimate killing machine, and will attempt to eliminate the others as proof of the quality of the training. As the party are eliminated one by one, the finger of suspicion points at Steed, and it becomes a case of kill or be killed...

117 A FUNNY THING HAPPENED ON THE WAY TO THE STATION

Written by Bryan Sherriff
Directed by John Krish
With John Laurie, Isla Blair,
James Hayter, Tim Barrett

An agent Steed and Emma plan to meet reckons he is on to those responsible for leaking secret documents. Unfortunately, he doesn't turn up for a rendezvous at a train station, and is found dead at his cottage. An analysis of timetables leads the duo to realise that the train Lucas was supposed to be on made an unscheduled stop before reaching them. They locate a disused station which had been made up to look like their rendezvous point. It's not long before a plot to assassinate the Prime Minister with a bomb aboard the train is uncovered. Steed and Emma take a trip on the express to try and find the bombers before they can carry out their plan.

118 SOMETHING NASTY IN THE NURSERY

Written by Philip Levene
Directed by James Hill
With Dudley Foster, Paul Eddington,
Patrick Newell, Clive Dunn

(A detailed synopsis of this episode is contained in a later section.)

119 THE JOKER

Written by Brian Clemens
Directed by Sidney Hayers
With Peter Jeffrey, Ronald Lacey, Sally Nesbitt

(A detailed synopsis of this episode is contained in a later section.)

Who's Who???

120 WHO'S WHO???

Written by Philip Levene
Directed by John Moxey
With Freddie Jones, Patricia Haines,
Peter Reynolds

Lola and Basil, two enemy agents, are working on an infallible way of infiltrating the Secret Service and eliminating its members. With a flick of the switch on a prototype machine, they will be able to swap bodies with Steed and Emma. Having captured our heroes and performed the exchange, the villains are able to cause all sorts of problems, knowing that Steed and Emma will get the blame. Meanwhile, the real Steed and Mrs Peel, trapped in Lola and Basil's bodies, are not able to convince anyone as to who they really are. Can they trick the inventor of the machine into believing the swap has been reversed, hence forcing him unwittingly to put things to rights?

121 THE RETURN OF THE CYBERNAUTS

Written by Philip Levene
Directed by Robert Day
With Peter Cushing, Frederick Jaeger,
Charles Tingwell

(A detailed synopsis of this episode is contained in a later section.)

122 DEATH'S DOOR

Written by Philip Levene
Directed by Sidney Hayers
With Clifford Evans, William Lucas,
Marne Maitland, Paul Dawkins

Britain's representative at a high-level meeting suddenly gets scared and refuses to enter the conference room. While journalists suspect that Britain may be on the verge of withdrawing from involvement, the representative thinks he sees a lion and falls under the wheels of an approaching car. A replacement is quickly found, who begins to suffer similar nightmares, which are taken to be premonitions of death. An Eastern Bloc observer is creating the dreams, but the reality is that the evil forces will stop at nothing to sabotage the talks...

123 THE £50,000 BREAKFAST

Written by Roger Marshall
Directed by Robert Day
With Cecil Parker, Yolande Turner,
David Langton

A ventriloquist and his dummy are travelling in a car which is involved in a mysterious accident with a hay lorry. While in hospital, x-rays reveal a consignment of diamonds hidden in the man's stomach. Returning the dummy to the ventriloquist's wife, our heroes discover that he was on his way to Zurich to perform for millionaire Alex Litoff. All is not what it seems, as Litoff is dead, buried in place of a dog at a canine cemetery. Litoff's assistant, Miss Pegram, is behind an attempt to make it seem as if the millionaire is still alive so that his assets can be disposed of, and now she wants to dispose of Steed and Emma...

The Positive-Negative Man

Mission...Highly Improbable

124 DEAD MAN'S TREASURE

Written by Michael Winder
Directed by Sidney Hayers
With Norman Bowler, Valerie Van Ost,
Neil McCarthy, Arthur Lowe

A secret agent hides a metal despatch box in a red treasure chest, while being pursued by enemy agents. Mortally wounded, he makes a rendezvous with Steed and Emma, but is unable to inform them of the chest's location before he dies. Steed is invited to compete in a rally organised by an old friend, only to find that the prize is the treasure chest they seek! The pursuing agents arrange rally entries for themselves and, after disposing of their allocated partners, go in search of the booty. Meanwhile, Emma's partner in the race also has his own reasons for wanting the contents of the despatch box...

125 YOU HAVE JUST BEEN MURDERED

Written by Philip Levene
Directed by Robert Asher
With Robert Flemyng, George Murcell,
Barrie Ingham, Simon Oates

(A detailed synopsis of this episode is contained in a later section.)

126 THE POSITIVE-NEGATIVE MAN

Written by Tony Williamson
Directed by Robert Day
With Ray McAnally, Michael Latimer,
Peter Blythe, Sandor Eles

Eminent experts who were involved in a shelved experiment to broadcast electricity on radio waves are being systematically killed off. Steed and Emma investigate the former head of the project, Cresswell, who is unable to explain why the remaining files on 'Project 90' have gone up in flames. The two agents then encounter a formidable foe, a masked man in rubber boots, charged with electricity, who can kill with one powerful discharge from his hand. The suit is occupied by one of Cresswell's henchmen, who sends him out on his next mission—to eliminate Emma Peel.

127 MURDERSVILLE

Written by Brian Clemens
Directed by Robert Asher
With Colin Blakely, Ronald Hines,
John Sharp, Eric Flynn

(A detailed synopsis of this episode is contained in a later section.)

128 MISSION... HIGHLY IMPROBABLE

Written by Philip Levene
Directed by Robert Day
With Jane Merrow, Francis Matthews,
Ronald Radd, Richard Leech

Professor Rushton, who works for the Defence Ministry, has invented a ray that is capable of miniaturising anything he chooses. His assistant, Chivers, intends to use the invention to sell prototype military vehicles to opposition forces. Chivers has already miniaturised and disposed of a Treasury official who was on his way to clamp down on the overspending incurred by the project. Hiding in a new tank, Steed finds

Mission...Highly Improbable

The Episodes

himself miniaturised along with the army vehicle, which will make it a little difficult for him to call Mrs Peel for help, especially when the telephone is almost the size of a house in comparison to him!

⟩⟩⟩⟩⟩⟩ Sɪxᴛʜ Sᴇᴀsᴏɴ — 1968/1969

Filmed in colour
With Patrick Macnee, Linda Thorson
With Patrick Newell as 'Mother'
Produced by Albert Fennell, Brian Clemens
Executive in Charge of Production: Gordon L. T. Scott
Story Consultant: Philip Levene
Script Editor: Terry Nation
Music by Laurie Johnson
Designers: Robert Jones, Wilfred Shingleton

129   THE FORGET-ME-KNOT

Written by Brian Clemens
Directed by James Hill
With Diana Rigg, Jeremy Young,
Patrick Kavanagh

A secret agent has been hit with a dart from an air pistol, and now has amnesia. Steed and Emma try to jog his memory at Steed's apartment, but without success. All he can mumble is that there is a traitor within the organisation. Steed goes to inform Mother, while Emma, left in charge of the agent, is hit by a knock-out dart herself. Mother assigns Agent 69, Tara King, to assist, but not before she's embarrassed herself by ambushing Steed by mistake. She gives Steed a note of her address, and he returns to his apartment. Emma is still there, but the agent has gone, and so has part of Mrs Peel's memory. Steed decides to take Emma to Mother, but he's hijacked en route and left drugged in a ditch. Now with amnesia himself, the only clue Steed has to his identity is Tara's address...

130   GAME

Written by Richard Harris
Directed by Robert Fuest
With Peter Jeffrey, Aubrey Richards, Alex Scott

(A detailed synopsis of this episode is contained in a later section.)

131   THE SUPER-SECRET CYPHER SNATCH

Written by Tony Williamson
Directed by John Hough
With John Carlisle, Simon Oates,
Alec Ross, Ivor Dean

Confidential documents are being stolen from Cypher headquarters, despite it being under constant surveillance. Tara is nominated to go to work in the establishment, and Steed takes an interest in the firm that has the window cleaning contract, particularly when the boss of the company which is supposed to be carrying out the work notes that they haven't visited the complex for months. The bogus cleaners are knocking out all the staff with a vapour that hypnotises them into a motionless state, and makes them susceptible to aural suggestion. They then proceed to photograph every secret paper they can get hold of. Steed decides it is time to apply a damp sponge to their scheme...

The Forget-Me-Knot

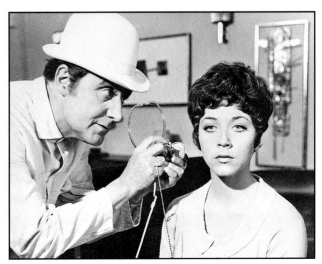

The Super-Secret Cypher Snatch

132 YOU'LL CATCH YOUR DEATH

Written by Jeremy Burnham
Directed by Paul Dickson
With Roland Culver, Valentine Dyall,
Dudley Sutton, Sylvia Kay

Ear, nose and throat experts are being murdered. An enigmatic chauffeur in a Rolls Royce carries a postman to the scenes of the crimes, then the postman delivers an empty envelope to the specialists. Upon opening the envelope, the men suddenly find themselves sneezing to death. Steed finds himself investigating the Anastasia Nursing Academy, who purchased a huge consignment of the unusual envelopes used in the murders. Tara, meanwhile, is just too late to stop another murder, and having seen the escaping Rolls, is abducted. Colonel Timothy, owner of a cold cure clinic, becomes a suspect, as the dead men were working on a new medicine which would have meant the end of Timothy's business. But then the Colonel receives one of the letters himself, and must stop his assistant, the real villain, from ensuring that Tara catches her death!

You'll Catch Your Death

133 SPLIT

Written by Brian Clemens
Directed by Roy Baker
With Nigel Davenport, Julian Glover,
Bernard Archard

The security of the Ministry of Top Secret Information is broken when an agent is assassinated at one of their country retreats. Even worse, the killer is a colleague of the dead man. Steed and Tara believe that the murderer has developed a dual personality. This schizophrenic condition begins to become apparent in many more people, and they all seem to have the same second personality, that of a foreign agent Steed encountered a few years before. Triggered by a simple phone call and a code word, the next target is Tara!

134 WHOEVER SHOT POOR GEORGE OBLIQUE STROKE XR40?

Written by Tony Williamson
Directed by Cyril Frankel
With Clifford Evans, Dennis Price,
Judy Parfitt, Arthur Cox

Steed and Tara are called in to find out why new supercomputer George/XR40 has broken down without reason. They help revive it by arranging a 'brain transplant' from Fred, the computer that preceded George. Their presence doesn't stop the continuing attempts at sabotage, however. Steed suspects that Pelley, the machine's creator, is behind it all when seemingly damning evidence comes from none other than George itself! However, on completion of the transplant, George reveals he was trying to communicate that Pelley is being drugged and interrogated by enemy agents. Meanwhile, Tara has put all her trust in the real traitor, leaving her in grave danger...

Whoever Shot Poor George Oblique Stroke XR40?

135 FALSE WITNESS

Written by Jeremy Burnham
Directed by Charles Crichton
With Barry Warren, John Atkinson,
Rio Fanning, Peter Jesson

Melville, one of Steed's colleagues, is suspected of being a double agent. He allows an associate to be caught red-handed when acting as look-out on a mission to collect evidence against Lord Edgefield, who is suspected of blackmailing Government personnel. Melville is convinced he did nothing wrong, and a lie detector confirms he is telling the truth. The

Legacy of Death

solution to the mystery can be found in bottles of milk—laced with a drug that makes people lie. Tara investigates Dreemy Kreem Dairies, is captured and drugged herself, which leaves Steed, who takes his coffee black, to tell the truth and save the day!

136 ALL DONE WITH MIRRORS

Written by Leigh Vance
Directed by Ray Austin
With Peter Copley, Dinsdale Landen, Edwin Richfield

Accompanied by agent Watney, Tara investigates a series of murders at the Carmadoc Research Establishment. With Steed in Mother's company as a potential suspect, Tara is left to wonder why a recently deceased astronomer had told his housekeeper to smash everything shiny in the house. Watney has a secret meeting with Seligman, who can crack the case wide open. However, Seligman is shot at the rendezvous point, and under the tree next to him is a shattered mirror. Tara discovers a telescope that can transmit and receive sound over vast distances, piggybacking a beam of light. As she works out how to use the device to contact Watney, she is attacked by two thugs...

137 LEGACY OF DEATH

Written by Terry Nation
Directed by Don Chaffey
With Ronald Lacey, Ferdy Mayne, Stratford Johns, John Hollis

Farrer, an ancient adversary of Steed's, sends our favourite British agent an ornate knife: 'the dagger of a million deaths'. Everyone believes Farrer is dead, and that this is his legacy. Steed finds himself in great danger from those in pursuit of it. Two criminals, Sydney and Humbert, are the most persistent pair on the trail of the dagger, killing several of their competitors. What they are all after is the location of a black pearl, Farrer's most prized possession, to which the dagger is the key. All the clues lead back to Farrer's house, but is he really deceased?

138 NOON DOOMSDAY

Written by Terry Nation
Directed by Peter Sykes
With Ray Brooks, Griffith Jones, Lyndon Brook

After a recent mission, Steed is convalescing in an agent's rest home, suffering from a broken leg. The exterior has all manner of defences to keep it secure. After being allowed to pass through, Tara comes to visit Steed. A letter she brings gives him a clue that Kafta, an agent Steed put away several years before, has escaped and is out for revenge. Together with two henchmen, Kafta sets about his task, cutting the rest home off from the outside world, with the aim of finishing the job off with a Western-style shoot-out.

139 LOOK—(STOP ME IF YOU'VE HEARD THIS ONE) BUT THERE WERE THESE TWO FELLERS...

Written by Dennis Spooner
Directed by James Hill
With Jimmy Jewel, John Cleese, Bernard Cribbins, Garry Marsh

(A detailed synopsis of this episode is contained in a later section.)

Legacy of Death

Legacy of Death

Have Guns—Will Haggle

140 HAVE GUNS—WILL HAGGLE

Written by Donald James
Directed by Ray Austin
With Johnny Sekka, Jonathan Burn,
Michael Turner

A raid on an ordnance factory is well worth it for the thieves responsible—they make off with 3,000 revolutionary new rifles, codenamed FF70. Steed visits Colonel Nsonga, who he suspects may be able to use the rifles to help his claim to the presidency of a newly independent African state. He is prepared to do business with the thieves, who intend to sell the weapons to the highest bidder. Steed sets himself up as a potential bidder in the auction, but before they begin, the thieves prepare a demonstration duel to show the efficiency of the new rifles, and one of the targets is Tara King!

141 THEY KEEP KILLING STEED

Written by Brian Clemens
Directed by Robert Fuest
With Ian Ogilvy, Ray McAnally,
Norman Jones

Steed is asked to be an official observer at a peace conference, but is kidnapped by Arcos, a criminal genius who has found a way to create exact replicas of any human face he cares to. He plans to use the technique to sabotage the conference by creating a double of the British agent. But Steed throws a spanner in the works by seeing to it that there are four replica Steeds at the conference. One after another, Tara finds three of the doubles dead, but when the original Steed escapes his kidnappers, she must decide—which of the remaining two Steeds is the real one?

142 THE INTERROGATORS

Written by Richard Harris & Brian Clemens
Directed by Charles Crichton
With Christopher Lee, David Sumner,
Philip Bond, Cecil Cheng

Colonel Mannering is in charge of a scheme to extract important information from trainee secret agents. Believing the interrogation is part of a training course, the agents give away their secrets in the bar afterwards, thinking that their trainers are working for their side. But then contacts of the agents who have been interrogated start to turn up dead. Steed fears for Tara when he discovers she has been sent on the training course, and Tara begins to suspect that something is amiss when she sees that Mannering's cigarettes match the butts that have been found in the homes of the dead agents.

143 THE ROTTERS

Written by Dave Freeman
Directed by Robert Fuest
With Gerald Sim, Jerome Willis,
Eric Barker

Sir James Pendred, an eminent specialist at the Department of Forestry Research, is assassinated in his office by two thugs with the power to make wood dissolve, leaving him with no hiding place. Steed and Tara find a photograph of Pendred with four other experts, who begin to turn up murdered, and realise that one of them must be behind it all. The five men had been working on a new strain of dry rot, one that could work almost instantaneously. The villain's plan is to blackmail Europe with the threat of releasing the chemical if his demands are not met, but what can our intrepid pair do about it?

144 INVASION OF THE EARTHMEN

Written by Terry Nation
Directed by Don Sharp
With William Lucas, Christian Roberts,
Warren Clarke

The disappearance of a Government agent leads Steed and Tara to the Alpha Academy, a training centre for young astronauts. Commander Brett, director of the institution, is in fact training the students to conquer outer space, and graduates find themselves cocooned in sub-zero temperatures, ready for the time when inter-planetary travel becomes a reality. Tara is captured, and used as the fox, with the cadets cast as the hounds who pursue her, thinking it's all part of their survival training. This is the least of her problems, however, as it looks like real aliens are after her, too!

145 KILLER

Written by Tony Williamson
Directed by Cliff Owen
With Jennifer Croxton,
William Franklyn, Grant Taylor

The ranks of Britain's Secret Service are being decimated by a new form of killer—an electronic one. REMAK (Remote Electro-Magnetic Agent Killer) is a supercomputer programmed to commit murder. While Tara takes a holiday, Mother assigns Lady Diana Forbes-Blakeney to assist Steed in cracking the case. As more bodies appear wrapped in plastic in a graveyard, one of them turns out to be the scientist who designed REMAK. His colleague reveals the location of the mean machine, and Steed and Lady Diana find themselves trapped in a factory where Steed must negotiate a succession of murder traps.

146 THE MORNING AFTER

Written by Brian Clemens
Directed by John Hough
With Penelope Horner, Joss Ackland,
Brian Blessed, Philip Dunbar

Merlin is an extremely dangerous quadruple agent whom Steed, unusually feeling the need to arm himself with a pistol, is about to bring in. The agent keeps a rendezvous with Tara and Steed at the latter's apartment, but he's stolen secret sleeping gas capsules, and in a skirmish one of them is broken. On waking, Steed finds that a whole day has passed and London is deserted. There's no answer from Mother, so, leaving Tara asleep, Steed and Merlin make their way through town handcuffed together. They encounter a military firing squad, and discover that martial law has been declared after a nuclear bomb was found beneath a trade commission building. Little do they know that a barmy Brigadier is behind the ruse, and is actually using the evacuation as cover for placing a real bomb in the city.

147 THE CURIOUS CASE OF THE COUNTLESS CLUES

Written by Philip Levene
Directed by Don Sharp
With Anthony Bate, Edward de Souza,
Kenneth Cope, Tony Selby

Why are two men investigating a murder that has yet to happen? The victim returns home, is shot by the men, and falls exactly into a chalk outline already drawn on the floor! Such

The Interrogators

Killer

a case, and the fact that Tara has broken a leg on a skiing jaunt, means Steed must call on a certain Sir Arthur Doyle(!) for assistance. With a myriad of confusing clues, the duo realise that they are dealing with hitmen who plan the workings of their assassinations to the finest detail. A photograph of Tara reveals she is the next target, with the plan being to frame Steed for the crime!

148   WISH YOU WERE HERE

Written by Tony Williamson
Directed by Don Chaffey
With Liam Redmond, Robert Urquhart,
Dudley Foster, Gary Watson

Tara's uncle is being held captive by a group of hoods who are gradually taking over his business empire. Tara visits the hotel where he has been taken prisoner, but she becomes trapped. Mother sends in his nephew, Basil Crighton-Latimer, to assist, and he too is captured. Although there is no obvious way in which they are all being held, anyone who tries to leave is the victim of bizarre accidents and has to return. Things become even more complicated when the prisoners realise that one of their number is in fact the mastermind behind their entrapment.

149   STAY TUNED

Written by Tony Williamson
Directed by Don Chaffey
With Kate O'Mara, Gary Bond,
Duncan Lamont, Iris Russell

Wish You Were Here

Steed is preparing for a vacation, unaware that he has already been on one for three weeks! His loss of memory is something he cannot come to terms with, and on a visit to Mother learns that he too is on holiday, and Father, a blind lady, has taken charge. Steed is removed from the active list and Tara sets about trying to help him restore his memory. What he doesn't know is that while he has been away, he has been hypnotised into killing Mother, and one of the villains responsible for Steed's condition is now invisible to him. This combination leads Tara to believe Steed really is losing his mind.

150   TAKE ME TO YOUR LEADER

Written by Terry Nation
Directed by Robert Fuest
With Patrick Barr, John Ronane,
Michael Robbins

A large briefcase has a mind of its own—literally—and a voice that reveals it cannot be opened by anyone but its owner. Steed and Tara get hold of the case from an enemy agent and take it to Mother. Once there, the case gives a series of orders concerning who it should be passed on to, which our agents decide to comply with. After being led a merry dance, the trail leads back to Mother. The spy who owns the case must be a member of his department, or could it be that the real villain is Mother himself?

151   FOG

Written by Jeremy Burnham
Directed by John Hough
With Guy Rolfe, Nigel Green,
Terence Brady, Paul Whitsun-Jones

Stay Tuned

In the fog-bound streets of London, Steed and Tara are stalking what seems to be a modern day Jack The Ripper, who is killing off members of a disarmament conference. They investigate a gentlemen's club, dedicated to a Victorian contemporary of the Ripper's, the Gaslight Ghoul. They confirm that the way the crimes are being committed are recreations of those carried out by the Ghoul in 1888. Steed believes the crimes are being perpetuated by someone who has a lot to gain from the disarmament talks failing—perhaps someone involved in the arms trade...

152   HOMICIDE AND OLD LACE

Written by Terrance Dicks
& Malcolm Hulke
Directed by John Hough
With Joyce Carey, Mary Merrall,
Gerald Harper

It's Mother's birthday, which he spends with his two elderly aunts, Georgina and Harriet. Being ardent fans of the spy genre, they ask Mother to relate one of his missions to them, and he chooses 'The Great Great Britain Crime'. Steed is once again pitted against Intercrime, his adversaries in the days of Cathy Gale. Their plan is to steal every single British art treasure, including the crown jewels, in one swoop. They panic the authorities, causing them to make the unwise move of hiding all the treasures in one location. Exactly what Intercrime wants them to do...

153   LOVE ALL

Written by Jeremy Burnham
Directed by Peter Sykes
With Veronica Strong, Terence Alexander,
Robert Harris

Why is it that a charlady can gain official secrets from civil servants so easily? How come they all fall in love with her at first sight? It helps that she is actually a beautiful woman in disguise, but in the game of love why not give yourself a real advantage—like a book that can place the hypnotic suggestion 'you will fall in love with the next person you see' into any reader's brain. Tara, in the course of her investigation, reads a copy of the book, just before being disturbed by the criminal mastermind responsible for the scheme. Can Tara cope with having her affections shunned by this man, especially when he suggests her best option is to jump out of the window?

154   GET-A-WAY!

Written by Philip Levene
Directed by Don Sharp
With Andrew Keir, Vincent Harding,
Peter Bowles, Peter Bayliss

A monastery becomes the makeshift prison for three captured Russian agents. One of them, Rostov, manages to escape and continues to evade capture by making himself invisible! Steed and Tara are holding a dinner party, unaware that the escaped agent's mission is to kill one of their guests. Steed is furious when the mission is accomplished, and visits the monastery only to find that the other captured men have made themselves invisible and fled. The only clue is a bottle of vodka found in one of the cells, and Steed knows the agent imprisoned there was teetotal...

Take Me to Your Leader

Fog

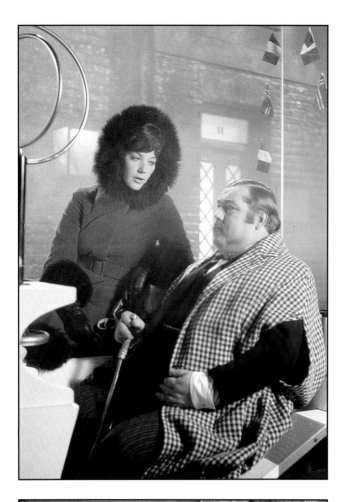

155 THINGUMAJIG

Written by Terry Nation
Directed by Leslie Norman
With Jeremy Lloyd, Dora Reisser,
Hugh Manning, John Horsley

The vicar of a village church is an old wartime colleague of Steed's and calls on him for help. An archaeological dig beneath his church has been the scene of a tragic death. A small, inexplicable burn mark in the victim's forehead, and the inscription 'It' marked in the dust next to the body intrigue Steed. Items incinerated within the cave indicate a white-hot discharge of electrical energy may have been responsible. Dredging a nearby stream reveals a black box which Tara discovers is actually an independently-minded instrument of death, part of a madman's plot to take over the world. Meanwhile, Steed must face a second deadly box, on the loose in the catacombs below the church...

156 PANDORA

Written by Brian Clemens
Directed by Robert Fuest
With James Cossins, Julian Glover,
Kathleen Byron, John Laurie

Tara is kidnapped by the Lasindall brothers, who need her to help discover the location of their Uncle Gregory's fortune. The old man is senile, and the brothers drug Tara to brainwash her into believing that she is Pandora, the lost love of Gregory's youth. Faking Tara's death in a road crash to stop Steed following their trail only serves to fire up our hero even more, and he goes in search of Fierce Rabbit, the codename used by a British agent in the First World War. Gregory was one of a trio of men who assumed that name, and soon Tara persuades him to reveal that the treasure is beneath his beloved painting of Pandora...

157 REQUIEM

Written by Brian Clemens
Directed by Don Chaffey
With Angela Douglas, John Paul, Dennis Shaw

Miranda, a young girl, is the principal witness in a court case against Murder International. An attempt is made in an underground car park to abduct her, but is foiled. Miranda is placed in Steed's custody for protection, while Tara finds herself kidnapped by the villains. Overhearing a plot to assassinate Mother at Steed's apartment, Tara escapes, only to arrive too late and be caught in an explosion. She awakens to find both her legs in plaster casts, but realises that they are a ruse, and she's unhurt. Tara discovers that the house she's in contains mock-ups of all the rooms she's been in since being kidnapped in the first place, and that everyone there has been an imposter. To add insult to her lack of injuries, she's told the gang where to look for Steed, putting both him and Miranda in great danger...

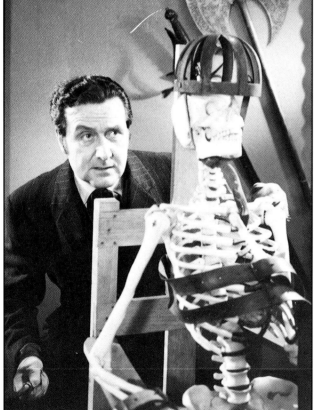

Fog

Get-A-Way!

Love All

Requiem

158 TAKE-OVER

Written by Terry Nation
Directed by Robert Fuest
With Tom Adams, Michael Gwynn,
Elisabeth Sellars, John Comer

Bill Bassett and Steed had been prisoners of war together, and on release celebrated Christmas in February. This has become an annual tradition for them. Unfortunately, this year will not run as smoothly, as hoodlums who wish to sabotage a nearby peace conference take Bill and his wife hostage. The couple have phosphor bombs implanted in their throats that can be detonated by a cigarette lighter, and then the gang move in their ultimate weapon—a rocket gun which is placed upstairs and targeted on the country house holding the conference. Steed appears, and quickly realises that something is wrong. His foresight makes him dispensable, and he becomes involved in a duel to the death...

159 WHO WAS THAT MAN I SAW YOU WITH?

Written by Jeremy Burnham
Directed by Don Chaffey
With William Marlowe, Ralph Michael,
Aimee Delamain

Steed has just twenty-four hours to prove Tara's innocence after she is accused of treason by Mother. Under orders, she had tested the security surrounding The Field Marshal, a tracking system that can tell the whereabouts and contents of all the aircraft in the world. Outwitting the defences, she had managed to take film of the War Room that contains the device. Circumstantial evidence suggests she has passed the information on to foreign agents, but nothing could be further from the truth. The opposition want Britain to switch off their defence system, thinking that its technology has been discovered and needs updating. In that time, missiles will be launched and Britain placed in grave danger. Meanwhile, Mother has given the order for Tara to be shot on sight...

160 MY WILDEST DREAM

Written by Philip Levene
Directed by Robert Fuest
With Peter Vaughan, Edward Fox,
Philip Madoc, Derek Godfrey

Jaeger is the brains behind a psychiatric technique to turn people into killers. First, they vent their frustrations on dummies in his surgery, before being programmed to go and commit the real act. It's all part of a plot to allow a disgruntled board member of Acme Precision Combine Limited to take control by eliminating the opposition. When Steed gets too close to the truth, Lord Teddy Chilcott, a jealous suitor of Tara's who has a burning hatred of Steed, is programmed to kill the one person who he believes stands in the way of his future with Tara.

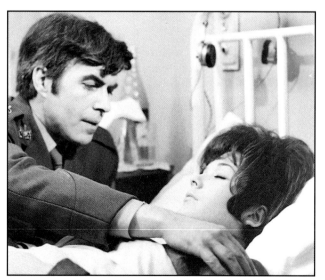

Requiem

The Episodes

Who Was That Man I Saw You With?

Who Was That Man I Saw You With?

Bizarre

161 BIZARRE

Written by Brian Clemens
Directed by Leslie Norman
With Roy Kinnear, Sally Nesbitt,
Michael Balfour, James Kerry

A corpse, mysteriously revived, attacks a young girl on a train. The body should have already been buried at Happy Meadows Cemetery. The proprietor of the graveyard, Happychap, is confounded that such a thing could have happened. The widow of the dead man reveals that he had spoken of taking a trip with Mystic Tours, who promise to arrange the ultimate way of getting away from it all. On checking the records, it appears that several people who were in trouble with the law are supposed to be buried at Happy Meadows. Steed decides to employ the Mystic Tours service, and wakes from his coffin after a faked death to find himself beneath the graveyard— living a life of luxury!

Take-Over

The Eagle's Nest

The Midas Touch

Cat Amongst the Pigeons

THE NEW AVENGERS

>>>>>> ## FIRST SEASON—1976/1977

With Patrick Macnee, Joanna Lumley, Gareth Hunt
Produced by Albert Fennell, Brian Clemens
Production Designer: Syd Cain
Music by Laurie Johnson

1   THE EAGLE'S NEST

Written by Brian Clemens
Directed by Desmond Davis
With Peter Cushing, Derek Farr,
Frank Gatliff, Brian Anthony

On a remote Scottish island, a monastery has become the base for Nazis intent on establishing the Fourth Reich. When an agent is killed investigating the place, Steed and his new associates Gambit and Purdey are sent to find out the reasons behind his death. The Nazis have kidnapped a cryogenic suspension specialist, and top of the list for a thaw-out is the body of Adolf Hitler! Our agents must fight to prevent the resurrection of the Führer, and stop his loyal troops from planning world domination.

2   HOUSE OF CARDS

Written by Brian Clemens
Directed by Ray Austin
With Peter Jeffrey, Lyndon Brook,
Frank Thornton, Derek Francis

Purdey, Steed and Gambit stop the Russian agent Perov from taking Vasil, a defector, out of the country. Knowing that shame awaits if he returns to the USSR empty handed, Perov fakes his own death in order to set in motion operation 'House of Cards', a way of activating sleeper agents who have been placed around the UK over the years. When they receive half a playing card, the sleepers have their orders to eliminate specific targets. Steed's name is on the King of Hearts, Gambit is the Jack and the Queen is Purdey. But Perov is now intent on assassinating Vasil, and Steed must break cover to protect him. Thankfully, Purdey and Gambit are not far behind...

3   THE LAST OF THE CYBERNAUTS...?

Written by Brian Clemens
Directed by Sidney Hayers
With Robert Lang, Oscar Quitak,
Robert Gillespie, Gwen Taylor

(A detailed synopsis of this episode is contained in a later section.)

4   THE MIDAS TOUCH

Written by Brian Clemens
Directed by Robert Fuest
With John Carson, Ed Devereaux,
Ronald Lacey, Jeremy Child

Professor Turner has produced a deadly creation—Midas. One touch from this young man means death. He is a carrier of every known disease in the world, and his services are well

sought after by the criminal element. The death of Hong Kong Harry, an adversary of Steed's, alerts our bowler-hatted hero to the power of Midas. Meanwhile, a foreign diplomat called Vann has employed Turner to eliminate a princess who is visiting Britain. Purdey goes undercover, but is soon rumbled by Turner, who promises to make a gift of her to Midas when the deadly youth completes his latest mission...

5 CAT AMONGST THE PIGEONS

Written by Dennis Spooner
Directed by John Hough
With Vladek Sheybal, Matthew Long, Peter Copley

Steed, Purdey and Gambit are investigating bizarre deaths apparently caused by flocks of birds. The Minister of Ecology is one of the victims. Handfuls of feathers are found at accident scenes—one a car crash, the other an air disaster. Purdey investigates the 'Sanctuary of Wings', owned by the discredited ornithologist Zarcardi. He has developed methods of training the birds, and demonstrates by causing a bird that has landed on Purdey's hand to draw blood. The birds guard her as she is kept imprisoned in a locked room. Steed and Gambit realise that the dead men are all former colleagues of Zarcardi, who has decided to use his faithful flock to reap vengeance for him on those who mocked his talents. Realising that Purdey is in danger, Steed and Gambit enlist an army of feline helpers to assist in a breakout!

6 TARGET!

Written by Dennis Spooner
Directed by Ray Austin
With Keith Barron, Frederick Jaeger, John Paul, Deep Roy

Five agents have mysteriously died. After medical analysis, the pieces fall into place and the department realises someone is trying to kill all Steed's colleagues, using curare poison. All the dead agents had just completed target practice at a high-tech range, little knowing that the 'enemy' targets' harmless blanks had been replaced with tiny capsules of poison that cause death within hours. By the time this is realised, Purdey is already on the range, trying to achieve Steed's never-matched 100 per cent score. She manages ninety-nine per cent, but that one per cent, a single 'hit' from an 'enemy' target, is enough to kill her. Steed is the next to fall victim, and it's up to Gambit to find the antidote before the whole department is wiped out.

7 TO CATCH A RAT

Written by Terence Feely
Directed by James Hill
With Ian Hendry, Edward Judd, Robert Flemyng, Barry Jackson

Seventeen years ago, secret agent Gunner was on the point of revealing the identity of a double agent called 'The White Rat'. The traitor got away, engineering an accident in which Gunner lost his memory. But now the agent's memory has been restored, and with it the determination to complete his mission. He sends an urgent message to Steed, which takes time to understand as it is in a long-defunct code. Those responsible for the double cross all those years before also find out that Gunner is back in action, and the race is on to see who will get to him first.

Cat Amongst the Pigeons

Target!

Faces

Faces

8   TALE OF THE BIG WHY

Written by Brian Clemens
Directed by Robert Fuest
With Jenny Runacre, Derek Waring,
George Cooper

Bert Brandon is about to be released from prison, and says he's stashed some stolen documents that, if revealed, could lead to the downfall of the British Government. Having made such unsubstantiated claims before, the attempted blackmail is not taken up, leaving Brandon to sell the papers on to the highest bidder. Before Purdey and Gambit can make contact with him after his release from jail, Brandon is assassinated by two foreign agents. The killers escape, but the hit could mean there is something to Brandon's claims after all. The answer to the puzzle may well lie within the pages of a Western novel—The Tale of the Big Why.

9   FACES

Written by Brian Clemens
& Dennis Spooner
Directed by James Hill
With David De Keyser, Richard Leech,
David Webb

Important government officials are being replaced by doubles. Recruited from amongst the homeless who frequent 'The Mission for The Distressed and Needy', a skilled plastic surgeon then gives them a new face and all the required training. When a friend of Steed's dies in a bungled swap, Gambit is sent to the Mission, playing the role of an alcoholic tramp most effectively. Purdey follows him into the group, and finally Steed gets in on the act when he hears that the group are looking for a double to replace him. Unfortunately, nobody's quite sure who's real and who's a fake, so the trio can't even trust each other!

10   SLEEPER

Written by Brian Clemens
Directed by Graeme Clifford
With Keith Buckley, Mark Jones,
Prentis Hancock, Leo Dolan

Our heroic trio assist in the demonstration of a new gas, S95, that is odourless, colourless and can put anyone to sleep for six hours. Unfortunately, several canisters are then stolen by a bunch of crooks, who use the gas to paralyse large areas of London and go on a robbery spree. Gang leader Brady is not expecting to see Purdey out and about, unaffected by the gas. As Purdey tries to locate her partners, Gambit and Steed find themselves on the run, and the thieves resolve to eliminate the only people who can identify them and put an end to their game.

11   THREE HANDED GAME

Written by Dennis Spooner & Brian Clemens
Directed by Ray Austin
With David Wood, Tony Vogel,
Michael Petrovich

Superspy Juventor is keen on getting his hands on 'The Three Handed Game', a secret document encoded by Steed. Unfortunately, it only exists as sections in the memories of three different agents, and only together can they make up the entire document. Juventor has a mind-transference machine

Dirtier by the Dozen

to extract the information, which can transfer the thoughts and skills of one person to another, leaving the donor a mindless vegetable. Steed, Purdey and Gambit each take responsibility for guarding one of the three agents with the photographic memories, but Juventor has all of them in his sights, and he begins to take control of the pieces of the jigsaw...

12 DIRTIER BY THE DOZEN

Written by Brian Clemens
Directed by Sidney Hayers
With John Castle, Shaun Curry,
Michael Barrington

Colonel 'Mad Jack' Miller is in charge of the 19th Special Commando Unit, which seems to be made up of all the worst recruits in the British military services. When General Stevens doesn't return from an inspection of the regiment, Steed and his colleagues are called in. Miller's troops have been turning up all over the world in places they shouldn't be, and the possibility of World War Three is looming. Could it be that they are now mercenaries, available to anyone for the right price? Gambit soon becomes the latest recruit to the Unit, but Purdey, who has been following her own line of enquiry, is caught and charged with espionage, and finds herself stranded in a minefield.

13 GNAWS

Written by Dennis Spooner
Directed by Ray Austin
With Julian Holloway, Jeremy Young,
Peter Cellier, John Watts

At the Ministry of Agriculture, the negligence of a couple of scientists has unwittingly caused a huge genetic mutation. While trying to find a formula that will grow plants to several times their usual size, some of the chemical that produces the growth has been washed down the sink and into the sewer below. As maintenance men start to go missing, Steed, Purdey and Gambit are brought in to investigate. The radioactive liquid has been consumed by a rodent, and the big rat now has a taste for human flesh. Purdey volunteers herself as live bait to flush out the creature, and everyone hopes Gambit can shoot straight!

 ## SECOND SEASON—1977

14 DEAD MEN ARE DANGEROUS

Written by Brian Clemens
Directed by Sidney Hayers
With Clive Revill, Gabrielle Drake,
Richard Murdoch, Terry Taplin

Steed's apartment is ransacked in what seems to be a wanton act of vandalism. His valuable porcelain and art collections have been ruined. When a bomb goes off in his garage, events take on a more sinister resonance. Crayford, an old foe of Steed's who was shot by the Avenger while trying to defect ten years before, has made it his life's ambition to bump him off. Time is running out for Crayford, as the bullet Steed lodged in his chest will eventually cause his death. To raise the stakes, he takes Purdey hostage, and sets up a showdown at a Victorian folly...

Dirtier by the Dozen

15   ANGELS OF DEATH

Written by Terence Feely & Brian Clemens
Directed by Ernest Day
With Terence Alexander,
Caroline Munro, Michael Latimer

Why are so many department staff dying of 'natural' causes? The only link between all four dozen of them is their visit to a health farm shortly before their death. When Steed's colleague Colonel Tomson succumbs too, the Avenger decides it is time to investigate, and checks himself in at the health farm. Behind the scenes, the establishment is run by the Angels of Death, attractive women who brainwash agents into revealing their secrets before sending them mad. Steed finds himself in the interrogation maze, a psychological tool in the battle for information, and Purdey also falls into their clutches. Can Gambit save the day?

16   MEDIUM RARE

Written by Dennis Spooner
Directed by Ray Austin
With Jon Finch, Sue Holderness, Jeremy Wilkin

The sudden death of one of Steed's closest friends is something his killers know will not be allowed to pass without investigation, so they decide their next mission must be to execute Steed himself! Victoria Stanton, a fortune teller everyone suspects to be a fake, actually discovers real powers when she foretells attempts on Steed's life that soon happen. While Purdey and Gambit are initially sceptical, evidence convinces them of the medium's abilities. Her interventions help Steed to keep one step ahead of his assassins. Behind the campaign is a department man who is using his informants for his own personal gain, and his potential income has to be protected at all costs...

Angels of Death

17   THE LION AND THE UNICORN

Written by John Goldsmith
Directed by Ray Austin
With Jean Claudio, Raymond Bussières,
Maurice Marsac

The Unicorn is a ruthless enemy agent, and his next mission is to assassinate a government minister. Steed is responsible for protecting the politician, and ends up following the killer to France. Purdey and Gambit join in the hunt, and manage to corner the Unicorn in his hotel. But the assassin is then mistakenly killed by his own men, who think they are shooting Steed (when in fact it's only his reflection in a mirror). Realising that it could cause trouble if the Unicorn's death is discovered, Steed makes it seem that the Unicorn is still alive. Matters become extremely complicated when the gang offer to swap a prince they have kidnapped for their leader. The exchange is all arranged, but the prince has been turned into a human booby trap...

18   OBSESSION

Written by Brian Clemens
Directed by Ernest Day
With Martin Shaw, Lewis Collins,
Terence Longdon

Steed and Purdey are asked to co-ordinate the security for a visiting Arab delegation. Larry Doomer, Purdey's former fiancé, is now a squadron leader involved in a plot to wipe out the Arab visitors. His father had been murdered years

The Lion and the Unicorn

earlier by Arab soldiers, and he wants revenge. Not wanting to meet Larry again, Purdey refuses to participate in providing protection for the delegation. Steed insists that she help investigate a robbery at an RAF ammunition dump. It soon emerges that Larry is planning to blow up the Arabs using a stolen missile while they visit the Houses of Parliament. Purdey finds the launch site, but it will be up to Gambit to win the day.

19   TRAP

Written by Brian Clemens
Directed by Ray Austin
With Terry Wood, Ferdy Mayne,
Stuart Damon, Barry Lowe

Soo Choy is a Chinese overlord, responsible for trafficking drugs to a large crime syndicate, but he falls foul of Steed and his friends, who are given information by a mortally wounded agent as to the location of his next drop. Their intervention leaves Soo Choy with a score to settle, as his failure to make a delivery is seen by him as a slur on his honour. He decides to take revenge, and baits Steed, Purdey and Gambit into taking a plane that will fly them to his jungle base. His plan is to behead the troublesome agents, and present them as trophies to the crime syndicate he has let down. It looks like Gambit will be first for the treatment, but why is the approaching soldier wearing a bowler hat?

20   HOSTAGE

Written by Brian Clemens
Directed by Sidney Hayers
With William Franklyn, Simon Oates,
Michael Culver, Anna Palk

Steed is just settling down for a delightful dinner for two with an even more delightful house guest, when the phone rings. An anonymous voice informs him that Purdey has been kidnapped, and that in order to get her back he must provide the top secret, full allied attack plans. Steed makes copies of the plans, and arranges delivery. His activities have not gone unnoticed, and before long he is suspected of treason. It is arranged for Steed to be followed, but one of the kidnappers has dressed up like Steed, and kills the tail. Gambit is ordered to bring Steed in, now suspected of murder. Can Steed use his wealth of knowledge to save Purdey and divert Gambit?

21   K IS FOR KILL — THE TIGER AWAKES, PART ONE

Written by Brian Clemens
Directed by Yvon Marie Coulais
With Pierre Vernier, Sacha Pitoeff,
Christine Delaroche

22   K IS FOR KILL — TIGER BY THE TAIL, PART TWO

Written by Brian Clemens
Directed by Yvon Marie Coulais
With Pierre Vernier, Sacha Pitoeff,
Christine Delaroche

Back in 1965, Steed and Mrs Peel came across a Russian soldier who, when accidentally killed, aged decades in seconds. Now, in the present day, Mrs Peel is in touch again to inform Steed of a young Russian soldier who has just murdered several

Obsession

Trap

Hostage

people and destroyed a garage in France. Steed goes over the Channel to investigate, and finds out the garage had been a military location in the last war. He is attacked by the Russian soldier, who then tackles Gambit and is killed. Just like a decade before, the soldier suddenly ages. It turns out that a satellite has accidentally given the signal to activate the 'K' agents, literally 'sleeper' soldiers who now believe a war has broken out. General Stanislav knows all about the men, but is not prepared to stop them until they have assassinated the French President and started the Third World War.

23   COMPLEX

Written by Dennis Spooner
Directed by Richard Gilbert
With Cec Linder, Harvey Atkin,
Rudy Lipp, Michael Ball

X41 is the code number of a top foreign agent called Scapina. Steed, Purdey and Gambit fly to Canada when a Russian agent there agrees to reveal the identity of the spy. Once in Toronto, their contact is killed and so is the murderer. It looks like the identity of Scapina could be found in a new, computer-controlled security building, and Purdey is sent to search files there to see what she can come up with. While she's down in the basement, the building is sealed and all the oxygen within is gradually removed. Purdey realises, perhaps too late, the true identity of the enemy agent—the building itself is X41!

24   THE GLADIATORS

Written by Brian Clemens
Directed by Claude Fournier
With Louis Zorich, Bill Starr,
Neil Vipond

Sminsky is a dangerous KGB agent, on a secret mission in Canada. He is in charge of a group of operatives trying to disrupt the Canadian Secret Service by destroying the computer files which contain details of all known active enemy agents. Sminsky has undergone extensive training in Siberia, and is using the knowledge gained there to endow his team with superhuman strength and powers. Two security men tailing the group are killed, and soon Steed, Purdey and Gambit, who were supposed to be on holiday, find themselves called upon to intervene. But how will they deal with capture and use as human targets?

25   FORWARD BASE

Written by Dennis Spooner
Directed by Don Thompson
With Jack Creley, Nick Nichols, Maurice Good

Still in Canada, Steed, Purdey and Gambit find themselves on the trail of a Mark VI guidance unit which, when incorporated into Soviet missile guidance systems, will put them ahead in the arms race. When a Russian agent's dying breath mentions a 'Forward Base', Steed goes fishing on Lake Ontario for clues. He uncovers a sub-aquatic community of enemy agents making ready for the third world war. Purdey is captured and taken prisoner, and Steed threatens to use depth charges to bring the true extent of their problems to the surface...

26   EMILY

Written by Dennis Spooner
Directed by Don Thompson
With Richard Davidson, Jane Mallet,
Les Carlson, Brian Petchy

*Steed has been asked to uncover the identity of a dangerous
double agent known as 'The Fox'. A trap at a petrol station
doesn't work out as planned, and the double agent escapes.
However, he did leave a hand print on Emily, a vintage car
belonging to an old lady called Miss Daly. She agrees to let
the Avengers take the car to the authorities so that the finger
prints can be analysed. Steed's hat protects the print from
the weather when it is stuck onto the roof, but this does not
help their anonymity, as the police have put out an APB on
the car, describing it as last seen wearing a bowler! The Fox
is only too aware of what they are trying to do, and together
with his henchmen sets out to destroy not only the car but
the interfering agents too.*

K is for Kill

Complex

Forward Base

The House That Jack Built

THE HOUSE THAT JACK BUILT

An air-raid siren sounds, and we see a man running across a field, pursued by two armed guards. This is Burton, an escaped convict. Both guards carry rifles. One of them is being dragged down a path by two bloodhounds, while the other is combing the woods. They are closing in.

Burton hides behind a tree as the guard without dogs goes past. He overpowers the guard and knocks him out cold, seizing his rifle and cartridge belt. Burton rushes off and climbs over a nearby wall, entering the grounds of a country house. He jumps down to the other side, and runs toward this possible sanctuary. It looks deserted. He gets to the front door, which is solid and locked, so he looks around the side of the house. Burton makes his entry through some French windows, smashing a pane of glass with the butt of his gun. Inside, two stuffed barn owls catch his eye, and he looks around. The place is covered in dust and cobwebs. Papers are strewn across a desk. There's a telescope, strangely placed on its tripod in the centre of the room. Burton listens at the door to the rest of the house. He decides to open it. This is met by the roar of a lion, and he looks up to see a jungle within the house. The lion leaps at him and, in his panic, he fires the shotgun ...

Steed takes a wrong turning

Emma holds the key to all

Emma arrives at Steed's apartment, carrying a large key. When Steed does not greet her, she assumes he must be busy somewhere. She looks in a back room, and finds him with his head under a thick black cloth. Steed's using his patent do-it-yourself portable darkroom to develop some holiday snaps. He won't be long—he'll finish the roll and take her out for lunch, as promised. Mrs Peel has bad news: she can't keep to the arrangement, as she has another appointment. Steed looks up to see Emma waving the large key at him and wonders if the Bastille has such a lock. Emma explains that an old uncle who died some time ago has left her his house, and she wants to take the

chance to inspect it. Steed is upset, and Emma placates him by saying she hardly knew the uncle. Steed, of course, was actually talking about the lunch date. He uses the confusion as an opportunity to ask Emma if she'll make him a cup of coffee, as he's got his hands full. Emma pulls the darkroom cover over Steed's head in mock frustration, and puts the key down on an envelope of photographic developing paper. As she does so, Steed's darkroom timer moves forward erratically, and then stops.

Emma tells Steed more about her new acquisition, called Seven Pines, in Pendlesham, which Steed immediately recognises as being in Hampshire. He's cycled around the area once or twice, and even knows the best route for her to take. She needs the B31, which he describes as a nice, quiet, leafy run. Emma gives Steed his coffee. She's a little unsure about her relative Jack's history, but reckons he's a knavish uncle twice removed. Emma goes to leave, almost forgetting her key. When Steed picks it up off the photographic paper, the timer spins backwards quickly, as he muses on whether there'll be any good wine in the cellar. Only when Emma leaves does he notice the erratic behaviour of his darkroom timer.

Mrs Peel gets into her car and, unseen by her, the dashboard compass spins. She drives off. Meanwhile, Steed has reached the final stage of developing his photographs, and pulls the papers from the developer mix. He looks at them, bemused. Where the key had rested on the papers, it has left a white outline indelibly etched in the prints. The key must have affected the photographic paper somehow. Steed is puzzled, and makes a call to Pennington, Emma's solicitor. He talks to him about Emma and her legacy, the house left to her by her Uncle Jack. Pennington is confused—he knows nothing of any such legacy, or who Uncle Jack is. Steed reiterates what Emma told him about Jack dying and leaving her his estate, all in a letter that the solicitor had sent. Pennington denies having written any such letter. Besides that he's been a lawyer for the Knight family for years and has

never heard of an Uncle Jack. With that, Steed rings Pongo, an associate, and says he has a job for him, to do with Mrs Peel being on her way to Hampshire, and a strange key with electrical properties...

In her car, Emma turns on the radio, but all she gets is interference. The key is in close proximity to it. She passes a house, just recently sold by Faulkner's, as the sign proclaims, and continues her journey along the B31. From a hillside, a scoutmaster is watching the landscape, and when he sees Mrs Peel approaching, he dashes for the road. He runs out into it, and Emma is forced into an emergency stop. She is not amused. He, however, says that he positioned himself exactly 150 feet away from her car, and the average stopping distance for a person with normal reflexes in such a car is 147 feet. He's very mathematical, you see. Still Emma is not impressed—what if she hadn't seen him? Sensing her indignation, the scoutmaster insists that if she had hit him, it would have been entirely her fault!

He tells her he'd like a lift. His bare-faced cheek amazes Emma, and she finds herself asking where he wants to go. He says as far as she's going. He's desperate to get a lift and is prepared to go as far as to recommend her for a scout badge for her trouble. Emma says that will not be necessary, and he and his scout flag-pole get in the open-top car. Sitting down, his attention slyly drifts to the large house key.

Emma wondered what he was doing—had he been acquiring his woodcraft badge? In fact, he'd been bird watching, something he is intensely fond of. They pass a sign that reads 'Pendlesham—9 miles'. The scoutmaster is amused to think that he has given Emma the fright of her life, but doubts that it's true. The miles roll by, and soon they arrive at Pendlesham. Emma asks where he wants dropping off, and he reaffirms that he'll go as far as she's going. He calls her by name, surprising her, but reveals he had seen the name on a letter on the floor by the passenger seat. Now he has her at a disadvantage, so he tells her his name—Frederick Withers.

They are just about to reach a crossroads. There's a sign to Seven Pines (also signposted are London—seventy-one miles—Pendlesham Ponds—two miles and one route marked No Through Road). As the car approaches the signpost, it passes a sensor in the grass by the side of the road—the car trips it, and it clicks into operation. At the signpost, the marker for Seven Pines revolves mechanically and faces the same way as the 'No Through Road' marker. The car passes and carries on down a dirt track, along which it activates another sensor, and the marker for Seven Pines turns back to its original position. Further on down the track, they trigger a third sensor. Behind them, and unseen to the duo, a post lowers across the track. From it hangs another sign—'Road Closed'.

They reach a narrow alcove in a wall, which must be the entrance to Emma's alleged legacy. She stops and lets Withers out, before continuing her journey down the long driveway, with acres of land either side of her. She pulls up at the huge house, and heads for the door. As she moves away from the car, she is unaware that the radio has started working again. Emma turns the key in the door...

Inside, a long hall greets her. On one side is a hat-stand with a bowler hat and an umbrella hanging on it, plus a coat that falls off as she walks past. Stopping to pick it up, she dusts it off and places the rather grubby garment back on the stand. A suit of armour further along has also seen better days. Then, there's the sound of a music box echoing down the hall, and she goes to investigate. She finds herself in the room where the barn owls are, and sees the music box, with a ballerina rotating on top of it. She closes it. Withers, meanwhile, has reached the front door.

Emma is studying some of the paperwork strewn across the desk. There is some Pennington & Company headed notepaper, and someone has been practising H.W. Pennington's signature, a blown up copy of the real thing on another sheet.

Mrs Peel goes to leave, and then the phone rings. It's an old candlestick-type model, and she picks it up. There's no one there, though. Outside, Withers has just managed to get into the house. Back inside, the internal door slams on Emma. She goes to it, gun already drawn, and hears a blood-curdling scream. Going through the door, she finds that the hallway has been replaced by a surreal new room, with a circular target motif on the floor, and an unusual contraption at its bullseye. It is a hexagonal structure, crowned by a clear dome with revolving diamond-shaped mirrors within, all tied to a central point by triangular pieces. Archways lead off into the darkness around the wall of the circular room. A low, bleeping sound can be heard, which quickly becomes very annoying. Inspecting the structure at the centre of the room, she hears the door close behind her, and finds herself locked in. She bangs on it, but to no avail.

In Steed's apartment, the phone rings. With a pancake on a plate in one hand, Steed answers it. It's not Pongo, as he thought, but a military type informing him that Pongo hasn't reported back yet. Should they contact Colonel Robertson, who could send the men in? Steed thinks not. He'll go there himself, and, grabbing his coat, bowler and brolly, he departs.

Back in the dome room, Emma is looking around, and decides to follow one corridor to a door at the other end. She opens it and finds another room with a dome in the middle, looking just like the previous one. She tries another corridor. Opening the door at the other end, she turns to see the dome behind her, then looks in front of her—it's another dome room. She enters it and looks around. The dome behind her has vanished. She's beginning to panic

and runs down a different corridor, finding yet another dome room through the door at the end. Emma takes out her lipstick, and marks a red cross on the dome for recognition, then goes down another corridor, through yet another door, and again sees the dome structure in front of her. She inspects it. It has her cross on it, so it must be the same one.

Suddenly, she hears an unearthly growling, and the sound of a man laughing. She goes down the corridor where she thinks the sound is coming from, and a wind begins to blow in her face. Emma looks to the floor, and finds an unstitched boy scout badge with a leaf and acorn on it. She takes it with her, and further on finds the scoutmaster's flag-pole. Beyond is a wall with a frosted glass window in it. She breaks it with the butt of her gun and looks through. Yet again, in front of her, is the dome room.

She runs back into the previous room. This time, the dome structure has gone, replaced by a staircase leading into the floor. Emma once again hears the man's laugh, then the roar, but this does not stop her descending the spiral stairs. What she doesn't see is the mud-covered pair of legs that move toward the staircase to watch her progress.

The staircase seems never-ending. Finally, Mrs Peel reaches the bottom and runs to a thin slit in the wall, which has daylight pouring through it. She's a fair distance up, and can see the countryside beyond, but this is no escape route. Once again, she hears the low, constant bleeping behind her and turns around. The dome room is back again, and she's inside it once more. She sits down and strokes her gun for comfort, finding hope when she hears the music box for a second time. Treading heavily, she walks along the corridor towards it, reaches the door at the end and opens it. Pulling back a pair of curtains within reveals the room that contains the stuffed owls. She rushes through this room, and finds the corridor beyond. Opening the front door, she escapes into what she thinks is the outside world, only to be met with the stuffed owl room again.

Before she can turn back, the front door slams behind her. Emma kicks it in despair, and turns to find the body of Withers sprawled across the desk. A bayonet on the end of a rifle sticks upright from his chest. She pulls back the curtain, trying to retrace her route, but behind it now is solid stone. She goes to a drinks table, puts her gun down and pours herself a brandy from a decanter, leaving the top off. Emma composes herself and begins to think.

Someone must be watching her. Every move she makes is being viewed. She puts her glass down and looks at the telescope in the middle of the room. There is a lead running from it, which she pulls out, and then throws the telescope across the room. Looking up, she sees a door handle move itself slowly back to its resting position. Emma grabs her gun. Reason is the order of the day. She's encountering rooms that move. Whole areas that disappear. How could it be done? Rollers under the floor? Some kind of motor as the driving force? If that's the case, there must be a trigger. She looks at the door, and opens it. An electronic button pops out of the frame between the hinges. Pushing it back in with a finger, she sees the room in front of her begin to move. But is it moving, or is she?

Looking around, she sees the decanter bung rolling about on the tray—it is the stuffed owl room that is moving. She takes her finger off the button, and the room stops.

The doorway has stopped at a maintenance area. Emma expects to find those responsible somewhere around. There are mechanical devices and electronic panels everywhere …

Back in the outside world, Steed has reached the crossroads and sees the marker for Seven Pines. He follows the dirt track road it points towards and finds himself reaching a dead end. He turns back, and gives the signpost a second look. The 'Road Closed' sign attracts his attention, and he decides to drive straight through it— and it shatters into several pieces. He has activated one of the roadside sensors, however, and a row of spikes comes out of the road ahead of him. They burst all his

tyres, and then just as silently disappear into the ground. Steed manages to control the Bentley and bring it to a halt. He decides to continue on foot.

Meanwhile, Emma has found a useful looking control panel. She inspects the gauges and spies a metal door. She takes a gun out and looks inside the room. A sign above a pair of closed curtains reads 'Welcome to an exhibition dedicated to the late Emma Peel'. She's not put off, though, and goes through the curtain. Within, she finds a doll's house, pictures of her as a baby, a photo of her parents, one of her childhood dolls and various items of clothing mounted on display panels. She sees a picture labelled 'Sir John Knight and daughter Emma', then a glowing head of a man with a moustache mounted to the wall. It bids her welcome, and hopes she finds the exhibition amusing.

The bust says she has been expected, and Emma demands that the voice show himself and tell her what he wants. She is told that she'll find out what she needs to know in section four of the exhibition. Emma goes through, carrying the doll with her. There are newspaper hoarding sheets on the wall, and the central one says 'Sir John Knight Dead'. A newspaper clipping next to it is from David Malbert's City News in the *Evening News*. The headline reads 'Emma Knight takes the helm of father's industries...twenty-one year old girl to head board'. There is a button next to the cutting, and Emma presses it. A ticker tape comes out of a slot in the wall. It reads:

'Knight Industries Soar + The Amazing Emma Knight Runs Company More Efficiently Than Ever +'. There's a tape player, too, and Mrs Peel investigates it. The recording is of a radio broadcast—the reporter announces he is outside the John Knight Building where Emma had just sacked an automation expert from the board of Knight Industries because she couldn't agree with his methods—his plans to carry automation to the ultimate degree, replacing man with machine and subjugating him. The man she had dismissed was Professor Keller. On another display board, Emma sees a couple of newspaper front pages, both from the *Evening News*. 'Emma Knight Dismisses Automation Man From Board', and 'Keller Sacked'.

Emma moves on to section five of the exhibition. It is entitled 'Obituary to Emma Peel'. The voice describes how he has waited so long for this opportunity. A television screen flickers into action. It is Keller. Emma had held him up to ridicule for equating man and machine, but she was wrong. He has proved that machine is not only equal to man, but superior. He'll do it without violence—the house will look after her and cherish her. It will keep her warm when she's cold, and feed her when she's hungry. She'll be kept quite safe from physical harm, as the experiment will take some time.

Emma looks around, and pulls open a set of curtains to find a large blow-up picture of her face. She hacks through it, and finds herself back in the control room. Up a level, she turns to see the dirty trousers and their owner, which had followed her earlier. She attacks, but it's not Keller, this is Burton, now on the verge of madness. Emma overpowers him and he hides in a corner, broken and disoriented, possibly regressed. He starts chanting a rhyme: "This is the horse that kicked the cow that chased the dog that bit the cat that killed the rat that lived in the house that Jack built..."

Outside, Steed has reached the house and sees Emma's car... Inside, Emma is still dealing with Burton. He's started another verse of the rhyme: "this is the bull that tossed the horse..." He cannot finish the rhyme easily this time, and has to stop to remember. Emma asks who he is. All he can relate is that he's a bad man, who ran away a long time ago and wants to get out. He holds out his hand, and she helps him up, at which point he takes the chance to try and strangle her. Emma pushes him aside. As she goes to escape through a door, Burton points a shotgun at her and laughs. Emma patiently asks him to give her the gun, if he wants to escape. But he'll have none of it, and shoots a hole in a wall. Emma skilfully removes the gun from him, and uses its butt to knock a larger hole through to the other side. There's another door immediately behind the wall, which leads to a master control room. The voice returns and congratulates her on finding a way to him.

Emma looks around and sees a man preserved in a glass cylinder. This is Keller, but he's long dead. The voice

The House That Jack Built

informs her that he has been dead for some time; now only the house is alive...Outside, Steed is looking at Emma's car. The radio is still playing, and he turns it off.

Emma is finding out the story behind what is happening. Doctors told Keller that he was going to die, that he had a year at the most to live. He used that time to great advantage. The house is a machine, indestructible, powered by solar energy and frictionless bearings. The machine's mind cannot reason and it has no breaking point, but at the end of the experiment Emma will undoubtedly be completely mad. She needs no further proof than what has happened to Burton. The machine will answer her questions if she has any, as it is tuned to her voice. The message ends.

Steed is looking around the outside of the house for a way in. Inside, Mrs Peel is studying a piece of the machinery labelled 'Programme Feed Card Slot'. Burton just looks dreamily at the pretty lights on the panels. Emma decides to ask a question of the machine. How will it know when she has been driven insane? It whirrs and splutters, and the electronic voice answers that she will kill herself. She's inquisitive as to how. The machine tells her that the key she carries will unlock a door at the far end of the machine, behind which is a small room that acts as a suicide box. Once inside, gas is released, but she will feel no pain in her death. Emma points out to the machine that it has just made a mistake. She knows what to expect now. The machine retaliates with its illusion of the lion jumping at her, and Emma shoots at it. She then realises there's nothing there—just a wall. Touching a control panel, she gets an electric shock. Controls and meters fluctuate around the room, and Burton laughs. Both Burton and Mrs Peel are then subjected to a piercing high-pitched noise, and Emma tries switching buttons and controls, but to no effect.

A car horn is sounded outside, and she realises help is at hand. The answer must be in the room—a way to get to the brain. She can't shoot her gun through the card slot, but perhaps a bomb would do it. Where can she get materials for one? The key fits in the slot as a start. Wadding and gunpowder may be a little more difficult. Maybe Burton has some shotgun shells left. She checks his belt—there is just one remaining. She extracts the gunpowder and pours it into the end of the key, which is hollow, and pushes it down with a hair clip. Burton grabs her handiwork and rushes into the suicide room. The door closes on him before Emma can stop it. The machine's LCD display flashes up a message: 'Suicide Activated—Identify—Not Target—Still Awaiting Target'. The chamber opens, and Burton is dead. Emma takes the key from his hand, and the computer brews up a heavy, howling wind. This doesn't stop Emma pushing the key

down the slot—on reaching the heart of the machine it explodes. Pandemonium breaks out, with smoke, electrical sparks and explosions everywhere.

Steed has managed to get into the hallway, and he sees the room spinning and stopping, out of control. Inside, Keller's glass chamber cracks up, just before the machine stops dead. In the hall, Steed takes a lance from a suit of armour and heads forward with it. Emma comes out of a door and meets him. "What happened to the shining armour?" she asks. Steed smiles, "It's still at the laundry. Never mind, I'll give you a ride home on the old horse." They walk down the corridor together to freedom.

Emma and Steed are on a tandem. It turns out that Withers was Pongo, sent to keep an eye on Emma. Steed told him to soft peddle Emma a little bit, which is why he didn't reveal his true identity and frighten her. With everything finally explained, they continue their journey at high speed.

(Note—This was a particularly well remembered episode, due in large part to the ingenious set. Its single dome room and corridor were filmed and lit from a variety of angles to excellent, disorienting effect. The designer, Harry Pottle, who also created the sets for Steed's and Mrs Peel's apartments, later worked on the Bond movie You Only Live Twice.)

ESCAPE IN TIME

Clive Paxton, secret agent, is looking around a country house. Life-like busts of several men, all from the same family, if their appearance is anything to go by, are placed on a high display stand in the centre of the room. Paxton walks through a door, and enters a chamber decorated with brown and ochre stripes. A switch is thrown, and he finds himself falling. Waking up, he is now in a room very similar to the one he had just left, except there is only one bust on display, and the surroundings are somewhat more antiquated. A man in Elizabethan attire appears, and shoots him...

Steed visits the barber

Emma has a close shave!

We see a card on a plinth—it reads, 'Invitation to a Grand Hunt Ball. We Request the Pleasure of the Company of Mrs Peel.' Emma is getting ready for the occasion. She puts on her silver shoes, and looks again at the invitation. Steed appears and turns it over, and on the back the card reads, 'We're Needed'.

We focus on a cabinet. The drawer we are looking at is marked 'C. PAXTON'. We're in a mortuary, and Steed and Emma, plus a civil servant, Clapham, are investigating the death of one of their best agents. At 3.45am his body was fished out of the Thames, where it had been dumped. He was shot with a sixteenth century gun of medium calibre, probably a sporting piece used exclusively by noblemen in the Elizabethan period. Steed is impressed by Mrs Peel's knowledge of the subject, and awards her ten points, putting her team into the lead, he quips. Clapham informs them that notorious criminals and men on the run are disappearing without trace. Someone has devised an escape route, and Clapham is sure that Paxton was on to it.

In Steed's apartment, Emma is looking through a file of missing persons. There's Kyle Bleschner, a German financier who embezzled half a million; Eubert, a French banker who disappeared with a cool million; President Bibi Gin, who arrived at election HQ, removed his hat and coat, and took off with the party funds. All of them were last seen heading for Britain, rather than South America, which would perhaps have been expected. Emma finds a picture of Tubby Vincent, but Steed informs her that he's on our side.

Tubby enters the room containing the busts and looks around. There's nothing of use in a desk drawer and, glancing out of the window, he sees a car. He checks a small notebook on the desk. It reads, 'Josino arriving from South America. Make contact 12.30pm, Mackidockie Court.' Beneath the writing is a drawing of a black crocodile. Tubby takes the paper and puts it in a pocket, but panics when he hears a noise from the corridor outside. Looking for somewhere to hide, he finds himself in the brown and ochre chamber. Someone pulls the handle of a fruit machine, Tubby falls, and the fruit machine stops, the dials on its face showing the year 1680. Tubby awakens, to find the room he was searching has changed again. There are three busts on the central display stand, rather than the five he had seen before. Looking out of the window, he sees a historical figure on a white horse arrive at the front door. The man comes up to the room, straight for Tubby, and stabs him with a Jacobean dagger, but Tubby manages to knock out his attacker.

Steed's doorbell rings, and Tubby stumbles in, mortally wounded. Steed looks at the note that was removed from the pad. Josino is an ex-dictator who absconded with half the treasury. Obviously another man on the run, he may just be their link to the escape route...

At Mackidockie Court, Emma and Steed follow a man who is carrying a blow-up black and green crocodile under his arm. This is Josino. He is wearing sunglasses, and a matching cream hat and coat. He stops next to a woman, Vesta, who swaps his crocodile for a stuffed giraffe. While Emma follows Vesta, Steed follows Josino. Josino stops at

a street stall, and swaps the giraffe with the vendor, Parker, for a brown and white striped kangaroo. He finds a message in the kangaroo's pouch, reads it and eats it. They walk past a newsagents, with an *Evening Standard* board and a *Daily Mail* headline sheet that reads, 'Where is Blake?', past J. Green tobacconists, and stop at a barber's shop, 'T. Sweeney—Shaving a Speciality'. Sweeney stops Josino at the door, and drags him in. Steed looks on from the shop window as Josino sits down in the chair, but he sees no more as Sweeney pulls the blinds down. Elsewhere, Emma is following Vesta in her car. Vesta has strapped the blow-up crocodile to the back of her vehicle.

Josino emerges from the barber's. He is now carrying a spotted elephant with a seat on its back. Josino has also acquired a black cross on one of his cheeks. Steed follows him to an Asian antique shop, with a statue of Ganesha, the elephant god, in the window. Later, Josino comes out of the shop, minus the elephant and the cross on his cheek. Steed's continuing pursuit is blocked by eight nuns, who congest a small alleyway on their way through. Finally getting past them, he has lost sight of his quarry. There's a ray of hope—but this is soon dashed when Steed realises he has seen a man wearing exactly the same clothes as Josino.

Emma stops her car in the road and gets out. In front of her car lies the black crocodile. Inspecting it, she heads down a nearby dirt track. She is being watched by Vesta and a man in red fox-hunting garb, Mitchell. As soon as Emma wanders into a clearing, Mitchell appears on a motor cycle, and tries to run her over. She rolls down the edge of a hill, keeping the crocodile with her. The chase continues; as Mitchell falls off his bike, Emma trips and drops the crocodile. He's persistent, and not realising that Emma is now standing at the edge of a cliff, he rides straight at her. She moves, and allows Mitchell to fall to his doom, the bike bursting into flames on impact below.

Steed is inspecting the deflated crocodile. It has seen better days. Emma is using her needlework skills to craft a duplicate stuffed giraffe, a talent which Steed was unaware of. "Our relationship hasn't been exactly domestic," Emma reminds him…

At Parker's street stall, Steed swaps the bogus giraffe for a kangaroo. Mrs Peel is keeping an eye on him from a safe distance. Steed walks off to the barber's, and Sweeney is in the doorway. He pulls Steed inside, and this time it's Emma's turn to have the window blind pulled down on her. Like Josino, Steed soon emerges with a black cross on his cheek and a stuffed elephant. He goes to the Asiatic emporium and looks at himself in the mirror within, puzzled by the cross. A lady in a sari enters—this is Anjali. She rips the black cross off Steed's cheek, and asks for his passport. Steed blusters for a moment, until she informs him that she's talking about the elephant. A

slight misunderstanding sees pearls fall from the toy, obviously the currency of the exchange. She puts the elephant in a storage trunk that contains several other similar stuffed toys. Emma, meanwhile, is still keeping look-out.

Inside the shop, Steed is told by Anjali about Ganesha the elephant god. He is a remover of all obstacles, and with his help one can surmount all barriers. She asks Steed what he would give for freedom, escape and complete liberty? Steed quips that he would give away half his kingdom. She nods: these are exactly the terms. She gives him directions to follow, and tells him that his height has been estimated at six foot two inches, his weight at 170lbs. She also insists that he continues to carry his umbrella in his right hand. Puzzled, he departs.

Steed follows the directions, back past the barber's, and Emma follows. She's blocked by two nuns, and just catches sight of Steed's figure passing by at the end of the alley ahead. Emma calls after him, but this is not Steed, just someone dressed like him. She reaches him, and realises he's a fraud. The impostor starts a fight, but is bettered by Mrs Peel. He doesn't get up.

Steed is being escorted into a car—a funeral hearse. He sees Vesta there, and then he is blindfolded. They drive along, and eventually reach the house where all the murders have taken place. Vesta goes inside and announces their arrival to Waldo Thyssen, who looks like a relative of all the busts seen earlier. Steed's blindfold is removed, and he looks around Thyssen's room. Waldo asks what Steed is escaping from, as he hasn't heard about his exploits. Steed says he just hasn't been found out yet. Waldo thinks this shows foresight, but what can he pay with? Steed says diamonds, and that he found out about Waldo's service from a friend of a friend of a friend. He's already aware of the terms, fifty per cent of the spoils. As Steed's problem is immediate, they shall therefore deal with it immediately.

Steed is treated to a film show. Users of the service have included Bleschner, Eubert, Bibi Gin and Colonel Josino, who Steed thought was in South America. Looking at a creaky black and white film of Epsom Derby Day in 1904, Steed is amazed to see Josino betting on the horses. Elsewhere, Emma is making up another stuffed giraffe…

Thyssen explains that he can send people back through the centuries. He is arranging a trial run for Steed to convince him that he is being honest. He will send him to the eighteenth century, and Steed asks if he will arrive at Waterloo. Thyssen clarifies the arrangement, saying he's travelling in time not distance, so he will therefore arrive at his point of departure.

Thyssen explains that the house has been in his family since the fifteenth century. Samuel Thyssen was alive in 1790, Steed's destination, and was considered a philan-

derer, a great one for the ladies. Steed is given a guided tour of the other busts on display. Bruno, with the goatee beard, was a sportsman; Edwin a duellist; Herbert was squire of four counties; while Matthew was the black sheep, an inquisitor and torturer who was said to have invented the rack.

Steed has changed into his costume and is shown through the door to the brown and ochre chamber. The handle of the fruit machine is pulled, and Steed feels himself falling…

He awakens on a sofa, a glass and a decanter on the side table. There are three busts on the central platform. He looks around the room, checking the back of the painting and the state of the furniture. It seems real enough, and he looks out of the window. A carriage and four horses pull up at the front door. A lady and a gentleman get out. Another couple rush through the room Steed is in, on their way to an intimate liaison. Steed has seen enough, and walks back through the door to the brown and ochre chamber. He wakes up safely in the twentieth century.

world. The double walks away and then stops—something is wrong. She rushes back to the hoarding, but it has already been replaced. It is solid, and cannot be broken through now…

Emma is in the hearse with Sweeney the barber and Parker the street vendor. They reach the house, Parker takes her blindfold off, and she is taken inside. Emma looks at the busts, and Waldo appears, looking annoyed.

Steed visits Emma's apartment, and rings the bell. There's no reply, so he presses the secret entry button at the top left of the door frame and goes inside. Emma's not at home, but he notices that she has been doing more needlework…Steed wastes no time in trying to find the house that he was taken to, and has Clapham join him in the Bentley. Clapham is struggling with the map to get some sense of bearings on where it might be—what can Steed remember? Hilly terrain, a church clock, a bridge. Not too helpful, but the memory of hearing turkeys does the trick. Clapham knows exactly which way they should head.

It is time for Steed to purchase a one-way ticket to the past, but he will have to arrange to get hold of the diamonds. Waldo instructs him that he must leave as he arrived, blindfolded.

Elsewhere, Emma has finished work on her second giraffe, and goes through the routine of getting a kangaroo from the stall, going to the barber's for an elephant, and visiting the Asian antique shop. Anjali is annoyed that they have sent a woman without telling her—she'll have to check with head office. Emma complains that this is not the sort of service she had expected, that she had heard good reports. She is then told her route—leave the shop, turn right, then left past the barber's, and there she will make her final contact. Emma follows the route, and walks past a hoarding with the headline, 'There is no substitute to 2001', with a row of four figures illustrated, holding hands. Hands burst out of the hoarding, and pull her through it, while her replacement smashes through another part of the same poster and into the outside

Emma has been told about escaping into the past. Waldo doesn't think the Victorian era would suit such a woman as Emma, nor the Elizabethan era, as Matthew was so cruel to women and Waldo wouldn't like to think of anything happening to her. The year 1790, in the Georgian era, seems ideal, and Mrs Peel feels there's no time like the present.

At the 'Yule Tide Turkey Farm', Steed and Clapham pass by in the car. Steed reckons they're close. The house must be behind the farm. Vesta, meanwhile, is just driving back to the house in her white MGB.

Emma is attired in a fetching purple Georgian dress, and is shown the door to the transfer room. Just as Emma disappears inside, Vesta turns up to warn Thyssen that Emma is the woman who followed Steed's escape route. Waldo decides to divert Mrs Peel to another era—Matthew's! He'll know how to deal with her. The fruit machine spins, and reads 1570. Emma wakes, and looks

around her. There's a large fire burning in the fireplace, and just one bust occupies the central podium. She opens a chest and finds Josino's body inside. She's been locked in the room, but her eye is drawn to the 'bust'. It rotates on its own, and springs to life. It is Matthew, in the flesh! Opening the door, Emma comes face to face with a hooded executioner…

Steed and Clapham have located the house at last. Creaking in the wind is a plinth on a frame featuring Ganesha the elephant god.

Emma has been put in the stocks. Matthew wants to know who she is, and why she is wearing strange clothes of the devil, designed to daze and bewitch a man's senses, to inflame him to lust. Emma quips that he should see her 400 years from now. Matthew's mind is made up—she's a heretic, a witch. Emma is amused, and Matthew roughly removes her Georgian wig. He will purge her secrets from her.

Sweeney the barber radios Vesta to inform her that Steed and Clapham have turned up. She asks him to deal with them. He knocks Clapham out, and then holds a shotgun to Steed, who releases gas from the end of his umbrella to subdue him. But Clapham is still out cold…

The executioner is heating a poker in the open fire—as soon as it's up to temperature, it will be used on Emma…Steed is inside the house and has reached the doors that lead to the brown and ochre time chamber. He looks around, puzzled. Vesta appears with a gun and a pair of handcuffs. Steed analyses the situation out loud, hopelessly trapped, and this is enough to catch Vesta off guard. He wrestles the gun from her, and handcuffs her to a nearby pillar. He then inspects the fruit machine, rips an external lead from it, and pulls the lever. He goes to leave, and the fruit machine comes up with four zeros, spitting out a gold coin in winnings. He continues looking around, carrying Vesta's gun for protection.

In another room, he finds an Elizabethan guardsman, apparently asleep on some steps. Steed disturbs him, and the pistol is knocked from his hand by the guardsman's rifle, flying into the air and embedding itself in the chandelier above them. Steed grabs a lance from a suit of armour on display, and does a merry jig with it, rotating it in his hands as he moves nearer. The guardsman is distracted by all this, and Steed knocks him out with a blow to the head. He then encounters Parker in Elizabethan costume, carrying a foil. They duel, but Steed's lance cannot be matched, and Parker is winded.

In the torture room, the hot poker is ready at last. Matthew puts on a glove to handle it. Steed enters and sees off the executioner, releasing Emma from the stocks in the process. Emma gleefully begins to deal with Matthew, slapping him to the floor. This defeat is too much for him, and if we hadn't realised before, we now

know that this is Waldo, who has been playing all his descendants throughout. He pulls out a twentieth century gun. Steed looks on, and comments, "A little ahead of your time, aren't you?"

Now at gunpoint, Steed and Emma discuss Thyssen's various masquerades. Emma liked his Matthew, but Steed preferred Samuel, a loveable little rogue. Steed, meanwhile, still has the lance in his hand, and Waldo orders him to drop it. Steed and Emma look at each other, and Steed does what he's told, after a fashion. The top end of the lance drops to Emma, and they move towards Waldo, carrying the lance between them. They rush him, and push him into the chest where Josino's body had been found. Emma sits on top of it to prevent Waldo's escape.

Steed reveals the secrets of the mystery. The 'time machine' is just coloured lights and cleverly placed mirrors, with the addition of a couple of canisters of sleeping gas. The trial run goes fine, but when the loot's been handed over, the game becomes much more lethal.

Steed and Emma leave through the various rooms, travelling through the 1690s, 1790s and into the 1960s. Emma sees Vesta handcuffed to the pillar and wryly notes, "Didn't we get the vote?" The duo depart, mission accomplished.

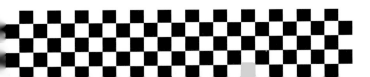

We are looking at a polished floor. One of Emma's silver shoes is on it, and chalk arrows have been drawn on the floor. They point to Emma's other silver shoe, and the arrows continue to a chair, where Steed is sitting. When Emma enters, he gets up and turns to face her.

He's prepared an escape route for her—it's not dangerous. He's taking her to a party, and has a taxi waiting. They leave to find a vintage red roadster outside. Steed opens the door so Emma can get in the back, and takes his place in the driver's seat. It will not start for him, so Emma takes over at the wheel while Steed looks around the back of the jalopy. The car backfires into action, and

Steed appears, his face covered in soot. They slowly drive off into the distance...

(Note—Peter Bowles, who played Thyssen in this episode, has enjoyed a very successful television career. He was in the pilot of Callan, *and a leading actor in such shows as* To the Manor Born, Only When I Laugh, The Bounder, Lytton's Diary, The Irish RM, Executive Stress *and* Perfect Scoundrels. *Geoffrey Bayldon, Clapham, later found fame as the star of* Catweazle, *and after that appeared as The Crowman in* Worzel Gummidge. *Rocky Taylor, who played Mitchell, turned up in* The New Avengers *episode 'The Last of the Cybernauts...?', playing the Cybernaut!)*

THE WINGED AVENGER

A cloaked figure is stalking through the undergrowth. He's approaching an office tower block, where half way up one light is on. A sign on the wall tells us that this is: 'Simon Roberts and Son—Publishers'. A gloved hand with huge talons appears, and the bird-like claw slowly traces the letters on the sign. It stops at the letter 'o' of Simon, and maliciously scratches it out.

Inside, Simon Roberts and his son Peter are agreeing that while business is always difficult, strength is power and the secret to success. An employee believes he is to be appointed to the board, but in fact he has become an unacceptable nuisance and is going to be dismissed.

The clawed figure is gradually climbing the side of the office block, gripping the concrete with its iron talons. Back inside, Simon informs Peter that he is going to be the one to give the bad news to the employee. Although reticent at first, Peter is soon sitting at his father's desk, waiting for the poor unfortunate. His father gives him one last piece of advice—these sort of things are best done quickly.

The employee with high hopes is shown in, but is asked not to sit down when he is presumptuous enough to do so. Peter tells him the bad news, just as his father had instructed him, and the ex-employee departs, a broken man. Simon is proud of his son, and suggests he goes out on the town to celebrate his baptism into the world of big business.

Roberts Senior is pouring himself a drink when he is alarmed by the sound of breaking glass behind him. Turning round, he sees that a window has been smashed, glass fragments falling everywhere. Looking out, there's nothing but an empty courtyard. What he doesn't know is that the threat is already in the room with him. It is a human figure in the costume of a blackbird, a huge beak hiding the assailant's face from view. Simon drops his glass of whisky as we hear the claws begin to slash, and he soon joins his tipple on the floor, dead. The bird flies the nest the same way it arrived...

Steed goes bird watching

Emma does a comic strip

Mrs Peel is working on an avant-garde painting, influenced by Picasso's blue period. Her name suddenly appears on the artwork, shortly followed by Steed popping his head around the easel. He informs her that they are needed...

At the crime scene, the duo interview Peter Roberts, son of the deceased. As there is no way into the room from either above or below, did the killer just fly in? Peter confirms that the door was locked, and his father's clothes had been torn to pieces, as if a huge bird had clawed him to death.

Steed and Emma consider possible suspects. Could it be an albatross, with its twelve foot wing span? Unlikely, as it isn't a vicious bird. Maybe a bird of prey. After all, there have been isolated instances of golden eagles attacking men. Simon Roberts was not the first such death, either—there have been four similar deaths recently. Steed wonders why successful businessmen always live at the top of buildings. In each case the victim had apparently been killed by a bird.

At the publishers, the Winged Avenger has returned to continue his work. As he leaves his car, we spy a comic

book on the floor which is obviously the inspiration for his name and costume. Once again he climbs, and now it is Peter in the office, exercising his father's ruthless streak. He is using a large reel-to-reel dictating machine, composing a letter threatening legal proceedings against a client. The window is open, but a vase is knocked over and smashes noisily to smithereens on the floor. Peter is obviously jumpy, wondering if he too has an intruder to face. He goes to the window and looks out. Again, there's nothing happening on the ground below. He closes the window, moving the dictating machine to his father's desk, where he continues to rehearse his hateful correspondence. The author he is concerned with is called Lexius Cray, and the threat of court action concerns a book deal that has already been struck. Suddenly, the Winged Avenger strikes again, making light work of the desk as well as his victim. We see the publishers' sign once more, and this time the birdman scratches out 'and Son' with his talons. Meanwhile, the dictation machine has recorded everything…

Steed and Emma look over the crime scene once more. Emma's eyes are drawn to the tape recorder, which needs respooling. She sets about the task, and soon they are listening to rustling noises followed by Simon's screams. Steed wonders jokingly if the killer did climb up the wall. Emma happens to know that the Lexius Cray mentioned on the tape is in fact a mountaineer—too good a clue for her to resist.

Mrs Peel joins Clay on the side of a mountain, the wind howling loudly, snow driving into their faces. Emma is posing as a magazine reporter chasing an exclusive. Clay suggests tea, which sounds like a fine idea. Pulling back, we discover that we are in Cray's office, and, as the snow and wind machines are turned off, that the whole mountainside is a mock-up for Cray's enjoyment. They will drink their tea on the terrace outside. Cray climbs down the side of the house while Emma uses the stairs. Meanwhile, Tay-Ling, Cray's butler, appears in the room, looks at a newspaper on the table, and smiles.

On the terrace, Mrs Peel tells Cray that the owners of her magazine, Simon Roberts and his son Peter, are dead. Cray knew them, and considered both to be blaggards—neither of them had a heart. They had published his memoirs and tried to swindle him out of the profits. Mrs Peel departs, and Cray remarks to Tay-Ling that he thinks they can handle her inquisitive nature. As Emma gets to her car, she watches a bird of prey flying overhead, which we see land on Cray's gloved hand.

Tay-Ling inspects the *Daily Mail* again, which has the headline 'Simon Roberts' Son Murdered'. He makes a phone call, noting to the person at the other end of the line that he has read all about his notorious exploits. Knowing that he has his listener's attention, Tay-Ling suggests that he knows how such strange things have been

carried out, and that a letter sent to his boss reveals all the evidence he needs. They talk business, and a midnight meeting is arranged.

Steed is in his apartment, inspecting a model of a high rise block with a magnifying glass, as he has decided to take a scientific approach to working out how the crime has been committed. Emma is not impressed, and wants to take action. She will pay a midnight visit to Cray to see what can be uncovered.

Time passes. Tay-Ling is pacing around the office nervously. Mrs Peel arrives in her car outside the grounds, wearing a burgundy and ochre jumpsuit. She vaults the perimeter wall with relative ease, but the Winged Avenger is already there, and the sound of a snapping twig alerts her to his presence. Both of them make for the house, the Winged Avenger using his usual method of entry, while Emma breaks in through the French windows. Cray has been watching her, however, with his bird of prey already in hand. He takes off the bird's hood in preparation.

As Emma climbs the stairs, the Winged Avenger has already found Tay-Ling, and is cutting him down to size. Alerted by the disturbance, Emma rushes to his aid, but is too late to stop the carnage. Tay-Ling is dead, the copy of the *Daily Mail* by his side, and an open window across the room. Emma is just about to check things out when suddenly Cray appears at the door, bird of prey ready to pounce. Emma immediately suspects that he is responsible, but Cray insists he has been out patrolling the grounds after hearing a disturbance. A copy of *The Winged Avenger* comic lies on the floor, and on the desk is a letter from Poole, an inventor. The professor had been seeking endorsement from Cray for a new product he had been working on. He had created boots that allow the wearer to walk up walls…

Emma takes the news back to Steed, who has been working on his scientific explanations for the crimes. He has narrowed it down to two alternatives. The first envisaged the killer inflating a small balloon, rising up the side of the nearest building, and then firing a rocket line across to the penthouse where his quarry resides. He then drops a trampoline, bounces on it, and in he goes through the window. The second alternative is that he bribed the doorman! Steed observes that the new boots Emma describes would take all the fun out of mountaineering. The Matterhorn during the tourist season would become packed with visitors—a beastly thought. Vertical tourists, vertical souvenir stall, vertical salesmen, vertical souvenirs. They decide to take the matter up with Professor Poole.

Arriving in Steed's Bentley, the duo make their way up a long flight of steps to an elegant country house. Studying the landscape, they spot Poole in a field, trying to fly with the aid of an aluminium framed cape. It isn't working, and after several attempts to get off the ground, he storms up

the steps, brushing straight past our heroes and through the heavy door into his home. Steed and Mrs Peel follow and find themselves downstairs, in a room full of model aeroplanes suspended from the ceiling and aircraft propellers on the walls. The man is obviously obsessed with aviation in all its forms. Steed and Emma try to ask him a few questions, but he never seems able to apply enough concentration in one direction to get to the end of a sentence, let alone complete an explanation.

He refuses to spare any more time for them, and marches off up his staircase. When Steed and Emma rush after him and call his name, he turns and greets them as if he was unaware they were still there. He's puzzled as to why they have come—Emma very smartly and underhandedly ventures that it's because he has promised to show them his new invention today. Poole scoffs at such a thought, and begins to praise the merits of ostriches and the miracle of birds being able to take flight. He wants to free man from his shackles through his work, explaining his activity in the field earlier! He carries on up the stairs with Steed and Mrs Peel following. They mention that they have heard of boots that help people climb walls. Evasive up until this point, Professor Poole gets even worse. Reminding them of what happened to the dodo, he storms into his study, slamming and locking the door behind him. They have to know what it is in the room that is of such importance, so Steed gives Emma a leg-up to see through the window above the door. Looking in, she is surprised to find Poole hanging upside-down from wooden bars on the far wall. They're not going to get anything out of him this time around.

Steed is sure that Poole is hiding some important information from them. He considers who the victims have been, and tries to look for a link. Yes, they had certainly all been businessmen, and ones with a reputation for

being completely ruthless in the pursuit of profit. Emma points to an article in the newspaper, about a similar tycoon. He is Edward J. Dumayn, a trendsetting business methods 'guru', who is in the process of making thousands of workers redundant by automating his factories. If ever there was someone who had set themselves up to be the next victim of the Winged Avenger, this was the man.

Dumayn is out shooting, a twelve bore under his arm. He bags one unfortunate creature, but when his gamekeeper Fothers appears, he is not too happy. Fothers is paid to keep the stocks of game high in this particular wood, but rather than grouse or pheasant, Dumayn's latest target is revealed to be a pigeon. He tells Fothers to try harder, and flush out something really big. Unfortunately, the next bird Dumayn sees is not one that can be bagged so

easily. It is the Winged Avenger, and in broad daylight the caped crusader despatches another victim to the great aviary in the sky, tearing his clothing to shreds and fatally wounding him.

Steed and Mrs Peel look through the items found at the scene of the crime. There is a page from a *Winged Avenger* comic, featuring an illustration that corresponds exactly to the photograph of the dead man's body. Surely not a coincidence? Our heroes don't think so, and decide to investigate the comic's creators.

Their enquiries lead them to Winged Avenger Enterprises, and a surprise awaits Steed in the offices of Stanton and Packer within the complex. He finds a scantily clad lady, Gerda, being menaced by someone in a Winged Avenger costume. Steed is about to rush to her rescue when he realises that this is a scenario set up to provide inspiration for artist Arnie Packer, who likes to use models to make his drawings as realistic as possible. Behind the mask of the Winged Avenger is Julian, obviously trained in the method school of acting, who is engrossed in playing the part of the costumed superhero. Right now, Arnie reckons that Julian could be acting with more feeling. The writer, Stanton, quickly composes some alternative dialogue and gives it to Julian. He will now squawk the blood-curdling cry of "Yuuuuurrp"! Practice makes perfect, and the scene is satisfactory. But this doesn't stop writer and artist arguing over who is the real creative genius behind the project, and which one has the most artistic influence over the concept. Arnie informs Steed that Stanton has been over-working, hence his fraught nature. But they are both puzzled as to why Steed is visiting them. He puts their minds at rest by saying he is after some back numbers of *The Winged Avenger* comic for a young nephew. Gerda doubles as secretary, and offers to help Steed with his query. He is happy to leave the two creatives to their bickering.

Steed reports back to Emma with his findings. Emma, meanwhile, decides that now may be the right time for her to visit Professor Poole again. In a fetching blue and magenta outfit, Emma returns to the inventor's residence and looks into his upstairs study. Finding it empty, a bookcase catches her eye—all the books have been put in upside-down. Looking up, Emma is intrigued to see that Poole is on the ceiling, sitting at a desk that is glued up there, on a chair that is similarly defying gravity. She prefers not to talk to the ceiling, so Poole agrees to join her on the ground, the right way up. This gives him a chance to demonstrate his silver boots, which we recognise as similar to those worn by the Winged Avenger. Once upright, he tries to take a step toward Emma and finds the boots are stuck. He takes a small electronic gadget out of his pocket, and presses the switch on it. The boots are instantly released. He explains that it is magnetic fields which give the footwear their amazing properties.

Poole admits that he had written to Cray about the boots, trying to get him interested in their potential, but that they were now off the market. An irresistible offer had meant that he had sold the only other existing pair, and was beginning to think of developing a far superior set, free of the imperfections they currently have. After Mrs Peel uses all the charm at her disposal to convince him, Poole agrees to tell her the identity of the purchaser, provided that she doesn't reveal that there are another pair of boots in existence—the buyer wanted shoes that were completely unique. Although he doesn't know the name of the individual who forked out for the boots, he does know who they worked for—Winged Avenger Enterprises!

Back at the drawing studio, Arnie the artist is putting the finishing touches to a scene that has the Winged Avenger surrounded by scantily clad ladies, wearing nothing but togas. Satisfied that he has captured the atmosphere, Arnie allows the models to have a rest. The break is spoiled by the arrival of Stanton, the writer, who is extremely annoyed. He points out that the Winged Avenger should be omnipotent, seeking out evil men, and disposing of

them. He doesn't see that happening in the present strips, and thinks the artist is taking the character in completely the wrong direction. At that moment, Emma appears, pretending to be a businesswoman. Her opening gambit is to ask whether the men have received a letter from her London office, which they both say hasn't arrived. After complaining about the poor administration prevalent in her company, she then reveals the contents of the alleged letter: her organisation has invested in boots that can make you walk up walls and across ceilings, and wondered if these could be incorporated into the Winged Avenger comic strips, as an exercise in cross-promotion. Stanton looks a little bleak at this, and Julian hurriedly takes off his Winged Avenger costume, while Arnie laughs in amazement.

Touching base, Steed and Mrs Peel analyse the evidence. Perhaps the fake Winged Avenger at the artist's studio is in fact the 'real' Winged Avenger—the murderer. Mr Julian E. Earp will need investigating at some point in the proceedings.

Back at the studio, Julian is putting his costume on after hours, admiring himself in the mirror in a vain way. But the real Winged Avenger is creeping up on him. Smashing the mirror, the crusader slashes at Julian, hacking him to the floor—another fatality.

Steed and Emma are trying to get inspiration and a key to the crimes from back issues of *The Winged Avenger* comic. While Steed decides to visit the studio again himself, Mrs Peel thinks it's time she put her feet up, and heads home.

At Winged Avenger Enterprises, Steed sees signs of a disturbance in the studio, and looks around. On the floor lies a huge piece of Winged Avenger artwork, with the character uttering the lines, 'And to those who stand between me and my purpose…' Steed lifts the artwork and finds Julian beneath it, another victim of the real vigilante. Putting a drawing board lamp on, Steed studies some of the latest pieces of artwork that have been left there. He finds drawings of each of the victims, illustrated in the positions in which they were found dead. The last

drawing he looks at is of Professor Poole, nervously sitting down and picking up a telephone.

Next we see Poole in exactly the same position. The person he is calling is Emma Peel. She's at home reading a book, and picks up her red telephone almost as soon as it rings. Poole asks her to come and see him immediately, and that she must not tell anyone where she is going. As he puts the phone down, a large claw appears in front of his face…

Steed has found an illustration depicting Poole being menaced by a large and sinister claw, one capable of doing great damage. Outside the office, passing the recently slashed sign which reads 'Winged Avenger Enterprises', is a man wearing soft blue shoes and carrying a gun. He sneaks up on Steed as he continues to study the revealing pieces of artwork, and places the revolver to Steed's left ear. Our hero quickly overpowers him, twisting his arm behind him and grabbing the gun; the would-be assassin is revealed to be Stanton, the writer. He had been alerted to the break-in and had come to investigate, coming armed for trouble. The writer is horrified to see that Julian is dead, but is even more shocked to see the series of drawings that Steed has been looking through, indignant that he hasn't scripted any of these artwork panels! The next one in the pile features a character called Elma Peem, which Stanton is a bit slow off the mark in realising is an anagram of Emma Peel! The illustration shows Emma walking up the steps to Poole's house—we cut to the scene happening in real time, followed by a picture of her climbing the stairs, which we see actually taking place. Realising that this is a storyboard of events that are gradually unfolding, Steed and Stanton jump into Steed's Bentley and rush to Poole's residence.

As time ticks by, the Winged Avenger already has Mrs Peel cornered at the entrance to Poole's study, just like in one of the cartoons in Stanton's possession. Emma slips inside the study and bolts the door. Luckily, her action buys her some time, as although the talons do some damage to the wood, the Winged Avenger is unable to break in and therefore opts to use the window to make an entrance. As Emma catches her breath, she looks up to the ceiling and sees Poole hanging down from it, lifeless, his boots keeping him up in the air. The threat to her life is once again approaching, as the Winged Avenger climbs across to the study window, so Emma drags Poole's body down from the ceiling and takes the silver boots from his feet.

Steed and Stanton hurry to the scene as the Winged Avenger smashes through the window in spectacular fashion, glass and framework flying in all directions. He looks around hurriedly, only to realise that Mrs Peel is above him, on the ceiling, wearing the same sort of boots as he is. Emma reckons that this will even the odds. The Winged Avenger announces that he is the eradicator of all evils, dealing out justice and vengeance to those the law cannot touch, and those who stand between him and his purpose.

He joins Emma on the ceiling, continuing to insist that he is creator and creation fused together in one being: indivisible, omnipotent, unstoppable. Perhaps Emma starts to realise exactly who she's dealing with. Her opponent is not prepared to let anything stand, or indeed hang, in his way. The pair begin to fight as Steed and Stanton pull up outside.

Stanton carries with him the artwork boards, and a noise from upstairs alerts Steed to where Mrs Peel is fighting for her life. He reaches the door to the study with Stanton close behind, struggling with the drawings. With one smooth kick, Steed has the door rattling off its hinges. They enter the room to the sound of the battle being played out over their heads, slowed down by the jerky movements required to hold the shoes to the ceiling. Music breaks out, rather similar to that from a TV series about another well known Caped Crusader… Grabbing a board from Stanton, Steed hits the Winged Avenger over the head with it. It has illustrated on it a cartoon word bubble saying, 'Pow!' Being a tough customer, it takes similar boards with 'Splat!' and 'Bam!' on them before Emma gets the chance to unhook her opponent's boots, the impact of the final board knocking the Winged Avenger straight out of the window he came in through.

Looking down to the ground below, we see that it is Arnie Packer who lies immobile, his Winged Avenger mask knocked off during the fall. "Really got his wings clipped," remarks Steed. Emma switches her boots off and comes down from the ceiling with Steed's assistance. "Yuuuuurrp!", Steed notes.

We next see our two principals enter Mrs Peel's apartment. Champagne is on ice, but that doesn't make a very balanced meal. Steed tries his hand with a charcoal pencil on a canvas as Mrs Peel uncorks the bubbly. What do they fancy? Oysters, turtle soup, a 1959 Chablis, *crêpe surprise,* tawny port and peeled walnuts, perhaps? Steed has visualised them in his work at the easel, and the reality is quickly wheeled in on a serving trolley. "The Benevolent Avenger strikes again," he remarks, as he brings together the lids of two serving bowls. They meet with a high-pitched ring, and a cartoon splash bubble appears between the two objects saying, 'Ping!'

(Note—the cartoon drawings in this episode were from the hand of the much-missed Frank Bellamy, a stalwart of the Century 21 *comic strips of the 1960s.)*

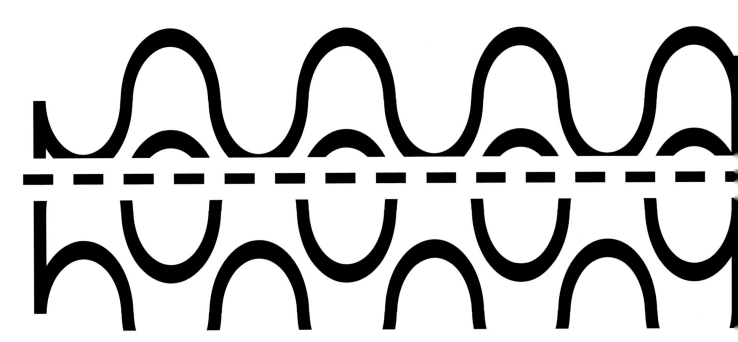

A fanfare is heard, and we see a prize statuette. It is a maiden holding a drape over her head, frozen in the motion of blowing in the wind. Looking down we find an engraved plate on the front, revealing that this is the 'Ollington Award, given to Z. Z. Von Schnerk for the Best Cinematograph Film of 1921'. Looking around the room we see a film poster. The star of the movie was Damita Syn, and the title was *The Bad Bad Lady*. The woman on the poster is obviously a vamp, with a long cigarette holder. To the right, we see the reality—this is Damita now, much older but still with the cigarette holder in hand. She moves towards a man who looks like the stereotypical silent movie director—this is Z. Z. Von Schnerk. A man is in the room with them, dressed exactly as John Steed would be in a similar meeting. Damita asks Z. Z. what he thinks of him. The director inspects him closely. He thinks him perfect for the part, but Damita asks for a second opinion.

We now see a man standing in front of another film poster, wearing a smoking jacket, and once again mirroring the demeanour of the actor portrayed on the poster. If his billing is correct, this is Stewart Kirby, former star of the film *Sophisticated Scoundrel*. Kirby thinks the man dressed like Steed is splendid, perfectly splendid, but maybe a bit tall. He checks this by reluctantly putting on a pair of glasses and taking them off again swiftly. Besides, the look-a-like has been employed for a non-speaking part, and the look is the most important thing. They decide it's time for a screen test. Z. Z. forms his hands into a square so that he can see what the camera will see, and Kirby takes out a gun. The double for Steed is shocked, and is about to say something before Damita reminds him that he has no dialogue. Kirby shoots him, and he falls to the floor, dead. A beautiful performance, Kirby reckons—he makes an excellent corpse.

Steed catches a falling star

Emma makes a movie

Steed rings an ornate doorbell with Mrs Peel's name on it, before looking above the door for the key. The door opens immediately and Emma exits in a great hurry, wearing a violet overcoat. Before Steed can say anything, she dismisses him, "Sorry Steed, I'm needed elsewhere." With that, she walks on. Steed follows, wondering where they are going.

"North to Whittlesham Farm. Find Fitzroy Lane, continue along it for five eighths of a mile, and stop," she says. What then? Steed wonders. Emma has had an anonymous phone call—a plea for help. Apparently, it's a matter of life and death, but Steed ventures that it could be a trap...

The duo arrive at the meeting place. It's on a road lined with fields, and in the one next to them are some ponies. A figure on a bicycle approaches in the distance, a local priest, who rides by them tipping his hat. Steed and Emma decide that this is obviously a false alarm and depart, passing the man of the cloth in their car. The priest stops and smiles. We recognise him—it is Stewart Kirby in a disguise. Checking the parcel rack of his bicycle, we see that the brown package has a camera lens poking out of the side of it. He pats it approvingly and smiles.

Back at Emma's apartment, she and Steed listen to the phone message again, with its abrupt conclusion. Steed thinks there is something vaguely familiar about the voice. Emma asks him to let her know if it comes to him in a blinding flash. Steed then reveals the reason for calling on her in the first place. He thought he'd drop by to ask her out for dinner, but perhaps they could start off with a ride over to the coast. Emma has to see a friend, but she'll be back by 5.00pm, so that's fine. Steed will call again to pick her up at 6.00pm.

Kirby is proudly showing Z. Z. and Damita the black and white film he has taken of our heroes in a screening room, when suddenly he orders that the film be stopped. He likes Emma: she has poise, looks and an animal vitality. Kirby likes the last phrase—it sums her up perfectly. Z. Z. wants Mrs Peel.

The bonnet of Mrs Peel's powder blue Lotus Elan S2 is up, and a pair of gloved hands cut a wire underneath it before putting it back in place. Emma appears around the corner, dressed in a light green trouser suit with white shoes. She gets into her car, but it won't start. A taxi pulls up, and an old lady dressed in black with an umbrella gets out, giving Emma the opportunity of an alternative form of transport. She asks to be taken to Victoria Grove.

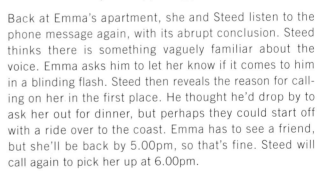

The taxi sets off, but it is Kirby at the wheel, in another one of his disguises. The old lady watches the taxi pass by—we see that it's Damita.

Driving along, they don't get far before Emma realises she is being taken the wrong way—they're heading out into the country. As she begins to protest, Kirby throws a switch, and gas floods the passenger compartment of the taxi through an air vent, sending Emma to sleep. The taxi proceeds to Schnerk Studios—'The Home of Z. Z. Von Schnerk Productions'. The gates open electronically, and we approach a studio that has definitely seen better days.

Kirby informs Z. Z. of Emma's arrival from a phone in an outhouse. Z. Z. is pleased, and throws a switch in a cabinet marked 'Electrified Wire System—Danger'. The box sparks into action.

Kirby gets into the taxi and drives around to the backlot. We go past sentry boxes, native totems, large vases and other bric-a-brac. They reach sound stage four, and the entrance door rises upwards to allow the taxi access. Inside, Emma falls out of the taxi onto the floor, still unconscious. Z. Z. is there with Damita, and they inspect their capture. The director is even more sure that Emma is absolutely perfect. Outside, a red light flashes below a sign on the soundstage that reads, 'No Entry While Red Light Is On'.

Time passes, and Emma wakes to find herself on a black and orange Persian carpet. She struggles to a sofa, and picks up a red phone beside it. There is no tone, and on checking the wire she finds that it isn't plugged in. Getting to her feet, she finds a decanter and pours herself a drink. It tastes alright, and she's obviously thirsty. Emma crosses the room to a window, pulls back the net curtain and sees another building across the street, but it doesn't look real. Inspecting an internal door, she finds a couple of film cameras and several arc lights pointing at her. She wanders through and finds that she's on a film set. Look-

ing to one side, she sees a street, with her Lotus parked on it. Emma leans against a wall, but her hand goes through it. She checks her car and then gets into the driving seat, but it still won't start for her. The taxi with Kirby at the wheel drives along the back of the set—Emma gets out of her car and follows it on foot.

Moving from one set to another, Emma finds herself looking at a church on a hill, the bells pealing merrily. In the foreground is a black wedding car, and something is attached to it. Examining it, Emma finds that it is a bride's head-dress. On the radiator mast-head of the Rolls Royce is a card. It reads: 'Wedding Invitation. You are invited to the wedding of Emma Peel.' She looks over to the graveyard next to the car, through an ornate gate. There is Kirby, now dressed as a bald vicar, looking like he's preaching an outdoor service. A wind machine is blowing leaves all over the set, conjuring up a heavy gale. The vicar beckons Emma towards him, and as she gets closer, distracts her by pointing into the distance, and pushes her down a hill. The vicar rubs his hands with glee as she rolls to the bottom of the slope. Picking herself up, Mrs Peel looks across the set to see a different car, a hearse. The bells of the church now chime mournfully. This car has a gold card with black writing on its bonnet. It reads: 'R.I.P. Emma Peel'. Emma looks around at the graveyard, and she can now see the faces of the headstones. They all say 'R.I.P. Emma Peel', in a variety of styles and typefaces.

She hears a voice call her name. The hearse now has a driver. It is Kirby again, with a pasty white face and an undertaker's outfit. They have been waiting for her. The wind machine stops, and Emma takes the chance to run off the set. Backstage, one floodlight after another illuminates her, until she is cornered under their intensity. Suddenly, all the lights are switched off at once. She looks around and sees a director's chair, with the name John Steed on the back. A figure in a bowler hat occupies it, facing away from her. On inspection, it is not Steed after all, but the body of the extra who was killed earlier. Emma is puzzled. Hearing voices on another part of the soundstage, she goes to investigate.

A queen, actually Damita, is sitting on a throne doing some knitting with very large needles. She notices Emma eventually, looks disgruntled, and carries on with her hobby. Mrs Peel enquires as to her identity and her part in the little tragedy that is going on, but is met with stony silence. Then, a fanfare announces the arrival of Kirby again, this time dressed as a Roman centurion, bursting onto the set through a pair of ornate double doors (behind him, offstage, we see a long blue sign that reads: 'Police Department—City of San Francisco'). Kirby tells Emma to stay away from his mother, who is pleased to see the return of her "son". Kirby is Alexander, home from the wars. The duo ham it up shamelessly, and Emma finds out that she has been cast as the wicked little sister. Alexander offers to kill Emma for his mother, which she approves of. A fight breaks out, but Kirby is no stuntman. Emma throws and kicks him into submission, but evil wins out when the queen hits Mrs Peel over the head with a scroll. Z. Z. appears, announcing his approval of how the scene was played, and Damita marks the scene with a clapperboard reading: 'The Destruction of Emma Peel, Director Z. Z. Von Schnerk, Slate 27, Take 1'.

Emma wakes again to find herself lying on a bed. A Western-style holster has been tied around her, with a six-gun in it. She inspects the gun, gets off the bed, and puts it back in its holster. She looks at a piece of modern art in the room, but is interrupted by hearing the sounds you'd expect to hear in a Western saloon coming from next door—there's even a piano tinkling away! She goes to investigate, entering the scene through a pair of swinging double doors. Kirby is at the bar, dressed in cowboy gear and toying with his own six-gun. Upon Emma's entrance the piano stops, as does the noise of the invisible crowd—the room is empty but for the two of them. Kirby spins the bullet chamber of his gun around, and warns her to get out of town. When Emma stands her ground, they face up for a shoot-out, a duel to the death. Emma is quicker on the draw, and Kirby falls across the piano, a patch of blood blossoming on the front of his shirt.

Emma takes the gun from him as he lies 'dead', and leaves the set, the noise of the crowd and the piano starting up again. On the rigging above the scene, Z. Z. and Damita look on. Z. Z. likes the results, telling Kirby he was marvellous. He reveals that he is creating his ultimate masterpiece, a compendium of all his films, a picture with passion, horror, danger and Mrs Peel as the lead! When Damita worries about Emma's departure, Z. Z. tells her not to be concerned—she cannot possibly get away from the studio. As Z. Z. escorts Kirby from the set to talk about the next scene, our attention is drawn to a silent movie text board on the set—'Meanwhile … back at the ranch'.

Steed lets himself into Emma's apartment, but is surprised that she has not yet returned. Not like her at all. He checks all the rooms, with no luck. He listens to the answering machine tape again, replaying the earlier message, checking it over and over, the answer he's seeking only just eluding him …

Back at the studio, Z. Z. is explaining how a great movie is a magnificent fabric, woven from the head to the eyes to the heart—the rest merely shadows. Kirby and Damita are listening, and are a little annoyed to be described as puppets. Z. Z. reminds them they are still under contract to him thanks to some ridiculous small print in their paperwork. The two thespians curse their agents. Z. Z. promises that this picture will restore them to the galaxy of stars in which they used to shine. It is time to change the com-

plexion of the movie—so far it has been confined and claustrophobic, but now it's time to open the story out …

Emma is looking for a way out. She finds the entrance, and a door slides upwards to allow access to the outside world. However, across from the door and behind some sandbags is Kirby, this time in the guise of a German Kaiser, cradling a machine gun. Emma dives for cover as he opens fire, managing to run once the hail of bullets has subsided. The Kaiser lines up for a bayonet charge instead, pursuing Emma down one of the studio's streets.

A soldier on horseback appears in front of Mrs Peel, wearing a bearskin hat and brandishing a sword. Emma runs for cover at the side of the street.

Z. Z. and his two actors assemble, the director carrying a handheld camera. He calls for a copy of the scenario, and Damita produces it from under her soldier costume. Z. Z. states that this is a very important part of the picture, a descent into the realms of terror, confusion and helpless efforts to escape.

Emma looks around the backlot and an arrow flies past her face, embedding itself into the side of a wagon. A Red Indian announces his presence with a war-cry—it is Kirby again. Damita the squaw had fired the arrow. Emma takes out one of the pistols she acquired in the Western set-piece and shoots Kirby. She does this three times, as Kirby keeps getting up, before she realises the gun is firing blanks. The pair move to the back of the wagon, Kirby brandishing a tomahawk. Emma beats him to the ground, breaking an arrow over him before running off. Z. Z. appears, annoyed. Kirby was scripted to win. This will mean pink pages! Time to start planning the agonising climax—the real death of Emma Peel.

In the projection room, Z. Z., Kirby and Damita are watching the latest rushes. The Centurion scene with the fist fight brings back unhappy memories for Kirby. Z. Z. is not happy—the film doesn't flow, they will have to do a retake of it all. Kirby compares Emma to an Amazon. Z. Z. scoffs, saying what they need this time is a last, desperate struggle. She will be captured, and they will kill her. Z. Z. orders his cohorts to find Mrs Peel.

Mrs Peel has reached the perimeter fence and pushes a prop street lamp against it. Sparks fly as Emma discovers the fence is electrified. As she gains a vantage point next to a large cat's head ornament, she hears whistling—it is a policeman with a bicycle. Emma rushes over, informing him that she has been kidnapped and a man has been murdered. She leads him to the body. Z. Z. and his actors have seen all this happening, but who cast the policeman, Z. Z. wonders? He will write him into the script, but write him out again—permanently.

Emma shows the PC the body of Steed's double, reminding him that the killer is still about, but he is a little obsessive about procedure. The constable mutters something about usually getting shot down and killed before he arrives at the scene of the crime, re-enacting a scene where he is shot from an upstairs room. Emma realises he is not a policeman at all—he's an extra, who prefers to be known as a 'film artiste'. He used to work at the studios, and often sneaks in to borrow his old costume and relive happy memories. As he knows where there is a hole in the electric fence, Emma asks him to escort her off the premises. He doesn't believe that she's been kidnapped, and suggests she leaves through the main gate—they must be making a film again, and he won't hear any other excuse.

Only when he realises the dead body really is dead, and there are no cameras about, does he agree to help.

Suddenly, Kirby appears, dressed as a gangster, carrying a tommy gun and flipping a coin in one hand. He recognises the extra, O'Reilly, and O'Reilly certainly recognises him, convinced once more that this has to be a movie in production. He relishes the chance to do a scene with Stewart Kirby, even though Emma tries to warn him that this one could be fatal. He walks toward Kirby, asking him to drop his gun, but Kirby guns him down, throwing the coin into the policeman's hat on the floor, quoting the appropriate cliché—"That's for the wife and kids!" He turns his gun on Emma. She ducks behind a shelf unit full of bottles, which is dramatically demolished by the gunfire.

Steed, meanwhile, is still puzzling over the answer message and its familiar voice. A speech from *Hamlet* plays in his head, and then, inspiration! It is the voice of Stewart Kirby!

The players in the film have returned to the queen's throne room set. Damita is once again knitting in her role, and Emma witnesses Kirby's entrance, this time as an American Confederate soldier. Re-enacting the scene, it is time once more to get rid of the evil younger sister—Mrs Peel. Kirby draws his sword, and gives it to the queen. The fight begins again, and this time he manages to overpower Emma. Z. Z. stops the scene, refusing to allow Kirby to run her through with his sword.

It's time for the climax of the movie. The heroine is trapped and the diabolical arch-fiend Z. Z. reveals his terrible plan. By now, Mrs Peel has been tied to an upright operating table by Kirby. Z. Z. introduces himself to his victim. He is making a movie, a downbeat film where the heroine dies. A tragedy. A drama that will place him once again among the ranks of the immortal film-makers. Confusion, desperation, fear, horror, death—all authentic and filmed as exactly as events happen. Z. Z. needs Mrs Peel, a woman of courage, beauty and action who could become desperate and remain strong, become confused but remain intelligent, who could fight back and yet remain feminine. Z. Z. hopes she will die bravely, for he will make her the posthumous star of his masterpiece, written, produced and directed by Z. Z. Von Schnerk! We see a close-up of Emma's face, surrounded by a ring of animated stars and the wording: 'A Z. Z. Von Schnerk Production'. Mrs Peel growls like a lion, right on cue.

Outside the gates of the studio, Steed has arrived in his Bentley. Inside, we are on the set of a mad scientist's lab, a half-moon guillotine swinging from the ceiling above. Emma is tied to a long table. Steed is looking for a way to get over the electric fence. He finds a set of wooden steps to lean against it. Climbing up the one side, he comes down the other on a spiral staircase left out in the open after some long-forgotten motion picture.

Kirby and Damita appear on the set, made up as leads in a horror movie, pale and drawn. Kirby has acquired a hunch-back, Damita a limp and the name Natasha. Time to carry out their experiment on human tissue they reveal, while Z. Z. films it all. Kirby must get his revenge, but he does not want to use his knives and scalpels—too crude. Mrs Peel's death needs more poetry—it will take time, but the end will be inevitable. Emma is asked what she thinks, and says she's in danger of becoming a split personality. The ad-lib is enough to stop the action, but it may have given Z. Z. an idea. There is a circular saw at one end of the long table. The cameras roll again and their work continues.

Steed is on the soundstage, and finds a script for the movie, which he reads with horror. Kirby is on the set, about to throw the switch to start the circular saw, but he is premature. They need to crow over their victim. Emma looks at them and says, "Gloat all you like, but remember, I'm the star of this picture." She has needled them, and Z. Z. yells "Cut." They need the body of the Steed stand-in now, and the actors go off to find it on the other film set.

But the real Steed is already there, and after skipping to the end of the script, he has found the body of his double. He hears Damita and Kirby approaching and hides. The body is too heavy, so they go to look for a wheelchair. This gives Steed the chance to substitute himself for his double, and, unwittingly, the two actors wheel him back to the action.

On the laboratory set, Z. Z. has started the saw rotating, and Emma is gradually moving towards it on a conveyer belt. It needs atmosphere, Z. Z. thinks, and he starts to play the piano in dramatic silent-movie style. The actors and Steed appear, and to their surprise Steed comes to life. They fight over the machine's on/off switch as the camera keeps filming. Steed overpowers them, and he's just about to switch the saw off when Z. Z. fires a warning shot with a pistol. Perhaps a change of title for the movie? *The Destruction of Peel and Steed*? Steed throws his brolly, causing the grand piano's lid to fall on Z. Z.'s outstretched gun hand. With this distraction he presses the button and stops the blade. Z. Z. rushes over, gun still in hand, and struggles with Steed. The gun goes

off... it is Z. Z. who is hit, but like the true professional he crawls to his camera and shouts, "Cut... Print!", before finally keeling over. Steed unties Mrs Peel, asking if she enjoyed the picture. She replies that at least it had a happy ending, but her favourite bit was people being hit over the head with a chair. She demonstrates on Steed, but this time it's a real chair, and Steed is out cold!

Steed and Emma are reading the papers. They're looking for a film to go and see. *I Was Napoleon's Nanny*, perhaps? An old Stewart Kirby film at the Plaza? What about *Nights of Abandon* at 'The Art'—unbridled and full of passion and sensuality, the winner of German and French awards. Steed's interest is piqued, but it closed yesterday. They decide to spend the evening at Emma's apartment. She pushes a foot against the wall, and it falls over. They're not at Steed's after all, but still on a film set!

(Note—Stewart Kirby was played by Peter Wyngarde, who went on to international recognition as author Jason King in the TV series of the same name, the character having evolved in a previous series, Department 'S'.) ◉

SOMETHING NASTY IN THE NURSERY

A man is running along a country road. He opens a big white gate leading to a house. Something has scared him. He gets to the front door and rings the bell, but there is no reply. It seems he is being chased by a skirted figure in an electric wheelchair, moving at high speed. He climbs in through a window, and locks it behind him. Taking out a gun, he locks the internal door and makes a hurried call on a green telephone. He asks the man who answers, Stockton, to urgently put him through to General Wilmot, owner of the house. We hear the sound of breaking glass, and a ball with yellow and blue stripes rolls along the floor. The man eyes the ball with suspicion and picks it up. It hypnotises him with its pattern, and he sees clockwork soldiers and toy monkeys, while he is suddenly in an oversized play-pen. The nanny in the wheelchair appears, but we still do not see her face. She says it is time for bed, takes the gun from him, and shoots…

Steed acquires a nanny

Emma shops for toys!

Emma wakes at her apartment in a violet two-piece outfit with a mustard polo-neck. A miniature merry-go-round is on a nearby table. A flag on one of the horses reads 'Mrs Peel'. Next Steed appears, stating that "We're needed."

At the Wilmot residence, Steed introduces Emma to the General. Also in the room is the dead man, Dobson, now under a white sheet. He has his thumb in his mouth, and a gun in the other hand. The leaking of defence secrets had been traced to one of three men—Sir George Collins, son of the attorney general, Viscount Webster, DS and Bar, or Lord William Beaumont, second cousin to a prince. Dobson had been investigating the men. Wilmot cannot believe that any of them could be a traitor. Steed points out that someone got to Dobson, so there could be a connection. Emma, who has been looking around, can smell lavender.

At Lord Beaumont's, a yellow and blue ball, similar to the one encountered by Dobson, is thrown through a window. Beaumont looks out, but there is no one to be seen. He picks up the ball, and he too is hypnotised, dreaming of clockwork toys and bubbles. He finds himself in a nursery with a spinning windmill and a big teddy bear. Once again, the faceless nanny appears…

Steed and Emma pull up outside Beaumont's residence, to see that Viscount Webster and Sir George have arrived before them. They cannot get an answer from the front door. Inside, Beaumont comes around from what he believes to be a dream to see the head of a stuffed grizzly bear staring at him from the wall. His eyes come into focus just in time to see Steed and entourage coming in through the French windows. He greets them all, but in the sort of excited way a child would. They are there for an important meeting, but Beaumont will have none of it, he'd prefer to go and play. When Steed mentions that there's been a leak of secrets, Beaumont shushes him by putting his finger to his lips.

Emma is looking around the grounds and finds the electric wheelchair, empty. Distracted by a disturbance in the bushes, she returns to find the wheelchair gone. Back inside, Beaumont doesn't believe the evidence on paper Steed has brought with him, so he screws it up into a ball and tries to throw it into the bin. He misses and goes to retrieve it from under the desk, muttering something about "Roberts." The other two men are a little disconcerted by the mention of the name. Beaumont gets up a little too quickly and bangs his head, knocking himself out.

Webster has things to do, and leaves hurriedly in his Jaguar. Emma follows, fearing that something is amiss. Sir George leaves very shortly after, as soon as Beaumont has come around. Beaumont is back to normal, but Steed wonders who this "Roberts" was he had mentioned while regressed. It turns out that she was his old nanny, and he recounts his recent dream about her, the nursery and the bouncing ball.

Webster gets back home, and Gordon, a man in a Mini, uses his radio to alert someone to his arrival, telling him to stand by. Inside, Webster gives James the butler his coat, and asks if he could get the pictures of nanny Roberts from the cellar. Obediently, James descends to the cellar, where he opens a trunk and finds the photographs. Unbeknownst to him, nanny is outside, as we can see from the ankle-high window at the top of the cellar wall…

Looking through the pictures, the pair recall how it must be thirty years since they've seen nanny Roberts. Webster finds it odd that Beaumont had mentioned her. Webster chooses a photo of the lady, and keeps hold of it. James returns the rest to the cellar, but someone is there waiting for him.

When James does not return, Webster follows him to the cellar—behind him a ball bounces down the stairs. Climbing the stairs with the ball, he sits down in a chair and looks at it, instantly hypnotised. He sees himself on a rocking horse, and, once again, the faceless nanny appears.

Emma arrives outside Webster's, and Gordon alerts his accomplice to her arrival. She finds Webster asleep, clutching the ball marked 'Martin's Toy Shop' and the photo of nanny. She hears someone in the cellar and goes to investigate. Down there, a gloved hand takes hold of a spear and throws it at her. A suit of armour falls over, revealing the body of James, slumped over a rocking horse.

Back at Beaumont's, Steed is asking about nanny. Beaumont remembers her smell of lavender and recalls she had set up a school for nannies.

Noting the origin of the ball, Steed pays a visit to the establishment, where its sign proclaims: 'Est. 1780. J. W. Martin & Son & Son & Son'. Inside, a train set is in working order, there are 'play' crown jewels, big building blocks, a sentry box and guard, and a jack-in-the-box on display. Martin appears, pointing out their reputation for supplying the nobility. Steed notices a tray full of 'Baby Bouncer' balls, of the blue and yellow variety. Martin says they are not for sale as they're a customer's own design. In fact, they're for G.O.N.N.—the 'Guild of Noble Nannies'.

Considering such a guild worth a visit, Steed locates the headquarters of G.O.N.N. (its sign reads: 'Unsurpassed

Childcare for the Nobility—Training School & Agency. Principal: Nanny Roberts'). Inside, in training room one, Steed finds eight nannies marching with prams. He is quickly surrounded, as the nannies pull out rattles from the prams, shaking them in unison. Goat, the tutor, greets Steed, thinking he must be an expectant father.

His secretary, Lister, appears, and Steed says he is here to see an old nanny of his, nanny Roberts. Goat reveals she is completely chair-ridden, and Lister is not at all enthusiastic about arranging such a meeting, especially at the moment, as she will be having her afternoon nap and shouldn't be disturbed.

Outside the room, Lister bumps into Gordon, who grumbles about how he hates playing nursemaid to a nanny, and Lister reveals she has to go into action again at three o'clock. Meanwhile, the trainee nannies take a break, leaving Steed to hold the babies—all eight of them—in their prams.

Lister is holding a blue and yellow ball. Their next target is Sir George. Meanwhile, Emma arrives in her car, and finds Steed still trying to cope with the children. She reveals that the babies are just sophisticated dolls. Steed tells her about the special balls at Martin's, and Emma shows him the picture of nanny Roberts. It's puzzling—she'll be in her eighties now. They wonder if Sir George could have had her as a nanny, too. Emma decides to go and ask him.

At Park Mansions, Sir George is going to his car, but a ball has already been placed there. He too is hypnotised, and finds himself in a nursery as nanny Roberts appears.

Emma arrives at Park Mansions, but Gordon spots her and tries to run her over in his Mini. She manages to get through a door and into a building to escape his violent ramming. She puts her head round the door to see a figure in a nanny costume jump into the back of the Mini as it speeds off. Emma finds Sir George in his Rolls Royce, regressed. He wakes from his dream, quickly returns to normal, and relates what has happened to him.

Lister wakes Steed to announce that nanny Roberts will see him now, but she draws the curtains, saying nanny finds the light a strain. Nanny is brought in, seated in her electric wheelchair. Steed tries to jog her memory as to who he is. Roberts is not sure. Outside in the office, Gordon is checking through the records. Steed says good-bye when he gets no recognition from nanny, but not before spotting a bottle of 'Old Lavender' on a side table. He finds his own way out, overhearing the course now in training room two, all about child welfare and health care.

Lister and Gordon tell nanny it was a mistake to see Steed—he never was in her charge, as Gordon's check of the records has revealed. This is the last piece of snooping Steed will do, Gordon muses.

Steed is in his apartment, putting champagne on ice and polishing glasses. Gordon arrives in his Mini, complete with a boxed 'Baby Bouncer'. Hearing an intruder, Steed grabs a gun from a desk drawer, only to see a black ball rolling down his spiral staircase. He picks the ball up, and hears a ticking sound. Hurriedly, he grabs his tuba from by the window, and pulls out the flowers arranged in it. He drops the ball inside it instead, and aims the tuba out of the window. There is a huge explosion.

Lister greets Gordon when he returns to G.O.N.N. headquarters. It's good-bye Mr Steed, they reckon. Lister has found out that the defence meeting has been cancelled, so they have another delivery to make. This time they go straight to the top. They also realise there is only one way Steed could have found out about their operation…

Emma arrives at Steed's apartment to find Steed picking himself up. He explains that he has been indulging in a little target practice. Emma tells him about Sir George, and her sighting of nanny Roberts. Steed decides to visit the toy shop again. Emma suggests they hurry, as every time they track down someone who can help them, somebody else gets there first.

At Martin's, nanny Roberts appears with a box. Martin thinks it's a repair job, as nanny says nothing. Outside the shop, Steed arrives just as nanny leaves in the Mini. Inside, he finds Martin lying on the floor, but he's just looking for something. Within the last hour someone bought his entire supply of 'Baby Bouncers'. Before Steed can find out who, the box that nanny brought in springs open, a hand holding a gun jumps up, and Martin is shot dead!

Back at G.O.N.N. headquarters, Lister is annoyed with Gordon. It's obvious he hasn't dealt with Steed, as he has turned up outside, and knows about Wilmot now. Gordon grabs a gun to make amends for his error, but Steed is nowhere to be found, so Lister calls for nanny.

Gordon runs through the woods trying to locate Steed, but only finds his Bentley. Gordon hides behind it, but Steed sees him crouching there when he returns. He vaults over the car and jumps on Gordon from above, knocking him out. At that moment, Steed sees the electric wheelchair and its sinister occupant coming towards him. Nanny pulls back her rug to reveal a machine gun. She fires it, but Steed evades her, jumping into his car and speeding away, bullets hitting the windshield as he makes it to safety.

Steed assumes that General Wilmot is next on the hit list. He visits him and tells the General so. After all, Wilmot planned the new missile bases. Wilmot says all his information is in his head, so there's nothing to worry about. Steed reckons precisely the opposite. If they could get to Beaumont, Collins and Webster, they could get to him.

Lister leaves Gordon in charge of HQ as she prepares to deliver another ball in the Mini. Enter Emma, who spies a

swing outside the training room, finding a hypodermic needle and a tray on the seat. Nanny Roberts appears, and although we think at first she's about to strangle Emma, she actually needs help. Gordon sees this liaison and opens fire, but Emma knocks him out, activating in the process a tape recorder which features the lecture that Steed heard earlier. She also finds shelves of the 'Baby Bouncer' balls, one of the trays marked 'treated'. Emma picks up one of them, and it begins to hypnotise her. Finding herself in an oversized nursery, she keels over.

Steed tells Wilmot about the crooks regressing all his associates back to childhood. Wilmot can't believe nanny Roberts is involved. Just at that moment a ball is thrown through the window, and Wilmot picks it up. He is hypnotised. Steed hides and watches as nanny appears with Lister, but 'nanny' is in fact Goat, the tutor from the school. Steed is spotted, but pretends he too has regressed. Goat explains that the balls are coated with a psychedelic drug that is absorbed through the skin. It produces immediate hallucinations of infancy, but the memory remains unaffected, even enhanced, and victims then tell their 'old nanny' anything. Picking Wilmot up, they show him a map, and ask him to place toy rockets where the missiles are kept. He does so willingly, and the villains mark up the map with a pencil.

Emma, meanwhile, comes to. Back at Wilmot's the General is given a gun, and told that he's a cowboy and Steed's an Indian. After nanny has gone, he can shoot him. Wilmot is very excited by the prospect. Emma, however, has regained her senses and is racing to the rescue. Steed takes the opportunity to grab the map between his teeth, pretending he's a dog. He rips it to pieces just as Lister realises he is wearing gloves. Emma enters and knocks Lister over, but Goat is back on his feet with a gun. Wilmot is still regressed and tries to shoot Goat. The noise of the shot makes Wilmot come round, back to the land of the living, but will he be able to live down the nickname of "Cuddles"?

After all that has happened, a little fortune telling is in order. Emma is looking into a glowing crystal orb. Steed is listening intently. She foresees a violent death, followed by another one and danger approaching. Steed is attacked by two large... things. Emma disposes of them. They are now in a dark catacomb, the headquarters of their adversaries. They enter the complex and fight, hopelessly trapped, seconds, inches from death. Then... the orb clouds over. Steed blows on it and the mist clears. Emma sees some writing... it says, 'Watch Next Week'. Steed's turn. He sees something absolutely riveting, leading Emma to cover the crystal with a black cloth.

(Note—The late Paul Eddington who played Beaumont, later made a career out of playing government officials, chiefly in the comedy shows Yes, Minister and Yes, Prime Minister. Yootha Joyce (Lister) later turned up as the deprived Mrs Roper in the sitcom George and Mildred. Clive Dunn (Martin) found huge fame as Corporal Jones, again playing a man greater than his years in the series Dad's Army.)

A kitchen. The ticking of a clock on the wall is the only sound that can be heard. A candelabra is set down on a table, next to a copy of the June edition of *Bridge Players' International Guide*. A page is marked, and the booklet is opened to an article by Mrs Emma Peel—'Better Bridge with Applied Mathematics'—a full page head and shoulders picture of her on the left hand side of the spread. The picture is lovingly caressed, a pair of scissors are taken down from where they're hanging on the wall, and the photograph is carefully cut out of the magazine. Then, an unseen hand cuts the picture into small, irregular pieces...

Steed trumps an ace

Emma plays a lone hand

The doorbell rings at Steed's, but in his haste to answer it, he falls down his spiral staircase. Emma hears the thud of the fall, and knows that something is wrong. Using a vase from a corridor table, she breaks the frosted glass to the side of the door and reaches through the splinters to open the lock from the inside. She finds Steed on the ground, obviously in pain, at which point he informs her, "Mrs Peel, you're needed..."

Later, Emma is preparing something medicinal for Steed—a scotch and soda. He has hurt his leg, but it's not broken. He may have damaged his tango though! Emma reveals her reason for calling on Steed—she had popped by to ask if he would drive her to Exmoor. Sir Cavalier Rousicana may sound like an opera, but he is in fact a bridge player of some repute. He has read Emma's recent article on the subject. Steed's read it, too—all bids, no trumps and applied mathematics—very confusing. Steed sounds almost concerned about Emma taking up the invitation of a stranger, even if he is famous. He need not worry. Sir Cavalier is seventy-five and his weekend entertaining should be seen as a privilege, as he hardly ever sees anyone. Satisfied that Steed can look after himself, Emma drives off to Exmoor.

Struggling with a walking stick, Steed is visited a short time later by military man Major George Wentworth. He has brought bad news—Max Prendergast broke out of jail two weeks ago. The German authorities didn't think to tell their opposite numbers in Britain until they realised that the fugitive was definitely heading their way. Intelligence suggests that he may be in London. Steed remembers his mad, warped sense of humour, recalling that Mrs Peel was more involved with him than anyone else. George is concerned that Emma is told as soon as possible about his jailbreak. Steed is also worried, but will tell her when she returns on Monday—after all, he wouldn't want to spoil her weekend.

Down on Exmoor, Emma has arrived at Sir Cavalier's country home, but someone is watching her arrival from the bushes. She rings the bell and knocks on the door. A woman eating an apple opens it, as Emma collects her bag from the car. She introduces herself as Ola Moansey-Chamberlain. When Emma mentions how hard the place was to find, she says she's not surprised—it's at the end of the world.

As Emma is shown inside, Ola reveals herself to be distinctly unusual. She is fascinated by her teeth and dentists—maybe that is Emma's profession? She reads Italian books, but doesn't understand them at all. When Emma asks where Sir Cavalier is, she is informed that Ola's uncle is on a jaunt down to London for the International Bridge Players Convention. He will be back later that night, and sends his apologies. Emma is shown to her room, and on questioning Ola further discovers that she is Sir Cavalier's ward—her mother was a good friend and now he looks after her. Moansey was the name of a pirate, and there is a family tradition of being judges, soldiers and nuns. Ola is an actress, but she'd rather be a nun, making Benedictine. Emma points out that monks do that, and she'd have to be smuggled into the monastery. Ola likes the sound of that—there have never been smugglers in the family, only pirates.

Emma's room has a four-poster bed, and Ola shows her around. Looking out of the window, the strange young girl sees a man in a tuxedo. She remarks that there's never been a murderer in the family, either. With that, she closes the window. Emma wonders where the staff are, and Ola explains that they are presently in between housemaids.

Ola leaves the room, walking along the corridor and through the revolving door at the top of the stairs. This door is rather unconventional—it has a picture of a playing card on each side. On one side is the joker, on the other the ace of spades, the traditional death card. Every time a person passes through it, the side facing the stairway changes...

In Steed's apartment, a coffee percolator is boiling. He pours himself a cup, but knocks the sugar over. Bending down, he looks up from the floor and sees a concealed tripwire on the stairs. His fall was no accident. He makes a call to George to explain what he has found out. The booby trap prompts them to fear for Emma, so Steed asks George to find out everything he can about Sir Cavalier, including how to get in touch with him.

In the kitchen of the Rousicana residence, Ola is enthusiastically hacking up a fish with a carving knife. Later, she climbs the stairs carrying a lit candelabra. Emma, meanwhile, is changing into evening wear. Ola continues along

the hallway to Emma's bedroom, lighting candles as she goes. Emma is not aware that there is a spy-hole in her bedroom and that someone is watching her as she changes. Looking around, Emma finds a cabinet full of records, but before she can inspect things further, a dinner gong sounds.

Entering the dining room, Emma is informed by Ola that dinner is always at 8.00pm. Sir Cavalier has asked that she start without him. Naturally, Emma thinks this must mean Ola has heard from him. Ola, brushing aside her forgetfulness, says that she has had a phone call from him. Emma takes her place at a long dinner table covered with a red table cloth. Surrounding it are large playing cards, acting as screens. The jack, queen and king of diamonds, the queen and king of hearts, and a joker are all present. Ola announces the contents of the meal—fish with red wine. Not an ideal combination, but she doesn't have the keys to the cellar to get a white. Sir Cavalier always locks the cellar if he goes away for any length of time…Ola stops talking abruptly, as if it was something she really shouldn't have mentioned. She makes an excuse for not joining Emma—she's slimming and has a lot of work to do. She has put out two portions, one for Sir Cavalier when he returns.

Ola leaves Emma alone in the dining room, putting on her coat as if to leave. Then, the phone rings. She goes to answer it. Reporting the contents of the call to Mrs Peel, Ola explains that her friend in the village has been taken ill, but it's five miles away, and she's worried about leaving Emma alone. Mrs Peel offers the use of her car, which Ola gratefully accepts, but on her departure she insists that Emma lock the door behind her. She stops, emphasising that she's been told to say that, and also that Emma won't like it here on her own. Mrs Peel reckons a book will occupy her time quite nicely. As the strange woman leaves, she takes her up on her suggestion of extra security, locking the door.

Mrs Peel moves back into the dining room, unaware that there is a light shining under a door elsewhere in the house, broken by moving shadows. The kitchen clock continues to tick steadily, breaking the silence. Ola, meanwhile, has driven the car away and parked it down the road…

Emma has gone back to her room. Someone is still spying on her. She picks up a book to read, then uses the opportunity to investigate the chest with the records in it. She picks one up, the label reads, 'Deutsche Phon, 78RPM, R326, Mein Liebling Mein Rose by Carl Schmidt'. Sifting through the records, she finds that they are all the same. She pulls back the curtain on the four-poster bed and finds a bunch of roses on each pillow. Flopping across the bed, she starts to read *Trump Hand,* the book she has found, and hears something squeaking nearby. She goes to investigate.

In another room, she finds a rocking chair, the source of the sound. In a single bed next to it, she pulls back the sheet to reveal a suit of armour, unaware that someone is beneath the bed. The doorbell rings, interrupting her search, and Emma goes to see who's turned up. She does not notice the door close behind her, apparently by itself…

A man wearing sunglasses is at the door. He takes them off, as if expecting Emma to recognise him without them. He acts strangely and doesn't answer her when she enquires who he is, instead working his way into the house. He suggests he may be Baron Von Duffy, in search of a stately home to purchase. Emma says this one is not for sale. She's giving him short shrift when he reveals his jalopy has broken down, but Emma cannot see it outside. He blames the fog. He's come to the house to use the phone, but is acting in a sinister way, asking if Emma is alone. As Emma hands him the phone, he suggests the reason she doesn't recognise him is his recent plastic surgery. As he goes to make the call, he looks at the phone closely—the wires have been cut…

In Steed's apartment, he and George are trying to ring Sir Cavalier's number, but with no success. George has found out that Sir Cavalier left the country four days ago for a holiday abroad. His house is officially empty. Steed puts his coat on as they consider risking the fog and driving down there. Taking Steed's bowler, George knocks a joker playing card from beneath it. He picks it up and cuts his finger—there's a razor blade on the back of it. Within seconds he keels over—the blade and its poison were obviously meant for Steed, who picks up the card carefully, smells it and frowns.

Back at the house, the strange man is accusing Emma of cutting the phone wires to keep him there. Mrs Peel, meanwhile, has ventured outside and seen his car in the driveway. What was he doing driving half a mile from the main road? He must have been on his way here. After offering a variety of spurious explanations for his excursion, Emma interrupts, telling him she's expecting company at any moment. He retorts that he's killed the owner, Ola and his alias, the Baron Von Duffy—and proceeds to pull out a dagger. What does she think of that? Emma is sick of his games, and wants to go to bed—the strange man offers to tuck her up. Mrs Peel has reached breaking point, and wrestles the knife from him, threatening to break his arm, before throwing him out of the house in one smooth move. He protests that he knows she isn't alone in the house, and that she only has to check the dining room. Locking the door, she heads straight there and sees that the second dinner setting has been half eaten.

Emma goes back to her bedroom, but before she can get there a hand takes the book from the bed and places it on a nearby chair. On opening the door, she finds other disturbances, too. The heads of her roses have been cut

off and placed in a semi-circle on the floor. Taking hold of the book, and going back to bed with it, she opens the pages to find the pieces of her picture from the bridge magazine…

Meanwhile, Steed has got quite a way through the fog in his car. He has reached a sign that says, 'From This Point You Have A Breathtaking View Of Four Counties'.

Emma has fitted the pieces of her picture together, and there's still someone watching her through the spy-hole. She lifts her suitcase down from a wardrobe and takes her gun from the handbag within. Emma goes to the room with the rocking chair and finds it locked. As she attempts to break it down, the telephone rings. She dashes downstairs to answer it, but finds that it is still disconnected. Hearing a disturbance from outside the kitchen, she runs through the house to investigate. She finds a carving knife embedded in the frame of the kitchen door and decides to boil a kettle for tea to steady her nerves.

Ola and the strange man are outside in the garage. She gives him some money, but it's only half of what he was expecting. She claims that it's because he hasn't yet given the scream. He does so half-heartedly, but when a man appears with a gun, it's a case of 'once more, with feeling'…

The scream alerts Mrs Peel. She dashes to the garage and finds a rag dummy at the wheel of the antique car within it. The kettle whistles as it boils, and Emma fails to sees the strange man's spectacles on the bonnet of the car…

Back in the kitchen, Emma sees that the swing door leading to the rest of the house is moving. Moving into the hall, she sees no one. The joker card side of the door is facing the top of the stairs. Going back into the dining room, she hears her name whispered. Checking the kitchen again, she hears another door slam. The ace of spades is now the card we see at the top of the stairs. She hears music playing from her room, and races upstairs. Opening the door, she finds her room covered floor to ceiling in roses. She angrily smashes the old record playing on the gramophone. The noise of the rocking chair takes over from the music, and breaking into its room she finds the chair occupied by the dead body of the strange man.

Steed has found Mrs Peel's car in the fog. Desperately, he calls for her…

Emma walks slowly downstairs, finding roses everywhere, and hearing her name whispered again. The music begins once more. A mirror is covered in lipstick drawings of a rose and a heart with an arrow through it. The voice seems to be coming from everywhere, proclaiming itself to be an old friend. The key to the door has gone—the voice declares that this is the point of no return.

Mrs Peel finds him at last in the dining room, lovingly stroking a photograph of her. The music, he recalls, is their song. He begins to cut her picture up with a pair of scissors. He translates the lyrics of the tune—'My love, my rose, my tender beautiful rose'. She recognises him—it is Prendergast. It was in Berlin that they met, the most exciting and most dangerous city in the world. He has thought of her often since then. He had been on his way to Rio, a long time ago, but had to see her before he left. Emma wouldn't let him go. She'd flattered him outrageously to stop him catching a plane. Roses had been in the room that day, and they played their tune over and over. She and Steed had planned it that way. And then the police. The handcuffs. Emma reminds him about the refugees, and the suffering he had inflicted on them. She also reminds him of the strange man upstairs that he has killed, but he says that he had to do it.

Prendergast begins to menace Emma, and her escape route upstairs is blocked by Ola, holding a gun. He has promised that she can watch him kill Mrs Peel. Emma wrestles the gun away from Ola, and Prendergast takes the chance to lunge at her with a pair of scissors. The fight moves back into the dining room. Prendergast has his back to the large joker card, which begins to move towards him. He turns in fear, and with one swift movement the card is used as a weapon to knock him out. Steed is behind it, coming to the rescue. He asks whether Emma would like to be taken home, or would she prefer to stay until Monday? It's morning, the fog has lifted and the fresh air is just what they need…

Steed is playing solitaire, with Emma providing unwelcome assistance. Emma tries a different tack, and shuffles the deck, asking Steed to pick a card. He looks at it, puts it back in the pack and she counts six cards out. She hasn't found his card though, as that's in his top pocket! Steed tries, asking Emma to take two cards. If she adds up the numbers, he claims, it will give the vintage of the champagne he has on ice. Unfortunately, both cards are jokers!

(Note—This episode is a revamp of the Cathy Gale story 'Don't Look Behind You'.) ◉

YOU HAVE JUST BEEN MURDERED

A man with an attaché case enters a room full of fine art paintings. This is Gilbert Jarvis. He takes his coat off and opens a drinks cabinet concealed behind a fake bookshelf. He notices a cigarette smouldering in a glass ashtray on a nearby table. Hearing footsteps outside the room, Jarvis searches quickly through a desk drawer, but before he can find what he's looking for a blond man appears in the doorway. It's Shelton, holding a gun. If it's money he's after, says Jarvis, he'll open the safe. Rings? His watch? There's no response. Perhaps it's the paintings that interest him? Nothing does the trick, and Shelton pulls the trigger. The gun is empty. Leaving the gun and a key on the desk, Shelton takes flight through the window, throwing a calling card on the desk as he departs. The card reads: 'You have just been murdered'.

Steed chases a million

Emma runs off with it

George Unwin, millionaire, has sent Steed and Emma an invitation to a party. Steed is a little reluctant—money will be the topic of conversation all evening. Steed has been asked by Lord Maxted, the famous banker, if he will be attending, and Gilbert Jarvis wants to meet Steed there too, having said that it's quite important, as he's just been murdered! Emma wonders how he will arrive at the party—in a hearse, perhaps?

Shelton pays a second visit to Jarvis, but this time Jarvis has a gun. It does him no good, though, and Shelton stabs him with a stage dagger, the blade retracting as he runs Jarvis through. Shelton leaves a second calling card—'You have just been murdered—again'. This time he's more conventional and leaves through the door. Jarvis is terrified, and phones Steed. Unfortunately, the line is bugged, and as he makes the call a red light flashes in the office of Needle, the bearded kingpin behind all the strange goings on. He listens in with great interest. Jarvis tells Steed and Emma what has happened, but is panicked when he hears a click on the line and puts the phone down.

At Unwin's party, Emma is wearing a low-cut, sleeveless, short white dress, while the waitresses are in top hat and tails. Steed and Emma look around at the assembled gentry and see Lord Rathbone, who made his first million before the age of twenty-one. Maxted corners Steed for a chat, and Unwin takes the opportunity to introduce himself to Emma.

Steed asks if Unwin has seen Jarvis. It's not like him to be late, believing as he does that time is money. Steed decides to call Jarvis to find out what is happening... At the Jarvis residence, we see 'You are about to be murdered' scrawled on the wall. Jarvis has picked up the phone to answer Steed's call, but as he does so Shelton appears with a gun. This time he shoots Jarvis for real, as Steed listens in.

At the party, Steed makes his excuses and leaves to find out what has happened. Emma is left chatting with Maxted the banker, who remarks that Jarvis had just asked for £1,000,000 in cash to be made available to him immediately.

Steed arrives at the Jarvis residence, to find him dead. He's intrigued by the number of bolts that there are on the doors. Steed rings Emma with the news, and she announces to the party that Jarvis has been murdered. This is enough to send Lord Rathbone scurrying away in a hurry, and as his vintage car leaves Unwin's grounds, Emma takes off in hot pursuit.

She arrives at Rathbone's house. A man named Chalmers, carrying a shotgun, is on the other side of the iron gates that bar Emma's way. When he is less than helpful, Emma decides to go over the wall to gain access. She finds herself in a tree on the other side, with an Alsatian barking savagely at her. Chalmers reappears to call the guard dog off.

Emma is escorted to the house, where a butler has to undo several bolts on the main door to allow them entry. It's a similar story with the inner door behind which Rathbone lurks; he's obviously a man preoccupied with protecting himself. Emma says she is there to talk about £1,000,000 in cash. More specifically, she has a journalistic assignment, 'How to become a millionaire', which she believes he can help her with. She finds that Rathbone has stolen cigarettes from the party, and concludes he must be a very thrifty man. Rathbone reckons such frugality breeds moral character. Emma wagers that the high security is not for seclusion, but because he's frightened. She tries opening a window, but Rathbone begs her not to.

Meanwhile, Unwin has received a visit from Shelton. Despite his efforts, he cannot escape, and once again Shelton pulls a gun and fires. Again, it is empty. Just like before, Shelton leaves one of his infamous calling cards—'You have just been murdered'.

It is dusk, and at Rathbone's, men with shotguns and guard dogs patrol the grounds. Rathbone gives the order that they are to shoot to kill if they encounter any intruders.

He locks himself within his inner sanctuary, and takes a sip from a tankard. He is startled to see a skull and cross-bones and the word 'Poison' at the bottom of the cup. The phone rings and he is informed that he has been murdered for the fourth time, which the caller says brings him up to his limit. It's time to talk business—if they don't, the next time will be for real.

Steed and Emma compare notes. Maxted the banker informs the duo that Rathbone is selling his government stock, as he needs £1,000,000 in a hurry. Maxted sees no way to delay the transaction, and Rathbone will be picking the cash up from the bank at midday. Later, Steed waits in Maxted's office as Emma keeps a look-out outside the bank. A car drives up; it is Rathbone, who picks up the money in a large suitcase. Emma follows him as he moves off, driving down country roads to a remote location. Rathbone gets out of the car with the suitcase, and checks a small map that he has with him. Through the woods, he comes to a river with a bridge over it. Downstream, a man with binoculars is watching him from behind a tree. This is Nicholls, another of Needle's employees. Rathbone gets to the middle of the bridge, and drops the suitcase over the side into the water, with some degree of trepidation. Rathbone departs, and Nicholls is about to make a move when he sees Emma approaching the bridge. He alerts Needle on his walkie-talkie, who decides that she should be dealt with.

Nicholls sneaks up on Emma and a struggle breaks out. He attacks with a sickle, and she resorts to defending herself with a long stick, which becomes steadily shorter as the battle continues. With her stick cut away almost to nothing, she throws it at Nicholls, catching him off guard, and he ends up landing fatally on his sickle.

At the offices of George Unwin Enterprises, a Jaguar drives straight at Unwin, stopping just short of pinning him to a wall. Shelton is at the wheel, and he delivers another of his cards. Unwin gets in his car and departs hurriedly, just as Steed arrives. Steed decides to follow.

Shelton briefs Needle over the radio, telling him that he almost damaged Unwin's prize orchid. He is now outside Unwin's flat in the Jaguar and the victim has just arrived home. Inside, Unwin pours himself a drink and opens the curtains, but Shelton is waiting there, armed with a samurai sword. Throwing the whisky in Shelton's face, Unwin tries to escape, but a fight is on the cards. Steed pulls up outside the flat just as Unwin is overpowered. Through the net curtains he can see the silhouette of Unwin sitting in a chair and being run through with the sword. Back in the room, we find that Shelton was just notching up another of his 'nearly' murders, but as he puts a card in Unwin's pocket, Steed appears at the window. Shelton advises Unwin not to say a word and hides, just as Steed breaks in. Unwin is obviously frightened, but tells Steed nothing, fobbing him off by saying the shadow dance he

saw must have been a trick of the light. Steed is shown the door after the pair agree to get together the following month when Unwin is not so busy. Heading back into the room, Unwin finds his 'You have just been murdered—again' card in his pocket and is shot with an arrow, but it only has a rubber sucker on the end. It falls away to reveal a circular inked legend on his shirt—'You have just been murdered'. Needle rings to suggest that Unwin watch television that evening, specifically Channel B at 10.00pm.

Steed and Emma are looking at a map. Bridge Farm is not marked, they discover, and is certainly bleak and deserted enough for a pay-off. Could it be a high class protection racket with a clientele of millionaires who won't talk? Steed is sure Jarvis was being threatened, but it's unlikely that Rathbone will fill in the details for them.

Just as he was told, Unwin switches on his television at 10.00pm. Needle appears on the screen as the phone rings. It is Needle on the telephone, too. He introduces himself, but advises that he's heard all the quips about his name, including the one about him being very difficult to find. He sees that as one of his natural talents, as well as being a natural parasite. Unwin has now been murdered four times over the course of the day. The price for them not to carry out the fifth and final assassination is £1,000,000, but they're happy to supply the suitcase for him to put it in!

Maxted the banker calls to inform Steed that Unwin has been in touch. He is to deliver £1,000,000 to Unwin's house. Steed has a plan in mind, and he and Emma depart to put it into action.

Steed calls on Unwin and sees the wads of bank notes in a British Banking Corporation bag. Steed tells him he knows he's being threatened, but Unwin insists that even if he was, he could take care of it himself, and asks Steed to leave. He begins to fill up the now familiar black suitcase.

Steed talks to Emma over the radio, telling her Unwin refuses to spill the beans. Hidden from sight, Steed watches Unwin leave his house and go to his car, and our bowler-hatted maestro fires a small radio transmitter which sticks to the suitcase. Checking his handy sized tracker unit, the bleeps he hears are working perfectly. He drives off in leisurely pursuit of Unwin.

Once more, the trail ends at Bridge Farm. Unwin gets out of the car with the case, and checks his map. He sees the bridge and walks towards it, Steed just behind him, keeping his distance and staying under cover.

Unwin drops the case over the bridge and leaves. A pair of hands appear from under the bridge to snatch the case. It's not the villains, though—it's Mrs Peel, dressed for action in her blue and magenta jumpsuit. She sees a snorkel heading towards her from downstream. A man surfaces, gun in hand, and they fight it out over the briefcase, Emma grappling him in a headlock until he passes out. She drags him out of the water, and as he comes to, Emma gets hold of the gun and orders, "Lead me to your taker!"

Steed intercepts Unwin, who says he needn't have bothered to intervene as, true to his word, he is taking care of things. He has put a bomb in the suitcase, and it will go off in fifteen minutes. Learning of Steed's plan, Unwin realises he has put Emma in great danger. Steed replies that although Unwin may have been murdered four times, there will be a fifth time if anything happens to Emma—he'll guarantee it!

Still using the homing device, Steed and Unwin follow Emma and her prisoner. As they pass a covered haystack in a field, Shelton emerges from a door in the hay to follow them!

Inside the haystack, Emma has been taken prisoner. Needle looks through her notebook (marked with her initials) and learns her identity. If he is always impossible to find, how did she manage it? Emma refuses to answer. He laments the death of Nicholls, one of his best men.

There is a spy-hole in the haystack, so Steed and Unwin can be seen looking around outside. They split up to continue their search. Inside, the suitcase is put in a Land Rover, next to all the other suitcases that have been collected. Needle explains the money will be put in safety deposit boxes, and then they'll be back for more. He will soon be the richest and most powerful man in the world!

Outside again, Steed finds Unwin unconscious. He has a quick look around, but when he gets back to where Unwin's body was, it's gone. Unbeknownst to Steed, it has been dragged inside the haystack. Steed is puzzled, but a clink from the haystack when he investigates it with a pitchfork reveals that things are not as they seem. He uses the opportunity to get on top of the stack and jump Shelton from above.

Realising that the game is up, Needle charges out of the side of the haystack, making his escape in the Land Rover. Rescuing Emma, Steed asks where the suitcase is. When Emma reveals it is in the Land Rover, they quickly rush outside, just in time to see the vehicle explode.

Needle ends up suspended half way up a tree! "Bang goes a million," quips Steed.

Steed is in his apartment stacking white boxes marked '10,000'. Emma is counting them for him as he brings them through, using her notepad to keep score. They are obviously quite heavy despite their shoebox size. Emma says she wasn't aware Steed was so rich—obviously he has been thrifty. Will he need an armoured car to transport it all to the bank? And then, tragedy! He only has 9,999—he's one short of being a millionaire. Emma provides him with what he needs—a 1947 halfpenny. Steed's done it—he's a self-made, fully fledged, halfpenny millionaire!

(Note—Simon Oates, who played Shelton in this episode, has another Avengers *connection. He played Steed in the 1971 stage production of* The Avengers! *He is also famous for his portrayal of Dr John Ridge in* Doomwatch.*)*

We focus on a sign: 'Welcome to Little Storping-in-the-Swuff, voted the best kept village in the country'. Below it is a smaller red sign: 'Please help us keep it that way'. The village is a vision of peace and tranquillity, down to the duck pond at its heart. Hubert and Mickle sit outside The Happy Ploughman, the local public house, rolling cigarettes, drinking beer and playing dominoes. They discuss the weather. It's a nice day. Yesterday was nice, too. We hear a crash, and look around to see a man being hurled out of the pub's front door. Another man stands in the doorway with a gun in one hand and a pint in the other. He shoots as the first man runs towards the village green. The locals are unconcerned, even oblivious, to the murder that has just occurred...

Emma marries Steed

Steed becomes a father

Emma appears at the door of Steed's apartment with Major Paul Croft, who has two large suitcases with him. He's two hours late, held up by an elephant on the runway at Karachi. Steed knows all about Croft because Mrs Peel has been talking about him all week. Croft, in turn, has known Emma since she was six years old. Steed is amazed, not at their length of friendship, but at the vintage of the champagne. His vittaler has sent him a '27, rather than the '26 he requested. Mrs Peel's friend Croft is resigning his commission to breed horses at a house just outside Little Storping. They drink the champagne as he informs them that he's sent Private Forbes ahead to prepare things, but knowing him, he'll no doubt stop off at the local pub on his way.

Forbes has done just that. He's about to leave when Jenny, the barmaid, tells everyone that there will be an event at twelve o'clock. Forbes is curious. Is it some sort of local carnival? They shrug it off by saying it's nothing really interesting. A man with sunglasses sits in a corner on his own with a pint. Forbes is encouraged to stay and have another drink, "on the house". He is easily persuaded. Landlord Prewitt gives the man with sunglasses a shotgun when he comes to the bar, and he takes it outside. Shots are heard. Forbes is concerned, but mysteriously none of the locals are. The man with sunglasses returns and gives the shotgun back to Prewitt. What Forbes heard must have been a car backfiring, they say. Forbes drinks up and leaves, saying he'll be seeing more of them as he's moving into the old house on the hill. The villagers look worried at this revelation...

Back at Steed's apartment, Major Croft is getting ready to leave. Emma is taking him to his new residence, as she

wants to see what it's like... Meanwhile, Forbes arrives at the house in his car and starts unloading. Mickle and Hubert stroll up. Forbes thinks they have come to help, and they start handling some of the vases and paintings, seemingly drunk from all their excesses. Hubert drops a vase, then Mickle puts his head through a painting—deliberately. They upturn a tea chest full of crockery and start to smash everything into tiny pieces. Forbes looks on, shocked...

Emma and Croft are approaching the village, and Emma looks at the occupant of a car they pass on the way in. It is Frederick Williams, a big financier whose empire had crumbled just a few weeks earlier. In the village, Emma's curiosity is piqued again. They pass Samuel Morgan in his limousine, the man who slipped the financial knife into Williams. Emma wonders what the chances are of two such deadly enemies being seen within a mile of each other—a coincidence, surely.

The pair arrive at the house to find all the art treasures smashed. Croft jumps to the conclusion that Forbes must be at fault, after getting blind drunk. He calls after him, but there's no answer. Croft decides to check the local pub—Forbes has probably gone back for more. He walks over there, leaving Emma to look around the house...

At the pub, Croft arrives to find Mickle and Hubert standing in the entrance. He goes inside and Jenny asks if she can help him. He enquires whether she has seen Forbes. She says they haven't seen any strangers all week. Mickle and Hubert confirm this. Croft goes out into the street and looks around. He sees a sign across the road: 'Little Storping Public Library & Reading Room. Museum of Local Antiquities' and goes to check it out.

The library is busy. Morgan is at the reception desk, informing Miss Avril the librarian that he was told to meet someone there who would be of financial advantage to him. Williams emerges from the library with a gun. The librarian asks Morgan to wait and, seeing Williams with the gun, points to the sign behind him that says 'Silence.' He nods and adds a silencer to his pistol. Morgan cannot wait any longer, and gives a calling card to Miss Avril. Croft enters, sees Williams with the gun, and is about to say something when Mickle and Hubert restrain him. Williams shoots Morgan, and life in the library continues as if nothing has happened.

Emma has found a sickle in the drive of the house, and follows her instincts to look in the woods nearby. She sees a head sticking up from behind a large felled tree trunk. It is Forbes—dead. Before she knows anything more, she is hit from behind...

Emma regains consciousness in the pub. She is being looked over by Dr Haynes. He says she's okay, but things would have been nastier if she'd hit the wall. Confused, Emma looks outside and sees that her car has ploughed through a garden fence and parked itself across the road in someone's garden. She says to the people there that she doesn't remember driving back into the village. Emma explains how she found Forbes murdered, and Haynes tells her to sit down, as she's obviously had a serious knock on the head. Emma knows she didn't imagine it. The villagers all deny that Croft had gone to the pub, too. Haynes agrees to accompany Emma to where she says Forbes can be found.

Emma relates her memory of things to Haynes as they drive toward the house. As they pull up, Emma is shocked to see that everything is tidy again—no smashed antiques, no car, nothing. They search in the woods and Emma finds the tree trunk, spotting a head resting on it facing away from them. It's not Forbes though, just Higgins the gardener, asleep. He wakes up to say that he has been asked by the estate agents to keep the grounds tidy, which is why he's there. Emma insists that the house has already been sold. Higgins reckons he's been sleeping there since 12.30pm, but he is a heavy sleeper. Haynes drives Emma back to the pub and offers to supply her with some pills to help. She declines.

Outside the pub, Mickle and Hubert are in Emma's car. It has been repaired. Emma looks at the watch on Mickle's wrist—it is Croft's. She frowns and, reclaiming her car, takes up Dr Haynes on his offer of pills, following him to the surgery.

A sign reveals the doctor's details: 'Dr J. F. Haynes, M. D. Surgery. Hours 9.00am–10.30am, 6.30pm–7.00pm'. Inside, Haynes gives out some pills. Emma reveals that she only wanted them as an excuse to get away from the villagers. She actually wants to use his phone. Picking it up, she tries to get an outside line, asking the operator to get her the police. She tells Haynes how she had seen Croft's watch on one of the villagers, but Haynes still believes she's imagining everything. On the phone, a Sergeant Banks answers, and Emma tells him she'd like to report a murder, possibly two. The policeman tells her to stay where she is, and he'll come to her. Putting the phone down, Haynes promises Emma that her accusations are ridiculous—he's known the villagers half his life.

The Sergeant arrives in his police car, and interviews Emma. He finds it a strange story, and of course Haynes cannot corroborate it. He's prepared to check the area out for himself, but insists Emma remains at the surgery. As he leaves, Emma remembers she hasn't told him about Croft's watch. Looking out of the window, she sees the Sergeant getting into the patrol car. He's wearing blue and white striped socks with gold and dark blue banding. They are certainly not police issue. Emma stops herself saying any-

thing else to the policeman and asks Haynes if he'd ever seen the officer before. She explains her fears that he's bogus, citing the socks as evidence. Haynes has had enough and locks the surgery door. He's going to call the hospital. Emma attempts to get out through a side door, but in the room beyond she finds Haynes pointing a gun at her. He is on the phone, calling for an emergency meeting to be held. Emma overpowers him, knocking him out, and is about to club him with the phone when she stops herself. She looks back into the side room. The bodies of Croft and Forbes are there, tucked under white sheets…

Emma drives back to the village and stops by the tea-room. She knocks at the door and looks in, but there's no one to be seen. It's the same everywhere, even in the pub. The whole village is deserted.

Everyone has made their way to the library. The villagers all agree that something has to be done. They bought some time by having Banks impersonate a police officer and having her stay put at the Haynes surgery. They've got Maggie the phone operator to thank for intercepting Emma's call and re-directing it. They must decide what to do with Mrs Peel, but are perplexed that Haynes is yet to turn up.

Haynes has come to, and makes his way to the library. Emma, meantime, is trying to find a phone that works… Arriving at the meeting, Haynes advises everyone that Mrs Peel has escaped. They leave *en masse,* and see Emma standing bemused in the middle of the village. The route to her car is blocked, and she's surrounded. They begin to close in on her. Emma runs, fights off a man with a pitch-fork, and evades capture by one after another. Even Mickle and Hubert cannot hold her. Haynes tells Mickle to get the helicopter. Emma has taken the opportunity to escape into open country.

Mickle and Hubert start up helicopter 'G-AVEE', and take to the air. Emma climbs over a fence behind some woods—the helicopter is fast approaching. Encountering another fence, she is snagged on some barbed wire, which slows her up. Mrs Peel stumbles into an open field, where the chopper begins to buzz her. One low pass follows another, and the down draft of the helicopter forces her to lie flat on the ground, captured…

At the Little Storping Museum ('Please obtain key from curator' a sign advises), amongst the various antique paraphernalia, we find Mrs Peel, trussed in a 1359 Chastity Belt, chained to the wall. She comes to and finds other people with her: Jeremy Purser, once the vicar, and George Miller, ex-police sergeant for the district, are both restrained in the stocks; Mr Chapman, the local magistrate, is chained upright to a rack; and Hilary, who ran the telephone exchange, has her mouth covered with what is described by the notice next to it as 'Scold's Bridle—used to chastise the nagging wife'. Emma looks outside the window and sees nothing has changed—a man is being mowed down with a machine gun out in the village.

Emma has the situation explained to her. Two strangers arrived one day and argued. One took out a gun and killed the other, an act committed in front of the whole village. The killer came back into the pub and offered a deal. He was a rich man and promised a million pounds to the village to keep their mouths shut. It was a tempting offer and a meeting was held to discuss it. The four people with Emma tried to talk the others out of the pact, but there were no other dissenters. Dr Haynes fixed the records to show that the man died of a heart attack. A whole town had been bought off. Then, the people became greedy and began to offer their service to others. The village is wide open now. Emma watches a car pull up by the duck pond, and a body is dumped out of it.

Emma tries to reach a display board of historic knives. She just manages it as the villagers enter mob-handed. They tell Mrs Peel she is to disappear. They've checked Croft's papers and realise he and Forbes will not be missed as they'd only just returned to the country. They know nothing, however, about Mrs Peel. And she's not prepared to talk…

The villagers take Emma outside and place her on a mediaeval ducking stool. They lower her into the pond and try and extract information by holding her head under the water. They immerse her once, twice, three times. But she's not giving in. A fourth time she is held under for much longer than before. Eventually she is brought up again and agrees to talk.

Back in the pub, she informs them that only her husband, John, knows she's here. She phones him. Steed answers and Mrs Peel calls him "darling," explaining she is Emma, his wife. The villagers cannot hear Steed on the other end, so don't hear him asking if she has had too much grape juice. Emma asks how the children are, and it is with this that Steed realises something is really amiss. He asks if she is being listened to. She confirms. Emma explains she's had an absolutely tortuous day (!). He asks if she is in Little Storping, which she confirms, but the villagers want her to make out that she's had some trouble with her car and has had to drive to Salisbury. Steed realises the truth, and Emma asks him to kiss little Albert, Julian, Gordon and baby Brian. He should take them to the museum after they've been to the pub. Steed ponders Emma's clues…

Emma is locked up again. She is told that she'll be taken care of after dark. A helicopter ride over the sea will lead to a long drop down.

Steed turns up at the pub and orders a pint from Jenny. He says he is just passing through, saw the museum, and fancied a look around. Prewitt the publican fobs him off by saying the curator is away. Steed suspects something. He says "Mrs Emma Peel," at which Jenny drops the glass she is cleaning. He smiles and says he just wanted to see their reaction. The publican goes for the shotgun under the bar, but Steed bangs his head against the counter instead.

Having made his way to the library, Steed sees the internal door to the museum. One shoulder charge and he finds himself sprawled in the middle of the room where Emma and the other captives are, before gallantly picking the lock of Emma's chastity belt.

Haynes, Banks, Mickle and Hubert enter the library with shotguns. Emma has resorted to protecting herself with the helmet from a suit of armour. The quartet fight with our heroes, and after the guns have been put out of reach, custard pies laid out on a table become ammunition.

Emma goes headfirst into the pies before Steed can overpower the resistance. Maggie and Jenny appear, and Emma goes after them with a loaded custard pie. Steed comments to Emma that this is something to tell the children—little Albert, Julian, Gordon and baby Brian! As Emma leaves, Steed hears the muffled cries of Hilary the telephone operator.

Later, in Steed's apartment, he has resorted to a can opener to help free Emma of her knight's helmet. The Ambassador will take it as a personal affront if she turns up in it, especially with his reputation. He releases her, saying she just hadn't adjusted it properly. Trying to demonstrate, Steed ends up with his head stuck—Emma shakes her head and feeds him a drink through a straw.

(Note—Tony Caunter, who played Miller, is a familiar face on British television, now best known for his role as Roy in the soap opera EastEnders.) ◉

A die is rolled. It's a one. Cooty Gibson is at the wheel of a racing car, number seven. Wearing a red helmet, he pulls down his goggles in preparation for a race. He is informed by an unseen voice that he has just one minute. We focus on a toy car racing set. It's a 'Scalextric', laid out with a miniature version of the same car placed on the track. It has the same colours, same number and same name on the side of it. The model car starts off, and Gibson finds himself driving the real thing in a simulator, gradually going faster and faster, bend after bend. Ater a while he cannot keep control and spins off the track. He lands on the ground, in a field, his racing goggles smashed …

Tara arrives at Steed's apartment carrying a present for him that she found on the doorstep. It has Steed's name on it, so he opens it. Inside is a board game—snakes and ladders.

The hands of an unseen man are once again rolling the die. It's a four this time. In front of the roller is a twenty-five square snakes and ladders board. Square four has a ladder leading upwards from it, and then we see a real person climbing an extremely long ladder in parallel to events on the board. This is Dexter. As he makes his way up, he is foolish enough to look down. A mistake, as even people without vertigo would feel queasy at this height. He finally reaches the top of the ladder and sees a square green shutter in front of him, marked 'Reward'. He pulls the shutter open and a plastic snake appears, making him lose his grip. He falls off the ladder into the dark void below. On the game board, a hand moves the red counter from square twenty-four, where the head of the snake is (just next to square twenty-three, which has the top of the ladder resting in it), and pushes it down to the starting square at the bottom left-hand corner of the board. This starting square is marked 'Revenge'. A butler asks the unseen figure sitting in a comfy chair if he may now serve tea.

Tara asks Steed if they should have a game of snakes and ladders, and opening the box she finds a note. 'Go immediately to the children's playground, Merton Park. What you gain on the roundabouts, you lose on the swings.'

In the park, a figure is seen in the distance, occupying one of the swings. It's Dexter, dead. Tara and Steed approach and stop the swing moving. Jigsaw pieces fall from his hand to a serving tray on the floor beside him.

Back at Steed's apartment, he and Tara are finding out a little more about Clyde Dexter. Steed was in the army with him, but hadn't seen him for years. Tara is puzzling over the jigsaw, but it's difficult as she's only got a few pieces from a large picture. Dexter was a zoologist, and seems to have died from a snake bite. Steed recalls that Cooty Gib-

son had been found dead the previous week in a field, his injuries suggesting that he had been killed in a car accident. He was a racing driver by profession. Other jigsaw pieces were found on Gibson, which are now in Steed's possession. He pulls a plastic bag from a drawer.

Meanwhile, Tara is checking up on 'Jig Creations'—perhaps they can help her with the puzzle. She speaks to 'The Master', and tells him her problem. It's not that she has just one piece missing, but that she only has a few pieces and cannot

find the rest. The Master concludes that this is indeed a problem, but cannot identify which puzzle the pieces are from. A few more and he might be able to help. He begins to contort his hands, and Tara wonders if he suffers from rheumatism. She is curtly told that this is training, and he decides to demonstrate his special skills to her, assembling a jigsaw in double-quick time. Tara asks what he does on long winter nights. Bemused, the Master tells her that he rides bicycles. As Tara leaves, the butler appears from behind one of the large jigsaw pieces that act as screens.

Steed is just getting off the phone as Tara enters his apartment. She's not had any luck so far with his far-fetched idea. He's been checking army records, to find out who else had served with Gibson, Dexter and himself, as that seems to be the only common link they have. He remembers it was towards the end of the war, and units were coming and going all the time. The cobwebs lift and he remembers Henry J. Averman, who served with him on several tribunals. He picks up the phone, then stops, realising that a phone call to him will be no good—he would have to book it at least two weeks in advance. The best approach would be to go and see him personally…

In Averman's residence, a phone rings as Henry glances over a computer printout. A second phone rings as he pulls another report straight out of the printer. His desk has half a dozen phones on it. Henry answers New York on a red phone. He tells them to buy at fourteen and a half, then changes his mind and says fifteen—thousand. As soon as he puts the call down, the same phone rings. It's Rome, and it sounds like they have a problem. With such bad news, Henry fires them. From outside Averman's French windows, the butler is watching all this happening, seeing Henry fill up his metal pill box from the rows of bottles on a side table.

Henry picks up a black phone. It's Cairo. They think they've fouled up too, but Henry tells them their action should help, and to take 1595. This carries on until the butler takes an opportunity to chloroform him. He has to hurry, though, as Steed has just turned up in his yellow Rolls Royce. The butler grabs Averman's pills, then hears the doorbell ring. With no reply, Steed goes round the back, and finds the French windows open, with Averman sitting motionless in his chair. The butler jumps Steed from behind, trying to strangle him with a phone wire. They fight, with Steed finally being subdued by a red ashtray to the head. The butler picks up Averman and leaves in a hurry.

Tara is preparing an ice pack in Steed's kitchen. Steed tells her that his assailant was no one he recognised, knew or would want to know. When Tara comes back with the ice, Steed thanks her—he wanted the cubes for his whisky. Putting such a large pack on his head would freeze his brain cells. Steed is obviously worried by events…

At the mastermind's headquarters, Averman comes round. He is being watched over by a television monitor, and the mastermind notes that he wishes him to be fully coherent—he would not want a game with an opponent who lacked any of his faculties, as there would be no joy in that. He says he is sorry to have abducted him, but he had turned down several of his dinner invitations, after all. Averman is facing a vertical board that reads 'Stock Market', with a share index graph listing the following on both axes: 'Peak, Boom, Rise, Fall, Slump, Collapse'. Averman is not amused—he is a busy man and cannot entertain such diversions. The mastermind finds him arrogant, and that's the cue to start the game.

Suddenly, Averman realises he hasn't got his pills, which assures the mastermind of his attention. They'll be returned when Averman plays the game to the best of his potential. The pills are hidden in the graph board. One end is sealed, the other, at the top of the graph's axis, is open. The pills will be ejected if and when the market reaches its peak. He has newspapers to give him current stock prices, and the phones and teleprinter will advise him of second by second changes. The butler lays out another game board in front of the mastermind, along with counters and a die. It has two columns either side of the centre of the board, each reading: 'Takeover' (in yellow), 'Gold' (green), 'Mines' (red), 'Oil' (sky blue), 'Silver' (light blue), 'Industry' (cream), 'Motors' (pink), 'Cotton' (ochre), 'Invest' (violet), and between the columns, at the bottom, in very large yellow letters is the word 'Lose'.

The mastermind concludes the game brief. Averman must buy and sell according to the information supplied, and his empire will grow or crash accordingly. The mastermind rolls the die. A four, indicating four minutes. The phones immediately start ringing, but Averman still stands motionless. The mastermind advises him of one final thing as an enticement to play. If Averman wins, he walks away a free man. If he loses, his pills remain where they are, resulting in the loss of his life.

This is enough to stir him into action. He looks at the paper quickly and picks up a red phone. "Buy Universal, sell Dale Iron," he advises. He picks up the black phone. "Sell, sell, sell, keep selling!" The blue-green phone: "Option. Take an option and hold." The green phone: "Sell, sell and keep on selling." The pills, which started to make their way up the tube on the graph, begin to slip. Averman panics, and doesn't know whether to buy or sell. The stress becomes too much for him and he keels over, dead.

Back at Steed's apartment, there is still no sign of Averman. Steed is sitting down with a glass of brandy. Through the window comes a rubber dart, with a note attached to it. Tara looks out of the window. The butler is in a car outside, and he drives off when spotted. Steed has unravelled the message from the dart. It reads, 'What you lost on the swings, you'll lose on the roundabouts.' Assuming that this note will follow the pattern established by the previous one, they make their way to the playground.

Averman's body is spinning on a roundabout. Steed and Tara find him, and lodged in his hand are yet more jigsaw pieces. They go back to Steed's and add these to what they already have. They have part of a house, trees and some sky, but still little else. They are definitely all pieces from the same puzzle and must therefore all be clues from the killer. The answers lies in the past…

There is a battle range, and soldiers march forward as explosions and gunfire ricochet around them. Through the smoke walks Tara, who jumps into a trench. Steed joins her, introducing Brigadier Wishforth-Brown. He informs them that the enemy are putting on a diversionary attack, which Steed finds unusual, as he thought the Brigadier was controlling both sides. Tea arrives and the Brigadier invites Steed and Tara to join him—after all, it's being served on a silver tea set. As the shells continue to land all around, Steed tells the Brigadier about the dead men and asks if he recalls anything about them. Unfortunately Steed is the only one carved in his memory, but that's probably because of the incident with the Colonel's

daughter at Montenegro. Steed asks the Brigadier to think of who else served with them, and he promises that he will, but in the meantime he really must take that hill by 5.30pm. They agree to meet at dawn the following day, as the Brigadier has a pressing engagement that evening.

Little does Steed suspect that the pressing engagement is at the mastermind's house. The Brigadier arrives, and the butler takes his cap and stick. They will dine immediately, and savour a brandy and cigar at their leisure afterwards, perhaps a little contest, too. The Brigadier says he is game for anything…

Tara nags Steed to hurry, as she thinks it's nearly dawn and they're still at his apartment. Steed points out to her that it's midnight, which means Tara's anti-magnetic shockproof waterproof chronometer has stopped.

The Brigadier has had a superb meal and thanks his host, Monty Bristow. He's puzzled as to why he was invited. Bristow emphasises that he is now something of a recluse, but makes a point of keeping in touch with various aspects of the outside world. It prevents his mind from becoming closed. "Broad horizons, broad base. Good thinking," comments the Brigadier. Bristow suggests a little game to relax, purely recreational. It's called 'Battle Stations', which is right up the Brigadier's street. Bristow notes that there is an even chance of winning, which is fair odds, much fairer than the six to one against which the Brigadier gave him… The Brigadier drowsily realises he has been drugged and passes out.

Waking up, the Brigadier hears the sound of a tank. A toy one is moving along a scaled down battlefield area. The Brigadier suggests that Bristow, or whatever he is called, cannot be serious. He hears the name of the other officers killed by Bristow's game. Then comes realisation. The trial. Now the Brigadier is told that his primary objective is to take the hill in the board game that surrounds him on three sides. It is a test of skill and strategy. Bristow rolls the die—a one. He has just one minute to do it. The Brigadier moves the game pieces forwards, as the sounds of battle continue all around. He's absorbed in the game and is doing well. He sets a jeep off towards the hill, and wins—he thinks. Bristow points out that he failed to scout out the land and overlooked the enemy artillery. The Brigadier moves a little to the left, and sees a toy cannon and soldiers hidden in a cave. The cannon fires and kills the Brigadier. The last post sounds.

Steed wakes Tara. His Aunt Emily's ancient, brassy, battered alarm clock with one hand missing tells him that dawn is fast approaching. They rush out of the flat to make their appointment.

They have reached the battlefield in Steed's Rolls Royce. The Brigadier is nowhere to be seen. A jeep approaches, with the Brigadier standing upright in it. The jeep ploughs past them and into a tree, which promptly splits in two.

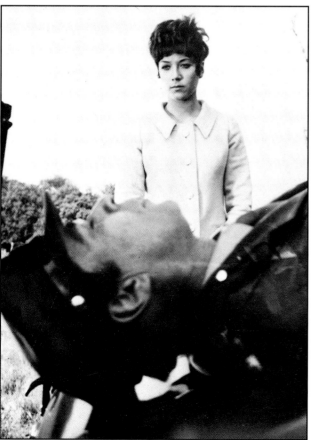

They rush to inspect the Brigadier and find more jigsaw pieces in his hand…At the apartment, Tara adds these further pieces to what they already have. Steed has been doing some digging, and has details on Sergeant Daniel Edmund, court-martialled in 1946 in Germany for playing the black market. He was tried by six officers, four of whom are now dead. His official status is missing, believed killed while trying to escape detention fifteen years ago. Tara questions the use of the term 'believed'. The fifth member of the panel was Professor Witney…

Steed and Tara pull up outside the Professor's workplace. They enter a library reception. Steed converses in Greek with the receptionist, who says Witney is in London, on a dinner appointment. Outside, the butler watches them leave.

The duo begin planning back at Steed's apartment. Steed will get a list of all the scholastic organisations in the country to help ascertain the whereabouts of Witney's appointment. If he's dining with someone, he is banking on it being with an academic colleague. Tara suggests she should cover the sixth member of the tribunal. Steed tells her there is no need—it's him!

Witney, unfortunately, has chosen to dine at Edmund's. They've already reached the brandy and cigars stage. It looks bad—they're talking philosophy. Did Edmund create himself or did others create him? Edmund has a vivid memory, and Witney is encouraged to take part in a word-making game. Edmund looks at Witney and tells him what he is thinking. Witney believes it to be child's play. Then, Witney mentions a phrase once used by Averman: "The luck of the game." Witney is struggling to remember the connection, and suddenly remembers his army days. At this point he slumps over, drugged.

Steed is still on the phone, trying to locate Witney. Tara has built a fortress of chairs around him and sits perched with her pistol, ready for trouble…

Witney will not play Edmund's game. He is in a large die, cut in half. Above him are seven dials that have letters on them, the starting position being XPPEIPR. He has to make a word of not less than six letters from the seven supplied. He has controls in front of him, round buttons marked I, P, E, Z, E, X, R, which will help him rearrange the letters. The game is called 'Wordmake', and the die reveals that Witney has two minutes to complete his task. Again, the player is reluctant, until he is told the forfeit. The ceiling of the die is coming down and will only stop when he finds the correct word. He starts pressing buttons madly, trying to find the solution, but he starts too late. The word 'Expire' appears, apropos Witney's current state.

Steed finds a toy Red Indian drummer outside his front door. It carries a note: 'Boys and girls come out to play, Witney's dead, hip-hip-hooray!' A visit to the playground reveals Witney's dead body propped up on a swing, leaving only Steed as Edmund's final target…

Tara is back arranging the jigsaw pieces. She's alone in Steed's residence, and asks herself the question: "When is a puzzle not a puzzle?" Suddenly, the butler appears at the door and answers, "When it's complete!" There is a scuffle between the two of them and Tara is chloroformed. The butler fits the final piece in the jigsaw and carries Tara away.

Edmund is shooting a rubber dart pistol at a series of stand-up targets on his desk. The butler appears, announcing that the lady has been accommodated. Edmund muses that there is only one to go now…

Steed returns home and finds the chloroform pad on the floor, plus the now completed jigsaw on a table by the window. He takes the puzzle to the jigsaw expert for evaluation. The Master says he has never seen a puzzle like it, and he knows all the ones produced in the country. His conclusion, following his lack of knowledge, is that the puzzle does not exist. He knows the house featured in the puzzle, though. The jigsaw convention of 1964 was held there. It's the residence of Mr Bristow, the games king.

Steed hurries along in his car, and finds the house… Inside, Edmund is drawing red lines through a list. It reads, 'Convening member of the court martial of: Sergeant Daniel Edmund. Captain "Cooty" Gibson. Major John Steed. Brigadier Wishforth-Brown. Captain Dexter. Major Averman. Major Witney'. The butler greets Steed at the door and talks about the weather, before telling him that Miss King is waiting for him. Steed is introduced to Edmund, who assures him that although he has changed his name and face, his mind still ticks on in just the same way. He advises that Miss King is perfectly safe, 'under glass' as he puts it. Steed is offered a drink, but decides to make his own choice from the row of six decanters he is presented with.

Edmund explains to Steed that he wanted him to be last. He wanted to play a little game with each of them, just as they had played a game with him. Steed reminds Edmund that he was guilty, got caught and paid the penalty, or should have, at least. Edmund appreciates the concern Steed shows for Miss King. If he wants her, he must win her in a game. Unfortunately, Steed's choice of decanter was wrong. He picked the brandy, which is exactly what Edmund expected him to do. That was the one that was drugged. Steed slumps to the floor…

Steed awakes, handcuffed, to play 'Super Secret Agent', another fiendish board game from Edmund's collection. Edmund rolls a six—lucky for Steed. That gives him six minutes to win or lose. This is one of Edmund's own games, involving courage, strategy, animal cunning and a damsel in distress. Steed sees Tara: she's in a giant egg timer. The sand will gradually fall from top to bottom as the game is played. Steed can reach her and save her, but only if he negotiates certain obstacles on the board.

The first one he lands on is 'You encounter fiendish Japanese wrestler'. Said man appears on a climbing frame and jumps down to confront Steed. He's easily beaten though, and Steed finds the keys to his handcuffs—the wrestler is wearing them as an earring.

The next square he encounters is 'You must disconnect time bomb'. Steed sees it, within a transparent safe. He's got sixty seconds to open it and throw the defusing switch. A huge clock ticks down as Steed goes about his task, completing the mission with just half a second to spare. The butler reminds Edmund that Steed must now get a reward. Edmund, obliging, puts the lights on above a doorway and Steed heads towards it. Going inside, he finds a six-sided chamber, each wall with a different number from one to six. There is a pistol on the floor in the middle. He is told that behind one of the six doors is safety, the other five are booby trapped. Steed opens doors three and six, directly opposite, together. The guardsman figures on both sides shoot each other, and Steed steps outside unharmed. Hanging from a string ahead is the clip for the gun, but no bullets.

Steed crawls through a metallic tunnel, with very little room. He sees Tara in the egg timer, but a guillotine falls in front of him—luckily, he was holding out his trusty bowler hat, which is chopped in half. He carries on, and at the far end of the tunnel picks up the six bullets for the clip. He is informed by Edmund that he now faces six assailants, dressed in nineteenth century sailor suits, but the added twist is that only one of the six bullets he has is

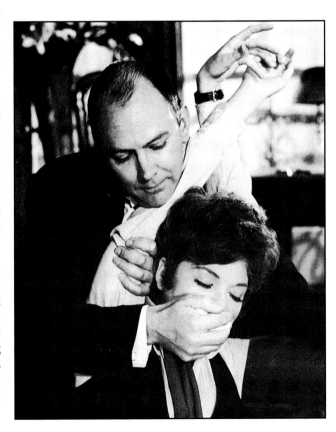

live. He fires the gun at the hour glass and it breaks, which Edmund sees as cheating. The assailants are knocked out one by one, and Tara joins in the fight.

Together, the duo beat all-comers and win the contest. There is a door in front of them, but Tara takes up a position behind it. The butler enters and she immobilises him.

Edmund has one final card up his sleeve, a razor-edged ace of spades, which he runs along the green baize of a table to prove its sharpness. He throws it at Steed, who bats it back with a fireside shovel, the card lodging in Edmund's chest. "Game, set and match," Steed concludes…

Steed and Tara are playing a game to some very strange rules being recited by Steed. He rolls the die, and Tara now owes a pound. He throws a six, now she owes him another pound. The game with such bizarre rules could only be: 'Steedopoly'!

(Note—Garfield Morgan, who played the butler, later came to nationwide fame in Britain as The Flying Squad boss Frank Haskins in The Sweeney.*)*

LOOK — (STOP ME IF YOU'VE HEARD THIS ONE) BUT THERE WERE THESE TWO FELLERS...

At the offices of the Caritol Land and Development Corporation, secretary Miss Charles is setting a conference table. She tells her boss, Sir Jeremy Broadfoot, that everything is now ready for the next day's board meeting, and leaves the building.

Two men in a black taxi cab watch her drive out of the car park in her Morris 1100. The driver of the cab is Jennings, assistant to 'Merry' Maxie Martin, who is in the back seat. They approach the building, but Jennings remembers they need their bag, and fetches it from the car. After a quick change, Maxie is now in clown make-up, with very long yellow shoes.

Sir Jeremy hears a horn peeping from outside in the corridor and goes to investigate. Under the door, he sees the tips of the yellow shoes. He opens the door and sees a gun pointing at him. Maxie pulls the trigger. A flag comes out of the

barrel saying 'BANG'. A second pull of the trigger and the gun goes off for real. The duo depart arm in arm, vaudeville style, to the accompaniment of some appropriate music.

Steed is inspecting the outline of the body, while Tara looks on. What have they forgotten? That it's 230 shopping days until Christmas? Steed asks her where the government would go in the event of a war. Tara is not quite up to speed on this case, and ventures the moon. Steed reveals the key to the puzzle—this is the company that has the contract for CUPID—Cabinet Underground Premises In Depth.

They look at the evidence. Exhibit one is a plaster cast of a footprint, long and thin. The shape of the impression is wrong as the person is of normal weight. They also have found a walking stick, which suddenly turns into a bunch of flowers.

Tara and Steed drive away from the scene. The flowers change into a bunch of bananas. Steed is bemused—

metamorphosis, tadpole into frog. Fancy swaggering down Bond Street suddenly finding that you're walking with a bunch of bananas. They then change into a sabre, which tears the roof of the car. Daffodils next, and then a top hat with a blue flower.

At Vauda Villa, Maxie and Jennings have reported back to... Mr Punch! He holds court from a puppet booth, and thinks the two of them have done well. Punch is worried that someone might have seen them. Maxie relates that it was like first house on a Monday, ie empty, and reminds them that only one director is gone—there's still more work to do. The next target is the Honourable Thomas Randolph Cleghorn. Punch and some puppets enact the death scenario they imagine...

Cleghorn is duck shooting. He lies in the rushes, blowing a duck call. Jennings responds with his own duck call, and Maxie appears, wearing a hat with a duck on it. Cleghorn fires and Maxie moves out of the way. Next, Cleghorn sneaks towards what he thinks is a duck, and suddenly the clowns rise up in front of him. Maxie hits him over the head with a caveman's club, which shatters on impact. Cleghorn stumbles backward and splashes into the lake—dead. The two indulge in another music hall exit.

Steed and Tara are playing table tennis, but there's not exactly a lot of room for it in Steed's flat. They discuss a red ping pong ball with a hole in it that was found at the latest murder scene. Tara wears the red ball as a nose, and gives Steed an idea—she's used it just like part of a clown's make-up. He goes to the encyclopaedia, to section 247—vaudeville. Steed looks up appendix G5—dying arts. A sub-section is entitled 'Eggs'. He reads from the tome and finds out that each clown make-up is copyrighted, then painted and preserved on eggs by a gentleman known as Marcus Pugman.

Tara goes to visit Marcus. He's not used to having visitors, even though his is supposed to be a public office. As he reluctantly opens the door, he points to the notice on it: 'EGGS—FRAGILE. Fragile Area. Take Care. Handle as Eggs. Tread Carefully. No—Handbags, Umbrellas, Packages. PLEASE TAKE CARE. Don't Knock. Please Don't Knock. Don't—Slam the Door, Talk Loudly, Vibrate, Even Breathe.' As Marcus reminds her of the 'no handbags' rule, Tara has to leave hers outside the door before being allowed in. He has spent twenty-two years of patient brushwork creating the collection, all rendered on large eggs. Marcus asks Tara to follow him along the white line between the open shelves. Eventually they get through, though not without problems.

Steed warns the remaining Caritol board members that he believes a red-nosed clown is responsible for the murders. Initially met with great scepticism, he points out that this would be a good disguise and could be part of a bigger plot to wreck project CUPID. It emerges that there had been differences of opinion between the directors. Broadfoot and Cleghorn argued about the choice of materials, Seagrave and Dessington about the choice of sub-contractors. Steed reminds them to be on their guard against comedians…

Marcus, meanwhile, has taken the sparse details from Tara and says it will take time to find the clown make-up she is looking for. When she offers to come back, he insists it will not be necessary for her to do so, as he will phone her. He leads her along the white line again, quickly locking her out and only opening the door a crack to allow Tara to hand him her card.

Back at the Villa, the performers are having a meeting. Brigadier Wiltshire, their next target, will have to wait, as Maxie left part of his make-up at a crime scene. It dawns on them that only Marcus can identify them, and they head off in his direction. Marcus, meanwhile, has identified the wearer of the make-up. The paper record confirms it—'"Merry" Maxie Martin, Reg 1931, 2739'. He telephones Tara, just as Maxie and Jennings enter his office. They drop a banana skin on the white line and begin to smash the eggshells on the floor. He asks Tara to hold, and rushes towards them, slipping on the banana skin, falling to the floor and toppling both shelf units over. The clowns shoot him dead, as Tara hears everything on the other end of the phone.

When Steed and Tara, all the eggs are broken and Marcus lies dead on the floor. Tara notices he is still clutching an egg in his hand. It is Maxie's.

In the Caritol car park, Maxie and Jennings slip something into Wiltshire's Rolls Royce. When the Brigadier finds it, he picks it up. It is black and round and has a burning fuse at the top, with the word 'bomb' on it, should he need any more clues. A Union Jack flag pops out of the side just before it explodes. Only Wiltshire's shoes are left, smouldering on the ground. Time for another showbiz exit…

Punch is delighted, quipping about the duo having "eggs-ecuted" Marcus. Maxie reminds Punch that he's the man of a million "cracks," and that maybe Marcus saw the "yolk"! Punch wonders if there is anyone else who might expose them to the authorities, but Maxie and Jennings don't think so. They set off on their next mission. Meanwhile, the Ventriloquist and his doll in Vauda Villa point out to their friend the Tenor that Maxie did not produce all his own material—he had a gag writer. Punch is angry, but between them they remember the writer's name: Bradley Marler.

Steed is on the phone, enquiring about Maxie with the Vaudeville Arts Information Bureau. In between bursts of difficult conversation, Steed tells Tara he thinks he's talking to the man who personally killed vaudeville. The chat resumes, with Steed insisting he doesn't want Hilarious Harry Housefly. Finally he finds out that Maxie is either retired or resting, and they may be able to find out where he is through his gag writer. In the meantime, Tara has been trying a card trick on Steed. He picks a card, looks at it, then puts it back in the pack. Tara tries to find it. As Steed puts the phone down and goes to leave, he informs Tara she'll find the card, the three of clubs, in her handbag.

Bradley is at his typewriter, struggling for inspiration, surrounded by screwed up paper. Steed enters and asks if he

is Bradley Marler. Bradley replies that if he isn't, he's having a great time with his wife! He is a little disappointed at the gag's reception. As Steed talks to him, he tries to find a joke that he will like. Steed tries to explain that he's not in the entertainment business, which Bradley takes to mean that he works in television! Steed persists, trying to find out the information they need, but is fobbed off with another gag, or promises of an excellent brain surgery routine. Steed asks about Maxie, and Bradley says he hasn't seen him for years. He was a quick change artist, fastest in the business, but then all the theatres and music halls began to close and he could not adapt to the new ways. His home venue was the Gladchester Palladium, but now it stands empty.

Maxie and Jennings return to the Caritol offices. Wreaths are laid at three of the seats in the boardroom, and Lord Bessington is hard at work in his office beyond, with the door ajar. Bessington walks into the board room and sees Maxie, who summons him forward and hits him in the face with a custard pie. Bessington struggles to wipe it off him. The clowns depart. Soon after Bessington manages to scrape the pie from his face, Miss Charles walks in and he asks her to call Steed immediately.

Steed and Tara have arrived on the scene. Steed samples the pie and concludes it is lemon flavour with fast-setting glue. He reveals the identity of their assailant, and perhaps a motive. Caritol bought the Gladchester Palladium along with thirty to forty other similar venues with plans to demolish them. People may think vaudeville is dead, but it looks to Steed like it might just have decided to fight back…

Punch is lamenting the failure of Maxie and Jennings to dispose of Bessington. A puppet ghost appears next to Punch, to say that someone else can reveal their location. The ventriloquist dummy reminds Maxie about Bradley, and the danger he could prove to be.

In his office, Bradley is still struggling with his new material. A horn hoots at the door, and Bradley immediately realises it's Maxie. He rushes to open the door, and greets him warmly, asking where he's been, as some feller has been looking for him. Hiding is no way to find work! Maxie hoots "Vauda Villa" to him. Bradley tells Maxie he knows why he's turned up: material! Maxie pulls out a knife, immediately reminding Bradley of the knife throwing routine he used to do. Maxie throws it, and it sticks in Bradley's chest. The shock has as much to do with knocking him over as the knife itself…

Tara is on her way to guard Bessington at his office. Bradley, meanwhile, reaches for the phone from the floor and calls Steed. He tells him about Maxie, and that he's been stabbed by him. Bradley had written the address down on a piece of paper on his desk, but with his last dying spasm, he knocks the paper off the desk along with the phone.

Seagrave leaves Bessington's office, having given him the CUPID papers, promising to phone in any messages to him. Tara turns up and informs Bessington that she's been sent by Steed to be his personal bodyguard. Once again, Miss Charles asks to go early, leaving Bessington alone with Miss King, a situation he finds uncomfortable.

Steed is at Bradley's. He finds him buried under a mound of his crumpled paperwork. He has died with a smile on his face. Steed searches the desk but doesn't find an address. There's nothing else for it—he'll have to sort through all the rejected material.

Punch informs the deadly duo that Bessington is the next target. Elsewhere, Bessington can't quite come to terms with Tara following him around so closely. Steed, meanwhile, is still looking for the address he needs, amongst a plethora of painful puns…

Maxie and Jennings pull up at the Caritol office block in their taxi cab again. Inside, Bessington takes a drink as Tara keeps an eye on him. To make conversation, she asks if he has been to Alaska. She went there when she was two years old.

The clowns get out of the lift, now in costume. They have brought a long red carpet with them. They get to the office door and start feeding the carpet through underneath it. Tara and Bessington don't see it as they've become engrossed in trying to find common areas of interest. He—cricket; she—skiing. They continue to alternate through stock exchange, fashion, golf, motor racing, glass walking sticks, before simultaneously saying, music! By this time the carpet is right between them, and they begin re-enacting a symphony concert they both once saw, each one of them being a different musical instrument. As the music reaches a crescendo, Bessington steps onto the carpet. The rug is pulled from underneath him and he falls out of an open window to his death. Tara looks out after him, then rushes to the door and has to struggle past the roll of carpet blocking it. She pursues the clowns, now out of costume, in her car as they make their escape in the taxi.

The chase continues into the country, and the clowns turn into the entrance to 'Vauda Villa—A resting place for artistes whose services are not in immediate demand.' Maxie gets out and hides behind a phone box. Tara pulls up at the gate and looks around, deciding to call for help. As she approaches the phone box Maxie, now disguised as a policeman, emerges, and asks her what the trouble is. As Tara starts to explain, he and Jennings overpower her and knock her out…

Steed is still at Bradley's office, struggling with endless amounts of suspect humour. He looks down at the chair he is sitting on, and finds the address.

Tara comes round, finding herself tied to a chair, bound and gagged, surrounded by the front half of a pantomime horse, the Tenor, the back half of the Horse, the Ventriloquist and dummy, Jennings, Maxie, and the Escapologist, still in chains. They all face the Punch and Judy stall, and Mr Punch appears. He decrees that Tara must be eliminated, but Maxie won't do it, he wouldn't feel comfortable killing a woman. Fiery Frederick appears and volunteers. He's wearing welding goggles and carrying an acetylene torch. He needs a new assistant. The other artistes don't like the idea, but Fred drags her away, still tied to her chair. Punch informs everyone that the final performance will be at six o'clock. Maxie wonders what is going on — there's still one director left.

Approaching the Villa in a Rolls Royce is 'Gentleman Jack—a Smile, a Song, and an Umbrella.' He looks remarkably familiar to us, as it's Steed improvising again. Inside the Villa, Fred drags a welding cylinder through to his room. He informs Tara that she will be the first woman to be burned in half. Outside, Steed has arrived at the entrance, and knocks on the door. Merlin the Magnificent Magician, principal of the establishment, answers the door. He informs 'Gentleman Jack' that they have no vacancies, but 'Jack' still insists on being shown around. Inside, he sees Fred dragging another cylinder to his room, as he's already begun his 'trick' with Tara. When Steed tries to look behind the main stage curtains, he is led away. Merlin says all the residents are eccentric, except him. With that, ping-pong balls start appearing in his mouth, which he takes out one-by-one.

Look—(Stop Me If . . .

Steed leaves, putting his case back in the car, but instead of driving off, he looks around outside. It's six o'clock, and Mr Punch is on-stage again. The artistes have congregated, and are none too happy when Punch tells them their work is done, especially as one director is still alive. Steed is inside the building and finds Fred at work. He knocks him out and takes off Tara's gag. Steed tells her what has been happening, that it's all an elaborate set-up to wreck CUPID. The artistes think they are getting back at the company that closed their theatres!

In the main room, it is bedlam following the announcement. A second pantomime horse appears on the scene and quickly despatches the original one. One by one, Steed and Tara deal with Merlin, the Escapologist, the Ventriloquist and the Tenor, leaving just Maxie and Jennings standing. They fight, Tara taking on Jennings, who keeps escaping through magic cabinets, while Steed encounters the miracles of Maxie's quick-change routine. He goes through the whole repertoire to try and deal with Steed—clown, washerwoman, male ballet dancer, cowboy, old time boxer, naval admiral and musketeer. They duel with swords, until one wallop from Steed sends Maxie back through all his changes, ending up on the floor in the room where Tara is finally getting to grips with Jennings.

Steed and Tara go back into the main room and see the Punch and Judy booth shuffling away. Steed asks if she's heard the one about the chap who wanted to clean up

with a foreign power. The duo punch through the fabric of the booth and it keels over. They reveal Seagrave to be the man behind it, the reason that Mr Punch didn't want the last director killed! With that, Steed and Tara exit vaudeville style, with appropriate music, of course.

Steed is in his apartment, reading the Tin Tin adventure *Le Lotus Bleu*. The doorbell rings and it is Tara in a party dress with a black choker. Steed isn't ready to go out, but he tries out his new quick change skills behind a pillar.

He goes through oriental gentleman, naval admiral, and Red Indian chief, before managing a tuxedo. Unfortunately, as he departs with Miss King, we see he has a neon sign on his back exhorting us to 'Eat at Joe's'!

(Note—Patrick Macnee remembers this as one of his favorite episodes, and singles out his climactic comedy duel with Maxie (the veteran comedian Jimmy Jewel) as the best of the innumerable fight sequences in the series' history.)

Heroes need villains, whether they're a recurring nemesis, an unstoppable computer or an organisation dedicated to changing the world for the worse.

Sherlock Holmes has the sinister Professor Moriarty, James Bond must deal regularly with S.P.E.C.T.R.E., Number Six in The Prisoner *has to tackle a succession of leaders calling themselves 'Number Two', and the Tracy brothers find that a lot of trouble is caused by The Hood in* Thunderbirds.

The secret agents in The Avengers *tackled one deadly force regularly over the years. Foes without emotion, with the instinct to kill embedded inside them.*

An inhuman force which would test our heroes right to the very limit...

THE CYBERNAUTS

We see a fountain pen on a desk, and hear a crash and the sound of a whip cracking. A man runs into an office and bolts the double doors behind him, taking the extra precaution of putting a sofa against them. He fires a gun at the doors as a fist comes through them, and tries calling for help on the phone, but it's too late. He loads a shotgun and fires both barrels, then all goes black at the sound of the whipcrack. The emergency services are on the phone, unanswered. The fountain pen lies smashed on the desk...

Steed receives a deadly gift

Emma pockets it

Steed looks around at the devastation. There is a chalk outline of a body on the floor. The shotgun's barrel has been bent upwards. Fire that and you'd end up shooting the ceiling. Emma arrives with the files. The first victim was Walter Carson, found dead in his apartment on the fifth floor, with a fractured skull. The second, Andrew Denham, died in his penthouse on the sixth floor, also with a fractured skull. Last night, here, Samuel Hammond died of a broken neck. Steed and Mrs Peel study the business interests of the two men. Carson was chairman of Convercial Imports, Denham head of Automatic Industrials and Hammond was on the board of Electrical Industries. Steed doesn't think that professional killers would use a battering ram. Looking for a strategy, they see that Hammond had one appointment booked for today— 2.30pm at Hirachi, a successful Japanese electronics manufacturer.

At Industrial Deployments, Bob Lambert is discussing the Hirachi deal. Unknown to him, a man is heading down the corridor towards him, the familiar whipcrack sound falling on a guard who stands in his way. Lambert is called to the phone to be warned someone has got into the building without a pass. He hears his secretary scream, and the noise of the door being violently attacked. He grabs a gun and fires all his rounds at the oncoming

intruder. They are useless and once more we hear the whipcrack. A fountain pen drops to the floor, similar to the one we have already seen, and the intruder smashes it to pieces with his gloved hands.

Emma arrives at the new murder scene. Steed turns up and Emma gives him a summary of statements from witnesses. The man was between 6' 2" and 6' 6" tall, and knew exactly where to find Lambert. He too had an appointment at the Hirachi Electronics Corporation in his diary, with Mr Tusamo, in London at 3.00pm on the twelfth. Hirachi have been in the news concerning the development of a new circuit element to replace the transistor.

The dead body had been hit from the front, without a trace of bruising on the face. Emma concludes that it is an advanced karate blow that breaks the neck like a hangman's noose. Only a handful of people in Europe would be skilled enough to do it, so Emma visits a karate class. The karate master is informed of her presence by a robed female assistant who takes the role of receptionist. Emma takes her shoes off, and is asked to state her business by the Master. He is Sensai, the knowledgeable one. She may one day meet Yamuko, the immovable one. Thinking he has to do a sales pitch to a potential new club member, Sensai explains that karate, unlike judo, is a science, not a sport. It means 'empty hand', as the hand can be more deadly than any weapon. You can shatter doors and smash pillars—maybe it's not suitable for a woman such as Mrs Peel. Emma would still like to join, so Sensai suggests that if she can get past his female assistant, she will be most welcome. Emma puts her handbag down and soon shows her worth. Sensai calls a halt when the assistant grabs for Emma's ankle. She attacked Emma as a woman, even though Emma has the skill of a man—a bad mistake. Having proved herself, Emma departs.

Steed has taken over an appointment with the Hirachi corporation. He goes to the secretary, Miss Smith, and announces he is from Industrial Deployments and has an appointment with Mr Tusamo at 3.00pm. He informs her that Mr Lambert is indisposed, and he is taking his place, producing a letter of authority. Steed goes in, while just behind him a bespectacled man carrying a briefcase walks up to Miss Smith and collects a written note, then leaves.

Steed and Tusamo begin their meeting. The circuit Hirachi have invented is ten years ahead of the opposition, and Tusamo will not say what other bids he has received for a piece of the action. "In darkness, the ceiling is always higher," he notes. They discuss the new age that is just around the corner, one of pocket TVs, wristwatch radios and continued miniaturisation. The intercom buzzes. Tusamo's next appointment has arrived. The shadow of one of our iron friends is at the door…

"He who talks too much forgets his listener," Steed imparts to Emma. They have in their possession Tusamo's appointment sheet: '2.15pm—Convercial Imports. 2.30pm—

Automatic Industrials. 2.45pm—Electrical Industries. 3.00pm—Industrial Deployments. 3.15pm—United Automation. 3.30pm—Jephcott Products Ltd'. They match the victims to the list—Carson, Denham, Hammond and Lambert. Emma wonders why they would not simply replace one negotiator with another, but Steed says that such talks require specialist knowledge. If what they think is happening is indeed the case, it leaves the last two firms on the list as suspects.

Emma has gone to Jephcott Products and is being shown a toy robot while she waits. They could supply them at a price that allows them to retail at £4 each. Jephcott appears and Emma states that she represents Widdle & Fentel, a chain of stores that are opening up new toy departments. Jephcott demonstrates a dog that comes to you when whistled for. Emma's own whistle does not do the trick, so she is passed one that will. Jephcott makes his apologies, as he must leave in a hurry to join a board meeting, but gives her a copy of their latest catalogue to look through.

At karate class, Emma is watching the students fight. Sensai announces a demonstration by Oyama, a fifth Dan in judo, a fourth Dan in karate. He breaks a block of wood with his hand, one thrust of his palm demolishing it.

Steed is checking a gadget within his umbrella. The doorbell rings—it's Gilbert, a ministry contact. He can only spare Steed three minutes, as his Minister wants some estimates. Steed gets right to it and asks about United Automation. Gilbert tells him what he knows, while rearranging Steed's trophies on a sideboard. They produce industrial and domestic appliances, their boss being Dr Armstrong. Gilbert knows him, as he worked under him for a time. Armstrong left the Ministry after refusing to toe the official line. He thought they should be constructive rather than destructive, and had a crazy idea about building a machine to clear debris from radioactive areas. He went ahead with it when the top brass said no to him and it led to an accident which wrecked the building he was in, killed half his staff and put him permanently in a wheelchair. Armstrong would choose an electronic calculator and equations over a pretty woman every time. Gilbert offers to pull a few strings for Steed to find out where he's based now.

Benson enters a control room and establishes a video link. Their girl on the inside has revealed that another two offers are to come. They know of one, but who can the other be? Tusamo keeps the names in a confidential file, so he can't say who is preparing to make a deal. Their contact will keep trying…

Steed enters his apartment and hears a clink from his kitchen. Mrs Peel is in there, although Steed thought she was supposed to be at Jephcott's. Emma explains that Jephcott will be in a board meeting until six, so she

circuits are built in triplicate, so any fault is automatically rectified without a haemorrhage. With the level of technology he uses, he has a trouble-free work force. Everything will eventually be computerised, Armstrong reckons. Even music will be composed by machines in the course of time. The new Japanese circuits will mean that further progress is only a matter of time. The computer will then be able to answer questions on any topic: science, finance, even military and political matters.

Benson calls Armstrong on the video link. He has found out that the rival offer to theirs is from Industrial Deployments, made by a man called Steed. Armstrong asks Benson to look behind him and identify the man, which he does. With that, Armstrong closes the meeting, but not before giving Steed a special pen. It runs on solid ink and lasts for ten

years. As Steed leaves, Benson enters. Armstrong picks up the phone again: "Roger, prepare for target assignment."

Jephcott is writing at his desk, using one of Armstrong's special pens. He puts it away after making notes while on the phone. He switches his lights off, and is about to leave for the night when he hears breaking glass and the whip-crack sound. Steed and Emma are waiting outside and think it strange that he's been so long coming out since his office went dark. They decide to go up and check.

They find Jephcott dead, lying behind his desk. Like the other victims, he was killed by a karate expert, who left by making a hole in the wall. Armstrong is in a wheelchair, so he couldn't be responsible. At that moment, a toy robot starts moving on its own—Emma and Steed look at each other incredulously...

Steed cuts notches in United Automation key cards with a pair of scissors. He's creating a set of skeleton keys as insurance for his next trip to see Armstrong. Emma takes one, too. It is time to get in touch with Tusamo at the Hirachi corporation. Steed gives Emma his number and says that if Tusamo isn't there she must try all the hotels in the area, in order to inform him that Steed will be making an offer in the morning. Steed puzzles over Arm-

thought they could compare notes. Steed feels his approach to United Automation needs a literary sheen—he'll play a journalist and talk of automation in modern society. Will the machine supplant man, or woman for that matter? Not if Steed has anything to do with it. United Automation is virtually impregnable, with admission by appointment only. Whatever he does, he must not forget his punch card, and he hands Emma a spare for safe keeping.

Steed arrives at United Automation and uses the punch card on the entry door to a lift. He runs his umbrella around the inside, just to check how solid it is. It leads to a high-tech office, which is empty but for a smattering of gadgets. Dr Armstrong appears in an electric wheelchair, stating that their meeting will have to be brief. This is the age of the push button, he begins, and his entire factory is automated, with just a few human maintenance staff. Humans are fallible, temperamental and so often unreliable. A machine is obedient and invariably more competent. Failure of machinery is unheard of in his factory. All

The Cybernauts

strong's motives—he's interested in getting the concession, but not in making profit. He jokes with Emma that if he's not back by 11.30am, he's stayed on for breakfast. Emma reminds him that he doesn't eat breakfast—she's holding the pen that Armstrong gave Steed...

Steed is at the automated offices. He uses his original card and gets in the lift. At the top, he looks around the office, searching the drawers. He checks over a silver-faced dummy with sunglasses and a hat. It doesn't move. He hears someone approaching, and goes into a chute to hide. Armstrong and Benson enter, and they look at the Cybernaut, harmless until programmed. Powered by solar energy, with a casing that can survive the blast of an atomic shell, one day Armstrong will be able to make one

The whipcrack sound is heard, and the phone keeps ringing.

The maintenance Cybernaut enters the same room as Steed. The robot stops, and Steed tries to tip-toe past again to the door. He thinks he's made it, but then the Cybernaut slashes backwards, catching him.

Emma proves not to have been at home when she was visited. She is speeding along in her car, the pen still in her pocket...

Steed regains consciousness, and is informed by Armstrong that the Cybernaut was programmed to capture, not kill. He talks of creating a complex computer, incapable of making a wrong decision. Steed asks if this would be the perfect politician, which is a mistake, as it sets

that can think for itself. The instinct to kill is directed by a simple radio transmitter in a pen on the person of its target.

Mrs Peel has tracked down Tusamo and makes an appointment at 11.30am the following day for Steed. Meanwhile, back at the control room, the frequency of Steed's pen, 0.113, is being fed into the Cybernaut's control computer. They find "him" on the tracker. It is at this point that Steed realises he doesn't have the pen any more, but Roger the robot goes out on his mission. Steed crawls through the passages, but comes across a metal grille at the other end that he cannot budge.

Emma picks up the pen to do a crossword. She watches the clock tick by, as it gets nearer to midnight. In the office block, Steed has found his way to the boiler room and turns the heat gauge up. Soon, a Cybernaut wearing a cap and a boiler suit appears to turn down the gauge, and Steed sneaks out of the door it entered through to another part of the complex. The maintenance Cybernaut reports back, its punch card revealing that the thermostat was altered manually. Armstrong and Benson realise they have had an intruder!

Steed tries to get to a phone, but he's too late. The Cybernaut is breaking in just as the phone rings in Emma's residence.

Armstrong off on a tirade about government by automation. Steed wonders what the voters will think, but they don't seem to be part of Armstrong's plans. When the new components from Hirachi arrive, it will be just a matter of time before an army of Cybernauts follow. The map reveals that the holder of Steed's pen has arrived at the factory. Armstrong wonders, if this is a friend of Steed's.

Emma uses the skeleton punch card that Steed gave her to get into the lift in the lobby. The control room can see her on its monitors. She won't be joining them, but she'll see how efficient an automated assassin is. Emma finds herself in a store room, and comes across the parts necessary to make up a Cybernaut's head. Back in the control room, Benson levels a gun at Steed as he tries to leave. He is forced to sit down in a control chair. Steed asks, "Is this your idea of progress? A cybernetic police state? Push-button bobbies, automated martinis, remote controlled olives? No, I'll stick to good old flesh and blood." With that he smashes his fist against the control buttons he has found concealed in the arm of the chair. Lights go out, music begins and the exit opens. He is shot at before bundling Benson over and making his escape.

Emma finds herself facing the Cybernaut. She hides behind packing crates as it approaches, marching through them to get to its quarry. Steed is on his way, but Emma is already cornered and starts shooting. Steed arrives and tells her to throw him the pen. The maintenance Cybernaut appears, followed by Armstrong who explains that this one can think for itself. Steed places the pen on this superior Cybernaut. The two robots fight each other to a standstill. Armstrong is horrified, and is killed trying to intervene. The brainless Cybernaut beats the thinking Cybernaut to a standstill, and then destroys the pen. Without any further orders, it remains motionless. Emma pushes it with a finger and it falls over...

Emma's car pulls up behind Steed's. He's reading the crossword and is stuck on nine down. "It moves in the dark, it leaves no mark, it's as hard as steel." Emma ventures "Cybernaut." It fits, and Steed is about to write it in when his pencil breaks. Emma offers him a pen. He refuses, as he doesn't hold with these new fangled things. Emma drives away...

(Note—After such an illustrious career, it seems a shame that Michael Gough, Dr Armstrong, will be best remembered for playing Alfred the Butler in the Batman movies.)

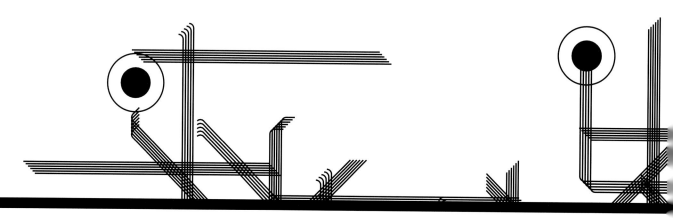

RETURN OF THE CYBERNAUTS

Computerised cards are being inspected. There is one each of Steed and Mrs Peel, and the remaining two are scientists called Chadwick and Russell. Russell's card is put into a machine. The scene changes to a country house. It is four o'clock in the afternoon and the sky is overcast. The front door is hacked open with the now familiar whipcrack sound, and an internal door is despatched the same way. Russell is in his study and on hearing the commotion tries to escape through the French windows. He is stopped and knocked out. The Cybernaut picks him up and carries him off...

Steed pulls some strings

Emma becomes a puppet

Steed and Emma are studying a bronze bust. It's a self-portrait and Steed is not altogether impressed. Their host is Paul Beresford, who is making a play for Emma. His business is booming, but he admits to feeding on other people's talents, a parasite of sorts. He invests in them, and likes to surround himself with beautiful things. He's inquisitive about Steed and Emma's business, but he

knows it's very hush-hush. Steed says they're working on finding Professor Chadwick, a scientist that the ministry officially describe as having been "mislaid."

The phone rings and the call is for Steed. They have to leave—another scientist has disappeared. Steed apologises for breaking up the evening, but assures Paul that there will be others. When they have left the building, a buzzer sounds and Paul responds by pressing a button. A secret doorway appears and the Cybernaut enters with Russell over his shoulder.

Steed and Emma have made their way to Russell's house. Emma comments on how much she likes Paul, and Steed admits he has a good line in clarets, particularly the '29. If Steed tries hard enough, though, he reckons he'll find something there to dislike. They look through the debris for clues, but there seems to be no link between the two abductions, as the scientists work in research areas poles apart.

Paul is talking to Benson, whom we met in the first Cybernauts episode, explaining the significance of Chadwick's presence. An eminent physiologist, he knows more about anatomy than any man alive. Paul has him locked in a cell, unconscious. He moves along to another cell which Russell is inside. He's as an engineer; give him any problem in his field and he'll solve it. Paul says all he needs now is an electronics expert and Benson has located one—Dr Neville. Benson demonstrates how the homing signal works. The computer cards we saw at the beginning of the episode are cardiographs, showing heartbeats which are as distinctive as a finger print. Pointing at the immobile Cybernaut in the lab with them, he claims that once it is programmed, it can find a person in a city of ten million. Neville's cardiograph card is placed in the machine, and the Cybernaut goes to work…

Neville is just leaving his laboratory when he sees the Cybernaut barging through a garden fence. He retreats and is backed up against a wall. Dropping his attaché case, he runs to his Jaguar. Getting in, he manages to start it, but the Cybernaut stops the car from moving. The wheels squeal on the tarmac, but the vehicle remains stationary. His car roof is ripped through and Neville finds himself being dragged from his vehicle through the hole.

Benson is using a television monitor to view events outside the house. It looks peaceful enough. He checks around. A Cybernaut is walking over the fields with its latest capture. Benson sees that Steed and Mrs Peel have just pulled up at the front door, however. They are spied on from a camera located in a bird box. Emma goes inside alone, Steed reasoning that now is not the time for claret, even if it is a '29. Benson reports on the phone to Paul that the Cybernaut is due back at any time, but when his conversation is cut short by Emma, Paul informs Benson that he'll have to deal with it. Emma has returned because she left her purse. A quick search recovers it, and Emma leaves again. Paul and Benson watch the two of them outside. Steed has had a message informing him of the latest victim, Neville, so they head for the crime scene, leaving just as the Cybernaut enters the grounds. Benson insists that it was not a good idea to cultivate Steed and Emma's friendship, but Paul reminds him that it's all just a game of cat and mouse…

As Steed stares at the Jaguar's slashed roof, Emma remembers the nine letter word beginning with 'C'. As Dr Armstrong is dead, someone else must have inherited his know-how.

The door to the lab opens and the three captives are escorted in to join Paul and Benson. They sit down, with piles of money on the table in front of them. Paul shows them film of Clement Armstrong, and talks of his work. They observe the manner of his death, courtesy of the video camera that ran continuously in the factory. He says that Armstrong was his brother, which is why they are all here. There is £100,000 in cash ready for each of them and he'll double this if they are successful in destroying those who killed his brother. He doesn't want anything

quick, which is why he hasn't hired assassins. The targets are Steed and Mrs Peel. Armstrong would have devised something more imaginative and creative if he were alive, so he wants the men to devise a rhapsody of suffering, a whole new idea. Russell thinks the idea is monstrous and barbaric. He refuses to help, so Paul tells him he is free to go. Russell goes to the door, which opens to reveal a Cybernaut. It chops him down. Paul will need another engineer.

Russell has been dumped back at his residence, his neck broken. Steed and Emma are checking things out. Emma recalls the trademark blow of the Cybernauts. If another one has been built, someone must have access to Armstrong's papers. Emma decides to check the files, and they agree to meet at Paul's, who has invited them over for a drink. Steed wonders who they will replace Russell with…

We are at the office door of Dr J. W. Garnett. The secretary outside, Rosie, is tittle-tattling on the phone. The Cybernaut enters and stands still outside the entrance to Garnett's office. The secretary makes a play, thinking it's a man with an excellent physique. When she tells the Cybernaut she likes men with big shoulders, it strikes her and she flies across the room. She's still conscious, and

her only concern seems to be that she's got a hole in her tights. When the Cybernaut starts battering down the door, she begins to scream.

The Cybernaut delivers its captive to Russell's former cell. Steed, meanwhile, has the unenviable task of interviewing Rosie. She expects that there will be hundreds of pictures of her in the newspapers, and wonders where the photographers are. She can see the headlines now: 'Ravishing blonde beauty defends her honour to the last'. Perhaps she ought to change into her bikini, the ever so revealing one, the one she's almost been arrested in twice. Steed disappoints her by saying there won't be any photographers for security reasons. No one has ever taken Dr Garnett away like that before, she muses. He didn't even have an appointment!

Paul enters the laboratory and talks to Dr Garnett, the two others having helped convince him of the sensible option. Paul informs the trio that whatever they need will be provided, no matter what the cost. Emma has arrived, and they observe her through a two-way mirror. Paul enters the room, and Emma informs him that Steed will be joining them later. Paul takes her coat and accidentally knocks the file she is carrying on the floor. Out pops a photograph of Dr Armstrong, and Paul pretends to stretch his memory to identify him. He remembers Dr Armstrong because he approached Paul the previous year for finance. He couldn't help him, but was most impressed by his brilliance. Emma says he was a megalomaniac. As Steed enters, the three scientists continue to watch. Garnett muses that he met Steed once—Benson rubs his neck and comments that so did he.

As Paul opens a bottle of wine—Louisville '28—Steed tells him he is expecting a call as a fourth man, Garnett, has disappeared. Emma informs Steed that Paul knew Armstrong. Steed has decided to talk to Armstrong's lawyer, in order to trace his next of kin. Paul smells the wine in the bottle and announces that it is "corked." He goes to fetch another bottle, using the opportunity to order Benson to organise a Cybernaut to deal with the lawyer. Steed and Emma discuss Paul. He and Emma had accidentally met at an auction, and he has taken great pains to get to know her—Steed isn't jealous, just thoughtful.

The phone rings and Steed picks it up. Paul dashes over to an extension line in the lab to listen in on the conversation. It's Conroy, to let Steed know that Armstrong's lawyer is John Hunt, of High Pines, Eddington. At this revelation, Paul activates the Cybernaut. In the meantime, he tries to delay Steed's departure, but the wine doesn't do the trick and Emma is left alone with Paul.

A Rover delivers the Cybernaut to its destination. Benson pushes a button on his car dashboard and off the Cybernaut goes, breaking the glass in the study door. Hunt has grabbed a gun to defend himself and fires all six shots, but to no avail. He is struck and killed. Steed appears, finding the damage and Hunt's body. He looks up to see the Cybernaut as it strikes him.

Emma leaves Paul after what she describes as a marvellous evening. Benson, meanwhile, is watching over the trio of scientists. Garnett has an idea, and needs some equipment. Benson looks at his shopping list, commenting that the gear is a bit costly, but he'll get what he needs…

Emma is nurse-maiding Steed at his apartment. He has a shot of whisky and takes off for the ministry, while Emma wrestles with Armstrong's file. Steed arrives at Garnett's office and Rosie informs him that Conroy is inside. Steed finds Conroy looking through desk drawers. He reveals that Garnett was an ideas man, keen on explosive devices and the like. Neville and Chadwick work in different fields, but have the same brief. Conroy finds something very odd about Garnett's medical file—his cardiogram is missing, as were Neville's and Chadwick's.

Garnett is working on a device, and presses the buzzer in his cell. Benson takes him to Paul, who asks what he has created. Garnett throws the device to the floor and clouds of smoke billow from it. The scientist uses the cover it provides to escape. Benson loads Garnett's cardiogram so that the Cybernaut can recapture him.

Emma is still file-bashing when she hears clicking footsteps outside the front door. It's Garnett, and he's there to warn Steed. As she is preparing a damp cloth for his head, the Cybernaut arrives. It breaks down the door, knocking Emma out of the way and collecting Garnett. Emma is out cold.

Garnett finds himself back in detention, and Neville and Chadwick are working together on an idea, a diabolically clever one. Paul is shown their plan, and he likes it. Steed and Emma won't die, but will wish that they had. To

The Cybernauts

complete the experiment, they need to know the skin conductivity and epidermal resistance of the victims. They have to arrange for them to touch a metallic object—Paul recommends the bust of Emma he has had made.

It is Steed's turn to nurse-maid Emma. They have realised the significance of the cardiograms as a guidance system. Garnett spoke of a threat against them, and as they ponder this, the phone rings. It is Paul, to say he has some information about Armstrong. They head straight over there. In the lounge, they see the bust of Mrs Peel, and Emma immediately picks it up. Steed holds it, too. Paul says he has discovered that Armstrong's factory was sold to a warehouse company and everything else went for scrap. He apologises for dragging them over just for that, but there's always the wine! The scientists are observing everything and take a picture of Steed's watch…

The scientists are making up an electronic gadget that looks just like Steed's timepiece. The control box for it will fit in Paul's pocket. Once activated, the device will jam the brain and the wearer will be unable to resist, although they will be fully conscious. The person will become like a human puppet, almost a human Cybernaut. Paul needs a practical demonstration, so he straps the watch to Garnett. Chadwick demonstrates the control device, and then Paul takes over. He can move him wherever he wants, and then pushes all the buttons together. It overloads and Garnett falls to the ground, dead. A full and successful test—Paul has a silver watch to give Emma, too.

Paul gives Emma the watch as a present. She appreciates the thought, but is a little hesitant. Paul turns up the charm so that she'll accept. All that he asks is that she will wear it for him tomorrow. More indirect methods are needed with Steed. Benson breaks in to Steed's flat and hunts for his watch. After an intensive search, where he disturbs almost everything, he finds it in a drawer and synchronises the time before carrying out the swap. Benson hears Steed approaching and makes his escape.

The following morning, Steed and Emma survey the mess in his apartment. Nothing is missing, which makes the whole affair even more puzzling. Emma has a lunch appointment with Paul at 1:00pm. Steed was initially reluctant to attend—three's a crowd and all that—but prefers to look at it as safety in numbers. He inspects Emma's gift and they get ready to leave. Elsewhere, Paul activates Emma's watch and she is instantly under his control. She leaves the flat, and in the rush Steed leaves his watch on the desk. Getting in her car, she nearly runs him over as she speeds away. Steed, puzzled, takes his Bentley and follows.

Paul is directing Emma to come to him. She enters his estate, smashing the white wooden perimeter gates as she drives through them. A camera on a nearby statue tracks her progress. She pulls up outside the house, but

Paul is confused as to where Steed has got to. He should be with her, commanded by his own watch. Emma enters the lab and Paul makes her stop. He speaks to her, thanking her for wearing his gift. It's a very special one. She can hear him—he can see it in her eyes.

Steed arrives and sees Emma's car. He looks around the side of the house. Inside, Paul is playing games with his puppet, Emma. Benson notices Steed lurking in the woods with the surveillance cameras, but a close-up shows that he is not wearing his watch. They have made a spare and Chadwick goes to fetch it. Paul sends Emma to go and draw Steed out. She is outside without her coat and Steed immediately goes over to her. He is baffled by her lack of response, and then feels the crushing blow of a Cybernaut.

Paul strokes a bust of his brother as Steed watches him in the laboratory. He reveals to Steed the secret of Emma's watch, and his scheme for revenge. Steed destroyed Paul's brother and the day of retribution has come, a day when Steed will obey Paul's every whim. He'll even come to envy the Cybernauts. The Cybernaut takes hold of Steed, and Chadwick reappears with the replacement watch, but a sleight of hand sees the watch put on the Cybernaut's wrist. Chadwick is knocked to the ground, and Steed uses the commotion as an opportunity to relieve Emma of her watch.

She's in command of her senses again and wrestles the gun from Benson. The Cybernaut then homes in on Paul, bear-hugging him. Steed and Emma try to pull the Cybernaut away from him, but it's too late. Emma stamps on the control box, and the Cybernaut stops with a jolt. It is Steed's turn to push the robot over with his finger…

Steed is trying to fix the toaster. He puts in two slices, and eulogises about how grateful we should be for living in the twentieth century: thermostats, computers, transistors, even automatic toasters. At the mention of its name, the appliance blows up, a hole in the ceiling showing where it has gone. Two pieces of burnt toast stand upright on the table. "That's the first thing Great Britain's ever got into orbit," they muse. Should Emma butter the toast, or preserve it for posterity?

(Note—The presence of Peter Cushing as Paul makes this an extra-special episode. His performance, while seeming to be that of a besotted admirer at the beginning, is tainted with a feeling that this is a man whose motives aren't as crystal clear as he would have us believe. Cushing would return to the series a decade later, helping to launch The New Avengers with his role as Von Claus in the première episode 'The Eagles Nest'.) ◉

THE LAST OF THE CYBERNAUTS...

We are at Steed's birthday party. A white cake with blue icing informs us of the occasion. Purdey is at the piano and Gambit is there, along with an attractive woman called Tricia. Their rousing chorus of 'Happy Birthday' is interrupted when Terry appears, injured. Gambit goes to him, and Terry tells them that they've found the double agent they were looking for. His name is Felix Kane, and they are making a contact at 10.30am the next day, in the same car park. Having done his duty, Terry expires.

Felix Kane gets out of his car at the rendezvous point, and is signalled by the flashing headlights of a second car. Steed is in his green Jaguar, Purdey and Gambit are close by in a white Range Rover. Kane goes over to the other man, and they exchange envelopes. Steed screams off in his Jaguar and blocks the exit. The second driver panics and tries to escape, smashing vehicles on his way, eventually ploughing into another car and coming to a complete stop, unconscious from the impact. The two Avengers vehicles manoeuvre Felix Kane's car into a dead end, a small hill running down toward a stationary petrol tanker. He smashes into it, and the resulting blast sends flames roaring into the air. It is an explosion of gigantic proportions.

We reconvene at another of Steed's birthday parties, one year on this time. There are a lot more revellers this year, and 'Happy Birthday' is sung with more enthusiasm. Steed wanders over to a corner, thoughtful. Purdey sees this and goes to him—she can tell he's thinking of last year. Poor old Terry. Their reminiscences are interrupted by Laura, one of the partygoers, who really needs Steed's attention.

At the gates of a prison, a man, Goff, is released. He's been inside for a long time. Before he can appreciate the outside world, a man intercepts him from the back seat of a car. This is Malov. They have business to talk about, and the gun he holds assures Goff's compliance.

Goff is taken to a room decorated with large black and white head shots of Steed, Purdey and Gambit. Goff should know Steed—after all it was Steed who put him away for ten years. Sensing Goff's reluctance, Malov insists that he's only in this for the money—if Goff plays along, there will be something in it for him, too. A man in an electric wheelchair approaches. It is Kane again, with a plastic mask covering his face. One fixed expression greets Goff as he is given what is described as a small down payment, the tip of the iceberg. Goff is offered a drink, and he asks for Scotch. Kane speculates that Goff must hate Steed. Kane's own loathing for the whole trio is all-consuming. He should really be dead, but his hatred of them keeps him going. Malov changes Kane's mask over so he wears

an expression of pleasure. We discover what Kane has found out: Goff worked with Dr Armstrong on building Cybernauts, but Steed and Mrs Peel foiled their plans. Kane's research has shown that Armstrong established a storehouse of Cybernauts and he believes that Goff knows its location. Kane will go to any lengths to find such a store. He pointedly tells Goff that he doesn't want to be forced to assume his mask of anger over such a thing...

Steed is playing a Stylophone. He's doing very well and you'd think him a professional. Mrs Weir, the housekeeper, appears, and Steed explains that he's had a birthday party and that the Stylophone was a present. He then reveals the secret of his virtuoso performance—a small earpiece is telling him which numbered notes to play. The phone rings. As Steed goes to answer it, he warns Mrs Weir that if she is a woman of high moral standards, she should leave the guest bedroom until tomorrow!

On the phone is Tom Fitzroy, a civil service contact. He tells Steed that it's just a routine call to let him know that Frank Goff has been released from prison. He thought Steed ought to know Goff was out and about, in case the man was bearing a grudge. Steed doesn't mince his words—he considers Goff small-fry and nothing to worry about. Putting the phone down, Steed hears Mrs Weir playing his Stylophone—her concert-hall performance made all the more remarkable by the fact that Steed has the earpiece in his hand!

At a half-demolished house, Malov is running a cable to Kane's wheelchair. He attaches it to a detonator, and Kane takes pleasure in turning the switch. An explosion opens up the vaults below the house and soon Malov, Kane and Goff are making their way to the stairs to see what there is down there. In the crevices of the walls are several Cybernauts. Goff made them and seems to know how to operate them. They can be preprogrammed, or manipulated by the use of direct radio control. They could even be directed from a wheelchair...

Steed is playing snooker with a lady called Laura, when he senses that someone is coming up behind him, through the door. Steed overpowers the intruder and is annoyed to see that it is Fitzroy. He was only approaching quietly so as not to spoil Steed's shot. He asks Laura to give them a few moments, which she willingly does. Fitzroy tells Steed that they've got trouble—Goff has gone missing, completely underground.

At Kane's studio, Goff has a Cybernaut working. It walks around the room, and then Kane has a go. He heads it towards Goff. Kane questions him further on his role in the creation of the Cybernauts. Goff was just a builder, not an architect, of the machines. Nothing more than a mere mechanic. Goff agrees that to take the designs further, you would need a cybernetics expert. Kane sees Goff's limitations and with one whipcrack from the Cybernaut under his control, disposes of another loose end. Malov and Kane take Goff away in a car and dump him in a field.

Steed is leading Laura through his country garden. She has a blindfold on and has not realised yet that Steed has a present for her. It's a horse, a fine specimen. Steed likes people to have what they desire and insists that she accept it. Suddenly, he hits out through the hedge next to them, surprising a spy. He hears a muffled cry and finds Fitzroy again. It's more trouble, he's advised. Goff has been found with his neck broken, as if he'd been hit by an iron bar...

Malov and a Cybernaut have driven up to a country house, the home of Professor Mason. He's well guarded, but not enough to resist an attack by a Cybernaut. The robot sets off on its mission and comes across a set of tall iron gates that are padlocked together. It pushes them apart. A guard with a shotgun fires both barrels, reloads and squeezes off one more shot before he is chopped, the whipcrack sound again signalling the victim's demise.

Mason is in his laboratory with an armed guard. He finds it intolerable that he has to be protected by men with guns, but the guard reminds him that whilst he is there, he is safe and no one can get at him. The guard leans against the door. We hear the whipcrack, and he is knocked out by a fist punching through the wood. The Cybernaut enters, and slices at Mason, not seriously injuring him. It picks him up and carries him back to Malov's car. Mason is set down across the back seat.

Steed is looking at the broken door of Mason's laboratory. Purdey is confused—if a man was not responsible for the damage, then what was? They question the guard. He saw nothing, but certainly felt it. Steed asks if he heard a swish, sort of like a whip cracking? The guard cannot help. He also can't advise them of what it was Mason was working on...

At Kane's studio, Mason regains consciousness and Kane introduces himself. Kane knows that Mason is working on secret cybernetics projects: remote control, automation and robots. Kane shows him a Cybernaut. Mason has heard of them, but has never seen one. Kane tells him that he has been brought there to progress Armstrong's work a stage further...

Gambit and Purdey are playing Scrabble. Purdey has created a word: 'Sighbernort'. Gambit insists that it is not spelt like that. Purdey is indignant and asks whether it matters. Both of them have looked up the old files about the Cybernauts. A kind of walking missile, capable of shattering doors, riding roughshod over any guards, impervious to bullets and very, very deadly. Gambit wonders why Purdey hasn't mentioned Mrs Emma Peel, then remembers she

never does. Purdey has noticed that Steed is worried, so it must be serious. The man who designed them is dead, Goff is dead ... so who exactly is controlling them?

Malov is lighting an acetylene torch in an effort to persuade Mason to co-operate. Kane thinks money would be a much more preferable incentive, and Mason just has to name his price. Kane tries another tack. We hear in great detail about the daily routine of a girl: the route she takes to college, the places along that route where she is all alone. They can pick Mason's daughter up at any time and have her annihilated. They have the means. Mason stalls, saying that what Kane is asking for is impossible. He cannot understand why he would do all this. Kane asks Malov to take off his mask, and Mason sees the full extent of his injuries. Kane tells of how the trio he can see in the pictures did this to him. Mason gives way and says that the materials he needs can only be obtained from Turner Laboratories. Kane reminds Mason that he has the means...

Steed has turned up at Turner Laboratories in an effort to find out what Mason was working on. An attractive woman, Dr Marlow, shows him around an area known to employees as Mason's Mandate. They don't just find ways of destroying things at this complex, they also find cures, though admittedly for bacterial infections that they themselves have created! In the Professor's den, Steed looks around. He still can't figure out what exactly Mason was working on.

Dr Marlow still insists that he cannot be told. Steed informs her that at that very moment 150 clerks are working on the paperwork to allow him to find out, but he doesn't have the time to wait. The regulations weren't drawn up to possibly save Mason's life. She cracks and tells him that it was cybernetics. From outside, Steed hears the familiar whipcracks approaching and takes the unusual action of locking the girl in a cupboard. A guard tries to shoot the Cybernaut, with the usual lack of effect. The Cybernaut breaks the door down, and from their television monitor, Kane and Mason can see what the robot sees. Mason points out the machine they require. The Cybernaut stands motionless. Steed approaches, and Kane can see him on-screen. With one swift movement, Steed is chopped.

Steed wakes up to see Purdey over him. He asks, "what happened?" Purdey is a little disappointed at this—she would have expected snappier repartee. Purdey relates that they found a hysterical woman in a cupboard, his action probably saving her life. He really must stop being so gallant, as women are liberated now. They have deduced that the Cybernaut came to the establishment with one purpose—to steal equipment, but why and for whom?

Meanwhile, Kane thinks Mason is stalling. He is wearing his beaming face, but if Mason looks into his eyes, he will see a twinkle of anticipation. Malov is then chastised for not covering all traces. A man called Foster links them, and three brilliant people will find that link. They must not find it, and so the Cybernaut is despatched on another mission.

Gambit is in bed, hiding under a sheet as Purdey enters. When he doesn't respond, she throws a switch by the side of the bed which retracts it into the wall. Mike is left in a heap on the floor. Purdey doesn't normally go in for slapstick and banana skins, she's more Coward and Molière. She wants Gambit to accompany her to J. B. Foster's. He's been working for the prison authorities, at the jail Goff was in. J. B. was one of only three people who knew Goff was going to be released a day early, and he has a weakness—he bets on the horses. If he loses money, he's bribable. Purdey reminds Gambit that he loses on the horses, too. Gambit replies that's because Purdey supplies him with the tips! He asks if she will wait outside, which she refuses to do as she knows he'll lock the door and go back to sleep. Gambit explains that his reason for asking is that he's not wearing any pyjamas. That does the trick...

Within the prison, the Cybernaut is climbing the stairs as Gambit and Purdey turn up outside. The duo split up, Gambit going in the front entrance, Purdey driving round the back. The Cybernaut has already found Foster's door, and Gambit hears the whipcrack sound while walking up the stairs just below. Purdey pulls up at the back of the prison and looks up to see the metal man hanging Foster over the edge of a balcony. The Cybernaut retreats, meeting Gambit on the steps. He ducks the robot's wild slashes and kicks it down a flight of stairs, but this is only a temporary respite. Gambit tries a hand chop to the neck and

hurts his hand. Purdey joins her colleague and together they push the Cybernaut over the staircase rails. It plummets several floors, smashing into pieces at the bottom. The head has come off and rolls away independently. Kane shrugs off the loss of the machine—it had served its purpose.

Purdey is bathing Gambit's swollen hand. Steed is examining the head of the Cybernaut. Fitzroy appears, having

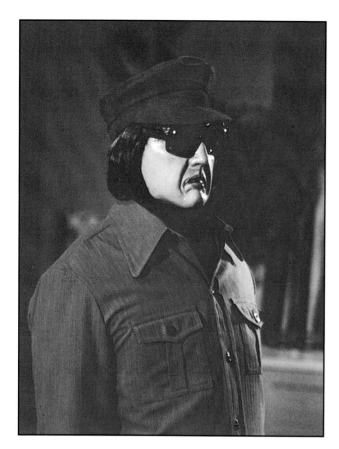

sides of a Range Rover. Kane pushes hard and shunts the car against Gambit, who is knocked out by the impact.

Mason picks up a phone and calls Steed. He tells him that Kane has gone to kill Purdey, and that he is now half-Cybernaut...Purdey hears someone at her door and thinks it's Gambit again. As she approaches, Kane smashes his way in. She knows who he is—the phoenix from the inferno. He chose her first as Steed will suffer so very much seeing the ex-dancer with her legs shattered. He lunges for her and they fight, crashing round the apartment. Purdey fires her gun, but it is useless.

Steed pulls up in his Jaguar and sees the handprint on the back of the Range Rover. He finds Gambit on the floor at the front of the vehicle, sandwiched between it and his XJS.

attached a white hankie to his brolly. He informs Steed that they got a thumb print off the head—just the one, and it's a pity that Steed is not wearing a hat because he could tell him to hold on to it. The print belonged to Felix Kane. Taking Gambit to one side, he asks him to keep an eye on Purdey.

At Kane's studio, Mason is ready. Kane is being fitted with Cybernaut technology. The limbs will operate by electronic impulse from Kane's nerves. Kane walks again, soon getting the hang of it. He has the strength of fifty men and is virtually bullet-proof. He is half-man, half-Cybernaut. Mason will have his freedom once Kane has completed his task. Kane cannot send a machine to do a man's work. He must eliminate them himself, and Purdey will be his first target...

Purdey is exercising, when she hears someone outside her front door. She approaches cautiously, but it's only Gambit, lurking. He says he's called to return a book, but has forgotten the book. He goes away again and heads back to his red Jaguar XJS, where he checks his gun.

Kane is dressed in a blue boiler suit with a blue cap, a brown scarf and sunglasses. He is ready for the outside world. After Kane has left, Mason asks Malov for a Scotch. Mason activates a Cybernaut, but Malov is wise to him and shoots just as the Cybernaut lashes out...

Kane arrives at Purdey's, but Gambit has spotted him. He gets out of the XJS, and they find themselves on opposite

Purdey is still holding Kane at bay, but then he grabs her. Outside, Gambit has recovered and checks his gun. Steed gives him an aerosol can—"Not that, this!" he advises. Kane is about to begin a chopping spree on Purdey when he has a brolly stuck in his back. Kane turns around and Steed sprays him with his aerosol can, straight in the face. He throws a can to Purdey, and starts on a second can himself. Gambit joins in. They are covering him from head to foot, and thus slowing him down. Suddenly he stops, motionless, and an arm bursts into flames. The only things still moving are Kane's eyes. Steed shows him the can's label, so that he can read it: 'Plastic Skin—Good for 101 Uses'. Steed adds cheerfully, "One hundred and two."

Which brings us to the end of the Cybernauts saga. There's no doubt that such unstoppable machines as these had their influence on modern-day creations, such as The Terminator, *maybe even* Robocop. *Whatever new versions are concocted, there is nothing that unsettles the nerves of* Avengers *fans more than that distinctive whipcrack sound effect, which warns you that death and destruction are just around the corner...* ♥

CREATING the AVENGERS

Brian Clemens

BRIAN CLEMENS

Throughout the world, "innocent" viewers, says Brian Clemens, have never forgotten The Avengers, *principally because of its characters: the elegant and cheeky John Steed and his seductive partners. The reality is not so simple. Even for those "innocents", doubtless nothing would remain of the series were it not for the exceptional quality of the many parts which went to make up the whole. As for those less innocent viewers, "whose spirit turned bad", as Brian Clemens puts it, they can discern, beneath the surface, a sophisticated social critique, which not only takes the British society of the era to task, but also the society of many other countries—perhaps a clue to the programme's world-wide success.*

So one question remains: why is this series, over thirty-five years after its first appearance on British television (in 1961), still as popular as ever?

It's a mystery worthy of The Avengers *itself.*

Brian Clemens has been at the heart of the production and realisation of all 187 episodes of the series. Naturally, it was Brian that we asked to tell us the story of The Avengers, *beginning with his own background. This he agreed to do, and in August 1990 he sent us, from Los Angeles, the comments that follow:*

I have always wanted to write. In fact I still have copies of books that I wrote and illustrated when I was five years old. When I was twelve I had my first short story published.

Unfortunately, the war meant that I had only about three years' schooling overall. I lacked academic qualifications, left school at fourteen and, hoping to be a journalist, became a messenger boy in Fleet Street for an advertising agency.

I then went into the army for two years' national service—and when I returned, entered J. Walter Thompson in a lowly position. I took the copywriters tests—one practical, one psychological—and gave them a problem: my practical test was the highest mark they had ever seen. My psychological test inferred that I was a dangerous lunatic! I became a copywriter.

I submitted a thriller to BBC TV, which they made. I then joined a very cheap company, run by the Danzigers, who were Americans, churning out low budget films and TV series in England. I became their contract writer, and had to write one half-hour TV episode every week—

although they would give me twelve days in which to write a feature movie!

It was terrific training in the old Hollywood style. Having no studio of their own, they moved around, and inherited other companies' sets. So I would be asked to write a movie with the Old Bailey, a gymnasium, the Albert Hall and a submarine in it!

I moved on, and wrote the pilot episode of, then script edited, the very first *Danger Man* series, starring Patrick McGoohan.

I was then asked to create and write *The Avengers*. The rest is history.

I first got involved on *The Avengers* as a writer of the very early episodes, which were made on tape, starring Ian Hendry and Patrick Macnee. In those days the premise was very much a spy/cop show.

It grew in style when Honor Blackman came on the scene with her leather clothing and so forth. Much of the style was due to economy. With no money left to build, say, a bank, we built a tiny portion, with bank notes in deep foreground and shot through them—thus the style began to form. During this time I contributed many scripts.

When it was to be *filmed,* they wanted someone who knew film and knew *The Avengers*. I was the only one qualified!

I began as associate producer for the first thirteen episodes with Diana Rigg, but I had *creative* control. I laid down certain ground rules—no women would be killed (although they could be bound and gagged and generally debased!). There would be no extras *per se*—everyone on screen would be a character. This was because our main characters, as outrageous as they were, would look ridiculous if placed alongside real, documentary-type people. Therefore, we never got involved in 'real' problems; there are no ethnics in the series, no blacks, no drug problems, no social problems. Ours was a fairy-tale world—the kind of Britain that outsiders like to imagine it is, even if it is not.

There was no conscious move into sci-fi—merely more outrageous stories. Remember that at that time, in *reality,* the CIA had a plan to poison Fidel Castro's boot polish, so we had to compete with real life outrageousness! We also predated the James Bond series of films by nearly three years, and indeed they eventually used three of our female stars (Honor Blackman, Diana Rigg and Joanna

Lumley) as well as Patrick Macnee. *The Man With the Golden Gun* was virtually an *Avengers* story we had done some seven years before.

The evolution came about because our audience not only liked our style, but wanted more, bigger and better, so we gave it to them.

The humour was always in the series—from its first inception we built on it. Also, underneath, we placed a great deal of sexual and Freudian implications. To the innocent, *The Avengers* was merely a happy pantomime of fast action and good humour. But, if you had a dirty mind, there were many more delights to be found.

Perhaps this is a comment on me and the others involved!

Nothing was an accident in the series. Clothes, sets, cars—every detail was discussed by the creative team and finally agreed by me. I have never worked so closely with art directors before, and they responded to this admirably. Our aim was to always keep the show ahead of its competitors—to keep it timeless. The fact that they have hardly dated at all is testimony to this. Most shows reveal their age by the cars and the clothing. We used unusual and old cars to begin with, and our clothes had a futuristic (or, in Steed's case, anachronistic) quality, which has kept them fresh even today! The series is still being shown all over the world, being rediscovered by new generations.

Producing the series, which I did after the first thirteen episodes, was an eighteen hours a day labour of joy. I took no vacation in five years. I was in charge of scripts, costumes, sets, editing, music and all creative elements. Of course, I was well supported by other talents.

Production was by *film*-makers—not TV people. Each episode was made like a little feature film, and each episode had a separate music score.

The key people were as follows: My partner, the late Albert Fennell, who oversaw finance, and was also very good at editing and dubbing, having made many fine feature films in the past.

Robert Jones, our art director most of the time, whose input and enthusiasm was terrific. He too had a long history of movie-making.

Laurie Johnson, whose music was the final icing on the cake, and again he was a movie man (his best friend was Bernard Herrmann, who worked with Welles and Hitchcock).

And Patrick Macnee, who has always remained loyal to the series, and never failed to give a professional, charming performance.

The stories developed in the following way. I would have a writer in and throw ideas at him. They would start to grow,

and when I had eight highspots (eight moments of action or intrigue), I then knew we had the foundation of a script. We were always looking to invert the cliché—thus duels were fought with wine, or feather dusters, and the settings for the fights were deliberately unusual and bizarre.

Also, we liked to attack the cliché, so that characters did actually *say,* "The natives are restless tonight." We liked to think that, once *we* had done a jungle story, no one could ever do one again and hope for it to be taken seriously.

The inversions were sometimes very funny. Thus a Sherlock Holmes character actually *planted* clues, and shot a man so that his body fell into the already chalked outline!

We liked to find a director who was sympathetic, and then tended to use him often. The ideal on such a series would be to have three directors alternating. Unfortunately, prior commitments never made this entirely possible. Directors had to be visual and have a sense of humour, plus a feel for suspense. Hitchcock would have been ideal—in fact, there is much in *The Avengers* that came from my long admiration of Hitchcock. He too used the unexpected setting, and his villains were always charming or unexpected: a dentist, a fisherman and so on.

Further changes came about when Honor Blackman decided to leave and go into movies. Then Di Rigg did the same.

About that time, I had a quarrel (not about the series) with Thames TV and left the show. During my absence, Linda Thorson was cast. She would not have been my choice, as she lacked style and, more importantly, humour. When I returned to the series, I created the Mother character as a means of bringing in some humour. Although Linda did her best, she was too inexperienced. But the character played by Jennifer Croxton (in 'Killer') was never intended as a possible replacement; her appearance merely enabled Thorson to take a vacation.

As for guest stars—well, of course we had a show with Donald Sutherland *and* Charlotte Rampling in it. Along the way we used the best British artistes, many of whom have gone on to become stars.

We never had any trouble getting anyone to play in the series. Everyone loved it—loved the fact that they could experiment with the crazy characters.

My relationship with the stars was fine, although, of course, there were sometimes disagreements. I welcomed suggestions and was quick to use them if they were valid.

The title sequences I designed and storyboarded for *all* the series, and the champagne one I actually shot.

The tag scenes at front and back were shot especially for America, where their TV format is such that, at the end of the episode are commercials, then afterwards, up come

Brian Clemens

the titles. I put in the tag scenes so the viewers would not switch channels—they became very popular for a while. We had fun inventing modes of transport for them to ride away in.

There were never any demands from US TV/ITV *et al.* I think it was because they regarded *The Avengers* as a house of cards, delicate and tenuous—no one was ever quite sure what made it stand up, what made it a success. All of them were reluctant to remove a single card lest the whole house toppled down.

As for the famous episodes: my favourite is 'The House That Jack Built', surely the only TV show where the villain who menaces the heroine is dead before the show starts!? I also liked 'A Touch of Brimstone'. (This, by the way, was banned in the USA as too sexy, but the ABC executives always ran it at all their parties!) 'Who's Who???' was a strange one. Patrick was ill and Diana was on vacation, so we had to make an *Avengers* episode without either one of the two stars! Naturally we did it with great aplomb. 'Pandora' is another favourite—I think Hitchcock might have made it. So too is 'Split', a scary one. In fact, many of our themes and stories have since, years later, been used in movies.

Then there was the one that spoofed *The Maltese Falcon,* and *High Noon,* and 'Too Many Christmas Trees', which is full of Dickensian atmosphere. In 'Honey For the Prince' we had to put a stone in Rigg's navel to get past the American censors! 'The Cybernauts' was so popular that we made two sequels to it. It could almost have become a series of its own!

Disasters? Just one—'Homicide and Old Lace'. During my absence in the Thorson period, three episodes were made, but none worked, so we had to reshoot material. But 'Homicide and Old Lace' was so dreadful that I finally decided to make a kind of joke of it, and make it an episode for Mother. It only half worked.

'The Forget-Me-Knot' was written and shot after I came back. I had to write it in one weekend, because we started shooting on the Monday! I am very proud of this episode because it cleverly enabled Steed to both lose and gain Rigg at the same time. He says goodbye, and watches her go off with a man who looks just like him (it should do—Patrick played both parts). So the viewers were not made too sad, because *The Avengers* is a happy show—an escapist froth of pure fantasy.

I tried too, in 'Bizarre', not to leave the viewers sad, which was why I had Mother promise that "they'll be back." And they were!

The New Avengers came about when Rudolf Roffi was making a commercial for French champagne, with Thorson and Macnee. At the time he wondered why the series was not still being made. We said because no one had put up any money to do so. He found the money, so we made it. It is a little different from the old series. I like to say that the old series had cardboard characters: in *The New Avengers,* I used thicker cardboard. This was deliberate, and aimed at capturing that section of the world who thought *The Avengers* somehow 'silly', or inconsequential. I tried to give the characters a little more depth. I think it worked. However, it fell down when Roffi ran out of money. Cuts were made, and finally we were forced to make episodes in both France and Canada. All these episodes had good scripts, but were badly made by countries who do not have a real tradition of *commercial* cinema. Neither country could quite capture the style of the show. I don't think the series was any different in story quality than the old one—we had action, sci-fi and bizarre stories, in equal proportions. I think that 'Dead Men Are Dangerous', 'The Midas Touch' and 'The Eagle's Nest' were as good as any episodes of the old *Avengers.*

Brian Clemens was one of the most important figures behind the creation of The Avengers, *but his prolific career has never been limited to that one series:*

Along the way, other things I've written include: *Sinbad's Golden Voyage, Blind Terror* (with Mia Farrow), *The Peking Medallion* (Robert Stack and Elke Sommer), *The Watcher in the Woods* (Bette Davis), *Station Six-Sahara* (Carroll Baker, Ian Bannen), *Dr Jekyll & Sister Hyde* (for Hammer films, which I also produced), And *Soon the Darkness* (a thriller set in France), and a number of other movies.

I created a TV comedy series, called *My Wife Next Door,* for the BBC, and also created and produced *The Professionals* TV series for LWT.

I have also written twelve stage plays, two of which have run in the West End of London (one of them was *The Avengers* stage version).

I have won awards from Cinema Fantastique, and two Edgar Allan Poe awards.

Brian Clemens continues to work in television and film; since writing these comments, he has helped to create and write the BBC series Bugs. ❤

A GLIMPSE BEHIND THE SCENES

Behind The Scenes

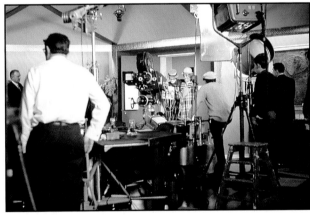

THE LEAD ACTORS

IAN HENDRY

Born in London in 1931, Ian Hendry died in 1985. In 1960, the series *Police Surgeon* was launched on British television, but only lasted a dozen weeks. Despite its short life, Hendry, playing Brent, a doctor working for the police, was popular, so producer Sydney Newman decided to revamp the concept. Taking into account what was fashionable at the time, an espionage series with plenty of suspense and humour was created, with Hendry in a similar role as Dr Keel. This was *The Avengers,* which raised the actor's profile still further.

After his departure from the series, he later rejoined Patrick Macnee in an episode of *The New Avengers,* 'To Catch a Rat'.

In the cinema, Hendry appeared in a number of horror and fantasy films: *Children of the Damned* (a follow-up to *Village of the Damned*), *Repulsion* (directed by Roman Polanski, with Catherine Deneuve), *Casino Royale, Journey to the Far Side of the Sun* (produced by Gerry Anderson, with Roy Thinnes, the star of *The Invaders*), *Tales from the Crypt* (with Peter Cushing and Joan Collins), *Captain Kronos Vampire Hunter* (written and directed by Brian Clemens) and *Theatre of Blood* (where he played alongside Vincent Price and ... Diana Rigg!).

On television, Hendry was seen in several series, including *The Persuaders* with Roger Moore and Tony Curtis.

PATRICK MACNEE

The future John Steed was born in Berkshire in 1922. Coming from an illustrious aristocratic family, he experienced a quintessentially English childhood: a strict private boarding school and an army of governesses at his service. After an incident-packed passage through the prestigious classrooms of Eton, he decided to become an actor, in spite of family disapproval.

His career began in the theatre and he quickly became one of the most promising actors in the West End.

Then came the Second World War, and service in the Royal Navy, after which he returned to the boards. He appeared in Laurence Olivier's film version of *Hamlet,* and later donned a naval uniform again for Michael Powell's war film *The Battle of the River Plate.*

After a short stint as producer on a documentary series about Winston Churchill, Macnee was asked by Sydney Newman to team up with Ian Hendry in *The Avengers* ... which brought him international fame.

Macnee was the only actor to star in every season of *The Avengers,* but his services to the small screen were not limited to the character of John Steed. He featured in other series like *Columbo, Battlestar Galactica, Love Boat, For the Term of His Natural Life,* and even... *Magnum!* He appeared in *The Return of the Man from U.N.C.L.E.* where, in an entertaining twist, he played the boss of Napoleon Solo (Robert Vaughn) and Illya Kuryakin (David McCallum). He was also Doctor Watson in *Sherlock Holmes in New York* (alongside Roger Moore as Sherlock Holmes) and returned to 221b for a series of Holmes TV films opposite Christopher Lee as Baker Street's most celebrated tenant.

In the cinema, Macnee has appeared in a number of horror films of varying quality: *The Howling* (directed by Joe Dante), *The Creature Wasn't Nice* (aka *Spaceship,* a parody of *Alien*), *Waxwork, Lobsterman from Mars* (with Tony Curtis) and Roger Corman's 1989 remake of *The Masque of the Red Death,* where he became the 'Red Death' in person!

Like three of his partners in *The Avengers,* he has appeared in a James Bond movie, *A View to a Kill* which, unfortunately, is a far from shining example of agent 007's adventures.

Today, after a rather troubled personal life (which he recounts with intelligence and humour in his autobiographies, *Blind in One Ear* and *The Avengers and Me),* he lives peacefully in California, still pursuing his career. In 1997 he appeared (as a retired secret agent!) in the series *Spy Game* and hosted the programme *Ghost Stories,* both for American television.

HONOR BLACKMAN

Honor Blackman was born in London in 1926. At an early age she appeared for Rank in a number of small British productions, acting alongside Dirk Bogarde in Terence Fisher's *So Long at the Fair.* Her popular success in *The Avengers* led to more widely seen films. In 1963, Blackman appeared in *Jason and the Argonauts,* directed by Don Chaffey, an epic film with some particularly remarkable special effects created by Ray Harryhausen.

In 1964, when, at the height of her fame, Blackman left the series that had made her name, it was to join Sean Connery on the set of *Goldfinger* (directed by Guy Hamilton). She worked with Connery once more in 1968, alongside Brigitte Bardot, in *Shalako,* a Western which failed to leave much of a mark.

Curiously, like many of the James Bond girls, she then experienced a quiet period in the movies. She did make two horror films of note, however: *To the Devil a Daughter* (a Hammer production, with Christopher Lee, Richard

Widmark, Nastassja Kinski and Denholm Elliott) and *The Cat and the Canary,* which only received a limited cinema release.

On television, Blackman appeared with Roger Moore in *The Saint,* and with Peter Falk in *Columbo,* as well as popping up in a variety of guest roles in British series, including *Doctor Who.*

Blackman has also made many appearances on the stage, in particular in a West End production of *The Sound of Music,* which had a successful run.

Best known in recent years for her scene-stealing role in the long-running comedy series *The Upper Hand,* she is still fondly remembered as the leather-clad Catherine Gale from the early days of *The Avengers.*

DIANA RIGG

Dame Diana Rigg was born in Doncaster, Yorkshire in 1938. After making her way through the Royal Academy of Dramatic Arts, she joined the prestigious Royal Shakespeare Company, where she distinguished herself in the famous dramatist's classic plays, peforming in *A Midsummer Night's Dream, Macbeth* and *King Lear,* among others.

After two years of stardom on television in *The Avengers,* she returned to the boards as Heloise in *Heloise and Abelard,* and Célimène in *The Misanthrope.* Among her many theatrical achievements, one should draw attention to her peformances in *Pygmalion, Anthony and Cleopatra* and *Medea.*

Rigg's appearances in the cinema are much rarer. One of her most memorable roles is certainly that of Tracy in *On Her Majesty's Secret Service*—the only woman whom James Bond has ever married. Unfortunately, it was a Bond film without Sean Connery, and the actor who replaced him, George Lazenby, only made the one appearance as 007. It is a shame that *aficionados* quickly forgot this film, denigrating it quite unjustly, because in fact it was one of the best adaptations of Ian Fleming's work. Then Rigg starred in *The Hospital,* alongside George C. Scott, and *Theatre of Blood,* a superb horror film in which she plays the daughter of Vincent Price's character. She appeared in *A Little Night Music* and *The Great Muppet Caper* (with Jim Henson's celebrated puppets) and also in *Evil Under the Sun,* adapted from the Agatha Christie novel.

On television, Diana starred in *Witness for the Prosecution,* a telefilm with Donald Pleasence and Ralph Richardson, and an adaptation of *Snow White,* where she portrayed the wicked witch, a role which few of her admirers would have thought fitting for her. She also played the title role in *Hedda Gabler* in a production for the small screen.

Finally, it is amusing to mention a curious 'sitcom' filmed in the United States under the title of... *Diana,* in which Patrick Macnee, who appeared as a guest star, hurls a mischievous, "Miss Diana... you're needed!" by way of homage.

Diana Rigg continues to work on both stage and screen, appearing in a critically lauded revival of *Who's Afraid of Virginia Woolf?* in London's West End, and on television in adaptations of *Moll Flanders* and *Rebecca*.

LINDA THORSON

Linda Thorson was born in Toronto, Canada, in 1947. Discovered by John Huston, she was engaged by John Bryce, then producer of *The Avengers,* for the role of Tara King, making her famous at the age of twenty.

If this role stuck with her somewhat, she was not held back unduly, working on British and American television, appearing in *The Caucasian Chalk Circle, Moonlighting* (with Bruce Willis and Cybill Shepherd), *Dynasty* (with Joan Collins and Linda Evans) and *Star Trek: The Next Generation*. On French television she played Maurice Biraud's partner in the telefilm *Palm Trees in the Metro*.

In the cinema, Thorson's appearances are rare and she is the only female star from *The Avengers* never to have featured in a James Bond film. She did appear however, in *Valentino* (a film by Ken Russell, with Rudolf Nureyev) and *The Greek Tycoon* (with Anthony Quinn and Jacqueline Bisset). She also had a role in *Joey* and the horror film *Curtains*.

On the other hand, she has acted in numerous stage productions, in plays like *Woyzeck* and *Steaming,* as well as in classics like *The Three Sisters, The Seagull, Bajazet, A Midsummer Night's Dream* and *The Merchant of Venice*. She has also played in West End plays like *No Sex Please, We're British* and *My Fat Friend*.

JOANNA LUMLEY

The star of *The New Avengers* was born in 1946 in Kashmir, India, where her father was a major in the Gurkha regiment. When she arrived in Britain, she failed to gain a place at RADA, consoling herself by becoming a celebrated model, making the covers of famous magazines like Vogue and Harper's Bazaar.

A role in *On Her Majesty's Secret Service* was followed by a leading part in the Hammer film *The Satanic Rites of Dracula,* with Christopher Lee and Peter Cushing.

After that came her most high profile role yet—Purdey in *The New Avengers*. Once the series had finished, she moved on to another television show, *Sapphire & Steel* (alongside David McCallum), which has since gained quite a cult following of its own.

More recently she has appeared in film adaptations of *Cold Comfort Farm* and *James and the Giant Peach,* but has of course enjoyed most success with her BAFTA award-winning role in the comedy series *Absolutely Fabulous.*

GARETH HUNT

Born near London in 1944, Gareth Hunt joined the Merchant Navy at the age of fifteen. After travelling for six years across the oceans of the world, he studied, like Diana Rigg, with the Royal Shakespeare Company. After minor parts in various television series, such as *Doctor Who,* he found fame as Frederick in *Upstairs, Downstairs.* It was that role which brought him to the attention of Brian Clemens.

After playing Mike Gambit, he appeared in the film *Licensed to Love* and *Kill,* a pale imitation of James Bond, and made some well remembered TV advertisements for coffee. In 1997 he appeared in the film *Fierce Creatures.*

THE VEHICLES

If the 'dream machines' used throughout *The Avengers* are 'stars', almost as recognisable as the lead actors, they know how to remain in their place and not upstage the characters in the foreground, as was too often the case in other programmes.

They are content to play their role, underlining the tastes and personality of each character with unequalled class. Today it seems impossible to summon up the dapper John Steed without envisaging leaping dynamically from one of his superb vintage vehicles.

As for his delightful and up-to-the-minute partners, one cannot imagine them at the wheel of anything other than their convertible sports cars, driving at breakneck speed along the narrow, deserted lanes of the English countryside (even though the first female star of the series wore her leathers astride a powerful motorbike).

Just like the series itself, these most beautiful 'stars' have still not aged. Out of time in their era, they have remained so in ours. As with all timeless creations, they will never grow old.

WHO DROVE WHAT?

In the early seasons, John Steed drove a white Vauxhall saloon, registration number 7061 MK, and a Bugatti (reg GK 3295). Then, with the arrival of Mrs Peel, he took to the wheel of two green Bentleys (one 1926, the other 1929) whose registration numbers were, respectively, UW 4887 and XT 2273. Steed remained faithful to his Bentley, but during some episodes of the Tara King season driving a superb yellow 1927 Rolls Royce Silver Ghost (reg KK 4976), as well as another Rolls Royce, still yellow, but this time a 1923 Phantom (reg UU 3864). For *The New Avengers,* Steed contented himself with an olive green Jaguar coupé (reg NVK 60P) and, quite often, a green Range Rover (reg TXC 922J) for travelling cross-country.

Steed's green 1926 Bentley

Cathy Gale rode a powerful motorbike: a Triumph (reg 987 CAA).

Emma Peel drove a blue Lotus Elan S2 for both of her seasons on the show. The registration number of the first was HNK 999C and the second SJH 499D.

Tara King drove a maroon AC Cobra 428 (reg LPH 800D) in some episodes and a red Lotus Europa (reg PPW 999F) in others.

Mother was driven around in a silver Rolls Royce (reg 3 KHM) or a Mini Moke (reg THX 77F), and even in a London bus.

Purdey had a yellow MGB Sports (reg MOC 232P), a

Steed later drove a Rolls

The superb 1927 Rolls Royce Silver Ghost

yellow Triumph TR7 (reg OGW 562R) and a couple of Honda motorbikes, one black and yellow, and one red.

Gambit mainly drove a red Jaguar XJS (reg MLR 875P), but also a white Range Rover (reg LOK 537P).

Tara King's AC Cobra

The green 1929 Bentley

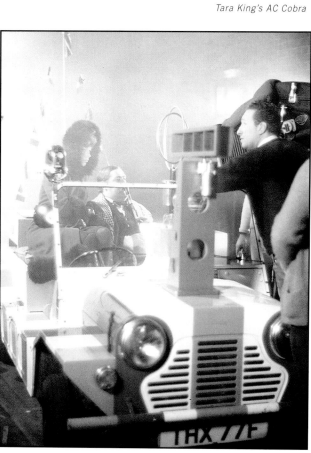

Mother's Mini-Moke

Emma Peel's blue Lotus Elan

The Vehicles

A TRIBUTE TO AVENGERS FASHION

The Avengers were all played by great actors of undeniable charm who drove exceptional vehicles. But the characters interpreted with so much panache by Patrick Macnee and his partners would not have remained in our collective memories to such a degree without their extraordinary clothes. The costumes were able simultaneously to dress (or rather 'mould', on occasion) the characters' elegant silhouettes and at the same time enhance the series with significance as well as style.

Cathy Gale's leather suits were a statement against the semi-Victorian values still prevalent in the Britain of the early sixties. Here was a woman ahead of her time: submissive to no one, independent and fully capable of looking after herself.

The feline Emma Peel continued the leather-clad look, and with her jersey and lamé dresses, boots and furs, she was another beautiful, desirable—and liberated—woman in control.

Tara King's thigh boots and miniskirts complimented the character's youthful cheerfulness perfectly.

One can imagine the refined John Steed, a glass of champagne to hand and a mischievous twinkle in his eye, explaining his penchant for immaculate suits from a bygone era: "Perhaps no one but me wears them any more, but to me, they symbolise the elegance of a time that has passed, and that is worth safeguarding as our traditions collapse around us, don't you think?"

A STUNNING PARADE

From the moment Honor Blackman arrived on the series, its producers knew that her character should become a fashion icon. To that end they called on the services of Michael Whittaker, who was at the time one of the most fashionable British designers. It was Patrick Macnee himself who suggested the use of leather. On the basis of that idea, Whittaker created four main suits to complement the already famous leather boots.

It was Emma Peel who brought *Avengers* fashion to the fore. The programme's producers immediately saw the need to modify the image of the female lead, to take into account Diana Rigg's own personality. It was John Bates, a top fashion designer, who took charge of operations and smoothly carried out the metamorphosis. If Emma continued to wear leather suits during the black and white episodes, she used them mostly for the fight scenes. They had to be particularly supple, to allow her body the freedom

A leather suit created by Michael Whittaker

One of John Bates' magnificent leather suits

required for the action, and moulded, in order to show off the classically trained star's considerable grace of movement. For Emma's everyday life, Bates created original day and evening wear, discreet and yet daring. Cut from silk and satin, in lamé and crêpe, they gave her the look of a perfect 'lady', her seductiveness belying her activities as an efficient secret agent.

As the series moved into colour, Diana Rigg herself suggested to her producers that her wardrobe be given a new style. It was Alun Hughes, another famous British fashion designer, who was charged with creating that new image. From then on, Emma was to wear a whole range of avant-garde clothes, and two outfits would be given main prominence: the miniskirt and the 'Emmapeelers'. The first shocked the Americans to such a degree that the distributors asked that Miss Rigg stopped wearing them, which she refused to do, with good reason. The second, so-named by Hughes himself, quickly became the symbol of action. When Emma appeared in that suit, one knew danger was imminent. "In her Emmapeelers," indicated Hughes, "Emma was like a cat, creeping silently towards the scene of her secret mission. You felt she was ready to face any assailant." The 'Emmapeelers' were made of crimplene jersey, complete with boots of the same material and colour. To underline still further Emma's cat-like aspect, Hughes also designed fur coats, one of them copying the pattern of a tiger skin.

When Diana Rigg was replaced by Linda Thorson, Alun Hughes took charge of dressing Tara King. Later, he admitted that Linda Thorson's personality had appeared to him as more complex than Diana Rigg's. Emma's avant-garde clothes were replaced with ones that emphasised Tara's more generous curves. Culottes appeared, and more trousers, but there were still as many miniskirts for Tara to wear with her charming and youthful innocence.

Generally, however, Hughes' designs weren't quite as eye-catching. The look came more from Linda Thorson's physique and personality than from a real concern for innovative design. However, Tara did wear more make-up and jewellery than Emma, such as sparkling earrings, as Mrs Peel was not particularly drawn to either.

Contrary to his female partners' modern garb, John Steed's outfits were, according to Brian Clemens, deliberately anachronistic. Until the end of Mrs Peel's era, they were often created by a young designer already well known at the time, but who was to become even more famous: Pierre Cardin. Although he was a Frenchman, he understood admirably well how to draw inspiration from the elegance of turn of the century Britain, helping Patrick Macnee as John Steed become the consummate figure of a gentleman, in itself one of the reasons for the success of *The Avengers*.

After that, Patrick Macnee helped to design his outfits himself. Although he did so with flair, it must nevertheless

Two creations from John Bates

John Bates' designs from Emma Peel's era

be said that Cardin's spirit was his guiding force. In *The New Avengers,* Steed's outfits remained the same. The setting of the series became more 'realistic', making his clothing appear even more out of time.

The ex-model Joanna Lumley wore her diaphanous and often low-cut dresses wonderfully, accentuating her ballerina profile, but her clothes were very much of their time, when the fashion world was calmer after the exuberance of the sixties. Another somewhat forgettable selection of outfits was modelled by the 'action man' Mike Gambit, who, as played by Gareth Hunt, was rather conventionally dressed. Curiously, Purdey's and Gambit's clothes seem old-fashioned today (far more in fact than those of their predecessors), if not resolutely unfashionable.

It has often been said that *The Avengers'* fashions influenced the creations of the 'Swinging London' designers. In fact, the principle contribution of the avant-garde clothes worn by Steed's seductive companions was to make those designers popular.

Many years later, the *Avengers* style seems fresher than ever, and one can still see ideas the programme pioneered on the streets today.

More of John Bates' designs

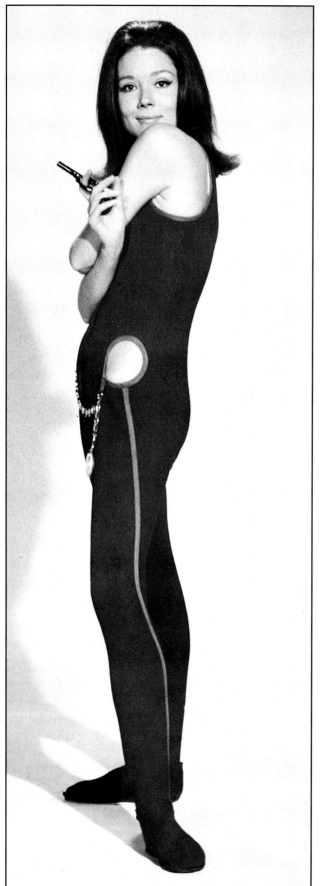

Three creations from Alun Hughes

Fashion

The feline Mrs Peel, ready for action

A typical Macnee/Cardin costume

Tara King, dressed by Alun Hughes

A diaphanous design for Purdey

THE DIRECTORS

Over the years, *The Avengers* employed the talents of a prestigious group of directors. As befitted a series where each episode was approached as if it were a 'mini feature film', many of the directors had thriving careers in the cinema. Here is a selection of those who worked most prolifically for the programme:

SIDNEY HAYERS (*Circus of Horrors, Night of the Eagle*): 'The Cybernauts', 'The Hidden Tiger', 'The Joker', 'Dead Men are Dangerous', and others.

DON CHAFFEY (*Jason and the Argonauts, One Million Years B.C.*, episodes of *The Prisoner*): 'Wish You Were Here', 'Stay Tuned', 'Requiem', 'Who Was That Man I Saw You With?'

DON SHARP (*Rasputin the Mad Monk, The Kiss of the Vampire*): 'Invasion of the Earthmen', 'The Curious Case of the Countless Clues', 'Get-A-Way!'

JOHN HOUGH (*Twins of Evil, The Legend of Hell House, Incubus, The Watcher in the Woods*): 'Fog', 'The Morning After', 'Homicide and Old Lace'.

JAMES HILL (*A Study in Terror*): 'Castle De'Ath', 'A Touch of Brimstone', 'Honey for the Prince', 'Epic', 'Something Nasty in the Nursery', 'Look—(stop me if you've heard this one) But There Were These Two Fellers...'

ROY WARD BAKER (*A Night to Remember, Quatermass and the Pit, The Vampire Lovers*): 'Too Many Christmas Trees', 'Room without a View', 'Split'.

ROBERT FUEST (*The Abominable Dr. Phibes, The Final Programme*): 'Game', 'The Rotters', 'They Keep Killing Steed', 'Pandora', 'Take-Over', 'My Wildest Dream', 'The Midas Touch'.

THE GUEST STARS

As Brian Clemens has pointed out, actors loved appearing in *The Avengers,* as it gave them the chance to play a role that was usually somewhat out of the ordinary. Here is a selection of the series' impressive array of guest stars:

BARBARA SHELLEY (*Dracula Prince of Darkness*): 'Dragonsfield', 'From Venus with Love'.

JOHN CARSON (*Taste the Blood of Dracula*): 'Chorus of Frogs', 'Second Sight', 'The Midas Touch'.

PATRICK MAGEE (*A Clockwork Orange*): 'Killerwhale', 'The Gilded Cage'.

ANDRÉ MORELL (*The Hound of the Baskervilles*): 'Death of a Batman', 'Death at Bargain Prices'.

LOIS MAXWELL (Miss Moneypenny in the James Bond films): 'The Little Wonders'.

SANDOR ELES (*The Evil of Frankenstein*): 'Concerto', 'The Positive-Negative Man'.

MICHAEL GOUGH (*Horrors of the Black Museum, Batman* and its sequels): 'The Cybernauts', 'The Correct Way to Kill'.

PATRICK CARGILL (A 'Number Two' in *The Prisoner*): 'The Murder Market', 'The Fear Merchants'.

CLIFFORD EVANS (*The Kiss of the Vampire, The Curse of the Werewolf*): 'Dial a Deadly Number', 'Death's Door'.

FRANCIS MATTHEWS (*Dracula Prince of Darkness, Rasputin the Mad Monk*): 'The Thirteenth Hole', 'Mission ...Highly Improbable'.

PETER WYNGARDE (Another 'Number Two in *The Prisoner, Department 'S', Jason King*): 'A Touch of Brimstone', 'Epic'.

RON MOODY (*Oliver!, Legend of the Werewolf*): 'Honey for the Prince', 'The Bird Who Knew Too Much'.

NIGEL GREEN (*Jason and the Argonauts, Countess Dracula*): 'The Winged Avenger', 'Fog'.

BRIAN BLESSED (*Flash Gordon*): 'The Superlative Seven', 'The Morning After'.

RONALD LACEY (*Raiders of the Lost Ark*): 'The Joker', 'Legacy of Death', 'The Midas Touch'.

ROBERT FLEMYNG (*The Terror of Dr Hichcock*): 'You Have Just Been Murdered', 'To Catch a Rat'.

FERDY MAYNE (*Dance of the Vampires*): 'Legacy of Death', 'Trap'.

BARRY WARREN (*The Kiss of the Vampire*): 'Too Many Christmas Trees', 'False Witness'.

CATHERINE WOODVILLE (who was married to Patrick Macnee): 'Hot Snow', 'Propellant 23'.

JULIAN GLOVER (*For Your Eyes Only, Indiana Jones and the Last Crusade*): 'The Living Dead', 'Two's a Crowd', 'Split', 'Pandora'.

KENNETH J. WARREN: 'Girl on the Trapeze', 'Intercrime', 'Epic'.

MELISSA STRIBLING (*The Brides of Dracula*): 'Hunt the Man Down', 'School for Traitors', 'Angels of Death'.

PATRICK NEWELL (in addition to his later role as Mother): 'The Town of No Return', 'Something Nasty in the Nursery'.

TERENCE ALEXANDER (*Vault of Horror*): 'The Town of No Return', 'The Correct Way to Kill', 'Love All', 'Angels of Death'.

REED R. DE ROUEN: 'Far Distant Dead', 'Removal Men', writer of 'Six Hands Across a Table'.

PAUL WHITSUN-JONES: 'The Wringer', 'The Man with Two Shadows', 'Room without a View', 'Fog'.

PHILIP LOCKE: 'The Frighteners', 'Mandrake', 'From Venus with Love'.

DUDLEY FOSTER: 'The Hour That Never Was', 'Something Nasty in the Nursery', 'Wish You Were Here'.

NIGEL STOCK (*The Lost Continent*): 'Concerto', 'A Sense of History'.

JOHN LE MESURIER (Sergeant Wilson in *Dad's Army*): 'Mandrake', 'What the Butler Saw'.

WILLIAM FRANKLYN (*The Satanic Rites of Dracula*): 'Silent Dust', 'Killer', 'Hostage'.

EDINA RONAY (*A Study in Terror, Slave Girls*): 'Removal Men', 'The Nutshell'.

PETER MADDEN (*Saturday Night and Sunday Morning*): 'One For the Mortuary', 'Room without a View', 'Pandora'.

BURT KWOUK (Kato, assistant to Inspector Clouseau in the Pink Panther series): 'Kill the King', 'Lobster Quadrille', 'The Cybernauts'.

ROY KINNEAR (*Help!, The Three Musketeers*): 'Esprit de Corps', 'The Hour That Never Was', 'The Invisible Man', 'Bizarre'.

PETER JEFFREY (*The Abominable Dr. Phibes, Dr. Phibes Rises Again*): 'Room without a View', 'The Joker', 'Game', 'House of Cards'.

JEREMY YOUNG: 'A Touch of Brimstone', 'Never, Never Say Die', 'The Forget-Me-Knot', 'Gnaws'.

WARREN MITCHELL (Alf Garnett in *Till Death Us Do Part*): 'The Golden Fleece', 'The Charmers', 'Two's a Crowd', 'The Invisible Man'.

EDWARD DE SOUZA (*The Kiss of the Vampire, The Phantom of the Opera*): 'Six Hands Across a Table', 'The Curious Case of the Countless Clues'.

PHILIP MADOC holds the record for guest starring in the series, in 'Six Hands Across a Table', 'The Decapod', 'Death of a Batman', 'The Correct Way to Kill' and 'My Wildest Dream'.

And not forgetting…

DONALD SUTHERLAND and **CHARLOTTE RAMPLING,** who were both in 'The Superlative Seven'.

CHRISTOPHER LEE: 'Never, Never Say Die', 'The Interrogators'.

PETER CUSHING: 'The Return of the Cybernauts', 'The Eagle's Nest'.

COLIN BLAKELY (*The Private Life of Sherlock Holmes*): 'Murdersville'

JOHN CLEESE (*Monty Python*): 'Look—(stop me if you've heard this one) But There Were These Two Fellers…'

IAN OGILVY (*The Sorcerers, The Return of the Saint*): 'They Keep Killing Steed'.

MARTIN SHAW and **LEWIS COLLINS** (*The Professionals*): 'Obsession'.

CAROLINE MUNRO (*Captain Kronos Vampire Hunter, The Spy Who Loved Me*): 'Angels of Death'.

FREDDIE JONES (*Frankenstein Must Be Destroyed, The Elephant Man*): 'Who's Who?'

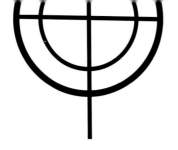

O THE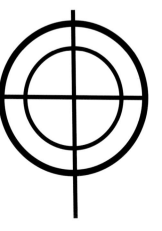

Эпо
- - - - - - - - - - - - - - - -